SELF-ATTITUDES
AND
DEVIANT BEHAVIOR

Howard B. Kaplan, Ph.D.

Baylor College of Medicine

Goodyear Publishing Company, Inc.
Pacific Palisades, California

Library of Congress Cataloging in Publication Data

Kaplan, Howard B.
  Self-attitudes and deviant behavior.

  Bibliography: p.
  1. Deviant behavior. 2. Self-perception.
I. Title. DNLM: 1. Self concept. 2. Social
behavior disorders. WM600 K17s
HM291.K18 1975   301.6′2   74–2955
ISBN: 0–87620–839–1

Library of Congress Catalog Card Number: 74-2955

ISBN: 0–87620–839–1
Y:8391–8

Current printing (last digit):
10 9 8 7 6 5 4 3 2 1

Printed in the United States of America

To Diane Susan and Samuel Charles,

who contribute in so many ways to my self-acceptance

Contents

Preface

This book sketches the outline of a general theory of deviant behavior and considers the apparent compatibility of the relevant research literature with this theoretical formulation.

The emerging theoretical structure, proposed in Part I, centers upon two core propositions dealing with the reciprocal relationships between self-attitudes and deviant behavior: first, that negative self-attitudes increase the probability of subsequent adoption of deviant response patterns; second, that the adoption of deviant response patterns increases the probability of subsequent increases in self-accepting attitudes. The theoretical structure generally appears congruent with the literature dealing with more specific categories of deviant behavior such as delinquency, drug abuse, alcoholism, aggression, suicide, and particular forms of mental illness. This compatibility is considered in Part II.

Hopefully the reader will find, as did the author, that this theoretical structure facilitates the integration of a number of diverse theoretical approaches to the study of deviant behavior, provides a framework for the incorporation of a vast array of findings stemming from empirical studies suggested by these diverse theoretical approaches, permits the simultaneous consideration of literature dealing with several different modes of deviant response, and serves as a prolific source of empirically verifiable hypotheses regarding why people come to adopt deviant response patterns.

PART I

TOWARD A GENERAL THEORY OF DEVIANT BEHAVIOR

Part I presents the outline of a general theory of deviant behavior that focuses upon the concept of self-attitudes. Chapter 1 provides a preliminary statement of the problem, defines deviant behavior, briefly describes the development of the outline of the theory, and describes the organization of the remainder of the volume. Chapter 2 considers the basic premise of the emerging theory of deviant behavior: the universality of the self-esteem motive. The self-esteem motive is defined, its development in the individual is considered, and empirical evidence for its prevalence is presented. Chapter 3 considers the classes of factors that influence fulfillment of the self-esteem motive through their effects upon the genesis of positive/negative self-attitudes. Chapter 4 contains a discussion of the influence of negative self-attitudes upon the adoption and stabilization of patterns of deviant behavior.

Chapter 1

Introduction:
Deviant Behavior
and its Explanation

In a general way the problem of the following chapters is the explanation of why people who had not previously adopted deviant response patterns come to adopt them. The true scope of the problem, however, can only be understood following a definition of deviant behavior.

DELIMITING THE PROBLEM

Deviant behavior is viewed from the perspective of both the person and his membership group. In any group the members of the group share normative expectations regarding how people with specified social characteristics will (not) and should (not) behave in specified circumstances.[1] The failure to conform to these shared normative expectations is greeted with reactions of surprise, negative evaluation, and the application of more or less severe negative sanctions by the members of the group or their surrogates. Deviant behavior is defined in part in terms of the failure to conform to the normative expectations shared by the group regarding how the subject will and should behave in given situations. However, this definition is understood here to imply the following qualifications.

A person generally holds membership in a number of groups — family, voluntary associations, work groups, peer groups, a community, a more inclusive society, and so on — each of which is characterized by a system of shared normative expectations. Deviant behavior thus is the failure of a person to conform to the specified normative expectations of one or more of the *specified* groups in which the individual holds membership.

Membership in a group is evidenced both by the person's prior (predeviance) acceptance of (conformity to) the normative expectations and by the application of the normative expectations to the person by other group members. If the person had *never* viewed the system of normative expectations as having any applicability to him, their application to him by members of the group would not establish his group membership; therefore, his failure to conform would not be deviant behavior. Nor would group membership be established or deviant behavior be judged to have occurred if the person judged himself to have violated group norms that the group members did not recognize as having applicability to him. Under this condition it would perhaps be more proper to speak of the person's reference (rather than membership) group.

Thus, if a person violates the norms of a specified *membership* group, his behavior is deviant even if it should (by chance or intent) conform to the normative expectations of some other group. However, if he no longer considers the normative expectations of one group as applicable to him but accepts those of another group and comes to be recognized by members of this group as one to whom the group expectations should apply, then a change in both his group membership and the deviant (conforming) character of his behavior occurs. He ceases to be considered a member of the former group and comes to be viewed as a member of the latter group; and his behavior that violates the standards of the former membership group is no longer characterized as deviant but rather is perceived as conforming to the standards of his new membership group. Indeed, any instances of subsequent conformity to the standards of the former membership group would now be regarded as deviant behavior by virtue of the failure of such instances to conform to the normative expectations of the new membership group.

The characterization of particular behaviors as deviant at a given time is in part a function of the person's various, multiple membership groups. The characterization of behavior as deviant may also change over time even within the context of the *same* membership group. Such changes may occur if a person changes positions within the group insofar as normative expectations may variously apply to different group positions. Alternatively, over time group definitions of normative expectations applicable to particular positions and in particular circumstances might change. This qualification also remains consistent with the general conception of deviant behavior as behavior by a person that fails to conform to the applicable normative expectation of his membership group.

In one further qualification to the general definition of deviant behavior presented above, instances of failure to conform to the shared normative expectations of the group fall into two categories. First, the person shares and therefore accepts as applicable to himself the normative expectations that the group applies to him at the time he deviates from them; that is, he is motivated to conform to the normative expectations regarding the desirable qualities he should possess and the goals he should achieve (and, of course, the undesirable qualities and goals he should not possess or achieve). Perhaps according to both group and personal standards he should be brave, industrious, well-born, physically healthy, occupationally successful, good looking, a successful thief, and so on, but for one reason or another, against his will, has been unable to display these hypothetically highly valued behaviors or traits. In that event he becomes the object of negative evaluations and sanctions by himself and others in his group (as he would be the object of positive evaluations and sanctions by himself and others in his group to the degree that he approximated the desirable qualities and achievements in question). Such instances of de facto deviations from normative expectations to which the subject was motivated to conform are specifically excluded from the category of deviant behaviors that is the concern of this volume. Rather, the concern of the volume will be the mutually exclusive category of instances of deviations.[2]

Unlike the first category, which contains instances of deviations from normative expectations that are essentially involuntary (whether due to lack of ability, circumstances of birth, illness, and so on),[3] the second category contains instances of deviant behavior that are essentially voluntary in the sense that the person either comes to lack motivation to conform (having withdrawn from, or substituted a revised set of, normative expectations) and/or becomes positively motivated to violate (that is, actively rejects or attacks) the normative expectations previously shared with others in his membership group. In summary, then, deviant behavior is defined as the failure to conform to the shared normative expectations of the subject's membership group in circumstances in which the person either ceases to be motivated to conform and/or becomes motivated to deviate from the normative expectations in question.

Within this definition of deviant behavior and the qualifications implicit in it, it is now possible to return to the general question posed at the beginning of this chapter: Why do people who have not previously done so come to adopt deviant response patterns? This question may be viewed as a general statement of more specific questions such as: Why does an individual who is a member of a group that condemns and punishes the use of specified types of drugs in any but specified situations adopt the use of such forbidden drugs in forbidden circumstances? Why does a person who is a member of a group that condemns such behavior patterns as theft, vandalism, and violence come to adopt such behavior? Why does a person who is a member of a group in which the permissible effects, amount, and circumstances of alcohol use are well defined come to adopt alcohol usage patterns that deviate from the permissible limits? Why does a person who is a member of a group which *characteristically* displays and approves "criminal" or "delinquent"[4] behavior patterns (for example, criminal organizations, delinquent "subcultures," informal prison inmate groups) come to reject these patterns and/or adopt patterns that deviate from the normative expectations of this group (but that may conform to the normative expectations of some other group, such as middle-class society)? This last question reemphasizes the point that judgments of deviant behavior are made relative to the standards of specified groups rather than with reference to a system of absolute moral standards.

FORMULATING AN EXPLANATION

For each of these, and similar, questions there is an abundant literature available that focuses upon the problem of why people adopt particular forms of deviant behavior. Each body of literature appears to be devoted to the development of more or less special theory that would account for the adoption of specific deviant patterns or some combination of such patterns. The end product would be a specific theory of alcoholism, of juvenile delinquency, of drug abuse, of paranoid schizophrenia, of aggressive behavior, and so on. Each of these theories would attempt to explain why an individual becomes predisposed to the particular forms of deviant behavior and the circumstances under which an individual is enabled to adopt the particular deviant pattern. However, when research efforts (particularly of a nonlongitudinal variety) focus upon a specific kind of deviant behavior it is frequently difficult to determine whether one is explaining why an individual is predisposed to *some* form of deviance or why he adopted that particular form of deviance. If, for example, alcoholic and nonalcoholic subjects were compared for the purpose of constructing a theory of alcoholism, the observed differences between the two groupings along a number of dimensions might or might not be observed in other comparisons between subjects characterized by some other form of deviance and nondeviant subjects. In order to distinguish between factors that predispose an individual to *some* form of deviance and those that account for the adoption of a particular form of deviance — an operation essential for the construction of special theories of deviant behavior — a variety of patterns of deviant behaviors must be considered simultaneously within the framework of a more general theory of deviant behavior. Such a general theory would identify the factors that were common to the adoption of one or another of a range of deviant behavior patterns and thereby would permit the distinction to be drawn between such common factors and those that were uniquely relevant in explanations of the genesis of particular forms of deviant behavior.

The recent literature associated with several patterns of deviant behavior suggested that common factors in the adoption of any of a wide variety of patterns of deviant behavior could be identified and that, therefore, the construction of a general theory of deviant behavior was feasible. More specifically, such factors were manifestly related to, or interpretable in terms of, the person's self-attitudes. From these suggestions the provisional outline of a general theory of deviant behavior began to emerge, centering around two propositions: (1) negative self-attitudes significantly increase the probability that deviant behavior patterns will be adopted; and (2) deviant behavior patterns function to change self-attitudes in a more favorable direction. This is not to say that the emerging theoretical model is a one-factor (self-attitudes) explanation of deviant behavior. Rather, the theoretical model suggests that the complex factors that influence the adoption of deviant patterns do so in interaction with, or mediated by, self-attitudes.

After a provisional outline of an emerging general theory of deviant behavior was formulated, another task was undertaken in preparation for empirical testing of the model: determining the "goodness of fit" of the model's core features with the existing research literature. The outline of the model was developed inductively during the consideration of an unsystematically selected number of studies of particular patterns of deviant behavior, so whether the central features of the theoretical model would be congruent with a more detailed examination of the literature dealing with specific modes of deviant behavior remained to be determined. If this congruence did not exist, then the model would have to be reformulated prior to rigorous testing of the theory.

It must be emphasized that the word "Toward" in the title of Part I of this book, "Toward a General Theory of Deviant Behavior," is used advisedly. The purpose here is not to present a fully developed theory of deviant behavior but rather to present a number of core propositions for such a theory. The more inclusive theory will be an outgrowth of the processes of seeking answers to the questions raised by these propositions on the one hand and previously formulated hypotheses and verified propositions dealing with deviant behavior on the other hand.

This book deals primarily with the reciprocal relationships between self-attitudes and deviant behavior, as well as those influences that are viewed as impinging directly on these relationships. Variables that appear to have less direct, but nevertheless appreciable, influence on these relationships will be less under discussion. Notable among such variables are social structural conditions, which are here recognized as having significant but indirect effects upon the adoption and stabilization of deviant response patterns.[5] For example, in the context of the emerging theoretical model, the condition of disjunction between culturally shared goals and institutionalized means for achieving the goals (Merton, 1957) might influence in turn the individual's failure, his consequent self-perception of failure, resultant self-rejecting attitudes, and the adoption of deviant modes of adaptation to his negative self-attitudes. With regard to the stabilization of deviant patterns, again from the point of view of the emerging theoretical model, the social structural variables subsumed under the "labeling" or "societal reaction" perspective (Becker, 1963; Erickson, 1968; Freidson, 1965; Goffman, 1963; Kitsuse, 1964; Lemert, 1951, 1967; Matza, 1969; Scheff, 1966) might influence the adoption of deviant patterns by either making the adoption of such patterns so apparently costly to his self-esteem that the person declines these potential routes to self-enhancement, or, alternatively, might effectively insulate the deviant from further normative influences (by severe reactions to initial deviance) so that the only apparently open route to self-enhancement is through commitment to, and effective performance of, deviant roles. However, although in the course of developing the core propositions in subsequent chapters frequent references are made to the points at which bridges with these social structural conditions and processes could be constructed, a detailed development of these relationships is beyond the purpose of this volume.

Nor, since the purpose of this volume is to point toward a *general* theory of deviant behavior, will much emphasis be placed upon the social structural conditions such as the nature of the illegitimate opportunity structure (Cloward and Ohlin, 1960) that might influence the adoption of particular modes of deviant response through making apparent the net self-enhancing potential of these patterns. Again, although reference will be made to such variables at different points in the following chapters (notably Chapters 8 and 9), the primary purpose of this volume is to consider why people come to adopt *some* form, rather than a *particular* form, of deviant behavior.

ORGANIZATION OF THE VOLUME

The results of the theory formulation and the determination of its compatibility with the research literature make up the substance of this volume. After a relatively brief presentation of the outline of the emergent general theory of deviant behavior in Part I, the literature dealing with selected categories of deviant behavior will be examined in Part II with a view to determining whether or not the existing literature is congruent with the central features of the theory proposed for explaining why individuals who had not previously adopted such behavior patterns adopt modes of behavior that deviate from the normative expectations of the group(s) in which the individuals hold membership. When particular categories of behavior are defined as deviant, the assumption is always made (though it is not always demonstrable) that the behavior in question deviates from the normative expectations of the groups of which the subjects were members *prior to adopting the modes of deviant behavior under consideration.*

SUMMARY

The purposes of the volume are described as twofold. First the core propositions of a general theory of deviant behavior address the question of why individuals are predisposed to adopt some form of deviant behavior, defined in terms of the failure to conform to the normative expectations applied to the subject by others in his membership group whether due to the subject's lack of motivation to conform or his motivation to violate the normative expectations in question. The second purpose is the discussion of the compatibility of the emerging theory, which places self-attitudes in a particularly strategic position, with the existing research literature dealing with specific modes of deviant behavior.

NOTES

[1] It should be noted that all or most members of the group are said to *share* normative expectations as to how specified types of people in specified situations will and should behave. It is not asserted that all group members will behave in a uniform manner. Thus, all members of the group (men and women alike) will agree that men should have certain attributes and behave in certain ways while, perhaps, women will and should have other attributes and behave in other ways; or, all group members (leaders and followers alike) agree that designated leaders will and should have certain attributes and behave in certain ways while, perhaps, followers will have other specified attributes and behave in other ways. While shared normative expectations *might* apply to all members of the group this is not necessarily the case.

2 The question to which this book addresses itself is why people who had not previously done so come to adopt deviant response patterns. This question implies that the adoption of the deviant pattern is indeed a *response* to preexisting circumstances that is under the control of conscious or unconscious personal (affective, cognitive, or conative) processes. That is, the deviant behavior is to be explained in motivationally relevant terms. The instances of failure to conform to the applicable normative expectations of the person's membership group(s) that are said to fall into this first category of deviant behaviors are by definition not motivationally relevant responses and are beyond the personal control of the individual (who presumably does not wish to be poor, ugly, weak, ill, and so on). As such they are not relevant objects of explanation within the context of the general question posed above.

However, this is not to say that the first category of deviations from shared normative expectations may not contribute to the explanation of motivationally relevant deviant responses (the second category of instances of failure to conform to shared normative expectations). The former deviations, for example, might serve as stimuli for motivationally relevant deviant responses as when the possession of stigmatized attributes influences the person to actively reject the group standards by which he is stigmatized and, rather, to emphasize the "virtue" of the stigma.

3 It may be argued that instances of involuntary deviance are not socially defined as deviant behavior, in that normative expectations applying to particular social categories implicitly assume the ability to perform appropriately. In the absence of such ability, the subject is assigned to a different social category, to which a different set of normative expectations apply. Thus, a paraplegic is not expected to perform up to the same standards of athletic prowess as apply to other adolescent boys. The report of Zahn (1973), for example, is relevant to this question. On the other hand it might be argued that those who are assigned statuses of "disabled" or "ill" are treated as deviant by virtue of their assignment to the "deviant status". For interesting discussions of disability as deviant behavior see Pflanz and Rohde (1970) and Freidson (1965). In a similar vein, an individual may be more disvalued and less rewarded by virtue of such involuntary "deviations" as being born poor and black in a society that values being rich and white.

4 Terms such as "criminal" and "delinquent" reflect the negative evaluations of such behaviors by some other group. Within the group under study, such behaviors may well be regarded as normative, and deviations from these patterns may be regarded as contranormative.

5 In Cohen's (1966:47) terms this distinction might be said to parallel the differentiation between psychological and sociological levels of explanation by which the explanation under consideration would be considered primarily psychological by virtue of its concern with variables relevant to motivation to deviance. The lesser emphasis on the variables and processes in the more inclusive social system that in their turn influence the variables involved in the psychological explanation would preclude labeling the explanation treated in this volume as a sociological theory. However, rather than labeling the exposition of the following chapters as a "psychological explanation" it might be more correct to say that the narrative emphasizes the psychological aspects of a theory that also incorporates sociological aspects. This volume explicitly recognizes the sociological input but has elected to expand upon the (in Cohen's terms) more psychological aspects of the explanation of deviant behavior.

Chapter 2

The Self-Esteem Motive

The theoretical model, the outline of which will emerge in the present volume, is based upon the premise that the self-esteem motive is universally and characteristically (that is, under ordinary circumstances) a dominant motive in the individual's motivational system.[1] In the present chapter the self-esteem motive will be defined, the individual development of the motive will be discussed, and the research literature that appears to relate to observations of the self-esteem motive will be examined.

DEFINITION OF THE SELF-ESTEEM MOTIVE

The self-esteem motive is defined as the need of the person to maximize the experience of positive self-attitudes or self-feelings and to minimize the experience of negative self-attitudes or self-feelings.[2]

Positive self-attitudes are referred to in the behavorial science literature by any of a number of terms, including feelings of self-respect, worth, approval, regard, acceptance, as well as esteem. In like manner negative self-attitudes might be noted by any of a variety of phrases, including feelings of self-derogation, rejection, hate. Whichever of these or similar terms are employed below, however, self-attitudes or self-feelings should be understood to refer to the affective or emotional responses of an individual to himself; they refer to the emotional experiences of the subject upon perceiving and evaluating his own attributes and behaviors.

Although in reality self-perception, self-evaluation, and self-feeling are so intimately interrelated that it is difficult to draw operational distinction between them,[3] these three modes of response by a subject to himself are distinguished for analytic purposes. Self-feeling refers to the emotional responses of an individual to himself. Self-perception (and related terms such as self-conception) refers to the individual's cognitive responses to himself. (The self as an object of cognitive awareness and structuring is referred to by such terms as self-image and self-concept[4].) Self-evaluation refers to the judgmental responses of an individual to himself regarding the degree to which he or particular aspects of himself approximate desirable qualities.[5]

Although, as will be apparent below, self-attitudes or self-feelings are profoundly and directly influenced by self-perceptions and self-evaluations, self-attitudes as providing the goals of the self-esteem motive will remain the focus of this discussion.[6]

DEVELOPMENT OF THE SELF-ESTEEM MOTIVE

The self-esteem motive is viewed as the normal outcome of the infant's initial dependency upon adult human beings for satisfaction of basic biological needs, among which perhaps the most apparent (to the infant) is hunger. From the base of biological dependency the person is said to pass through the stages of learning to need other people, to need the expression of positive attitudes toward oneself from others, and finally to need the expression of positive self-attitudes.

The Need for Other People

Since the infant is in fact dependent upon the parent or parent surrogate for the satisfaction of basic biological needs, in time and with the development of increasing discriminative ability the infant may be expected to subjectively associate need satisfaction with the presence of specific adult figures. For example, the infant will come to perceive a relationship between the instances in which his hunger is assuaged on the one hand and the presence of the mother on the other hand: the probability is far greater that the infant's hunger will be assuaged if the mother or mother surrogate is present than if she is not present. As the presence of the adult figure increasingly becomes associated with need satisfaction, the former phenomenon comes to evoke the same kind of responses as the initial need satisfaction. Just as the total need satisfaction experience (feeding) or intrinsic aspects of it (the nipple, the taste of milk, the stomach filling up) evoke feelings of pleasure, tension reduction, and so on, so does the associated phenomenon, the presence of the adult figure, come to evoke pleasurable experiences. Just as the presentation of a stimulus associated with the feeding experience (the sight of the bottle or breast) evokes positive excitatory emotional responses in anticipation of need satisfaction (feeding) so does the presentation of the parent come to evoke similar emotional responses. In short, the perception of the mother's presence evokes pleasurable emotional responses in the infant. Thus, the mother's presence becomes an intrinsically gratifying experience for the infant where formerly it was only gratifying to the infant in conjunction with the satisfaction of the infant's biological needs. The mother's presence is now said to be an acquired need (independent of its association with satisfaction of the infant's biological needs), to have positive motivational significance just as the satisfaction of biological needs is said to have positive motivational significance. Just as the infant cries for relief of his hunger so will he (given his newly acquired need) cry for the presence of his mother whether or not he is aware of current biological needs.

The Need for Positive Attitudes From Others

Insofar as the mother and/or other adults[7] have become motivationally significant features of his environment the infant is likely to become extremely sensitive to their presence and to phenomena associated with their presence — that is, the range of behaviors manifested by the adult figures. In her continuing role of ministering to the physical needs of the infant the mother or mother surrogate will produce a variety of such behaviors, including facial expressions, body postures, physical gestures and completed acts, and vocalizations. At times her facial expressions take a form that an observer might describe as a smile and at other times assume a form that might be described as a frown; at times her body posture might be described as relaxed and at other times rigid; on occasion her gestures and acts might be described as expressing approval or love and on other occasions as expressing annoyance or disapproval; on some occasions her vocalizations might be harsh, loud, and frequent while on other occasions her vocalizations might be soothing, quiet, and infrequent. The mother will tend to display some rather than other of these culturally patterned behaviors depending upon the concrete circumstances; and which of these behaviors are performed might well be associated with the degree to which the infant experiences need satisfaction. Thus, during the acts of feeding or washing the infant the mother might characteristically be relaxed, smile, and speak softly, while during periods in which the harassed mother must delay feeding the hungry infant she might characteristically speak in loud and harsh tones and handle the infant roughly.

The mother's behavioral responses toward the child that accompany (or result in) the child's experience of need satisfaction (pleasure) or need dissatisfaction (pain) might be responses that are unrelated to the child's behavior, as when she expresses annoyance toward the child because she had an argument with a friend or behaves kindly toward the infant because her husband complimented her. Or, perhaps more probably, the mother's behaviors toward the child that are associated with the infant's experience of pleasure or pain might be responses to the infant's behavior, as when the mother claps, smiles, and hugs the infant who has displayed a new ability, or when the mother yells at or slaps the infant for overturning a vase. In either case, to the extent that certain behaviors by the mother do in fact consistently appear in conjunction with, or result in, the infant's experience of need gratification the infant will likely come to subjectively associate these behaviors with these experiences of need gratification (or need frustration).

These behaviors by the mother, which in fact are displayed in conjunction with the acts of satisfying (or frustrating) the infant's needs (such as hunger or the otherwise avoidance of physical pain) and which are subjectively associated by the infant with his experience of satisfaction or frustration, might be described briefly as expressions of parental attitudes. That is, if an observer or the mothers themselves were asked to interpret the meaning of these maternal behaviors they would likely interpret them in terms of expressions of positive or negative emotional responses.

As these maternal attitudes become increasingly associated in the infant's awareness with experiences of satisfaction or frustration of his physical needs the expressions of attitudes themselves come to evoke the same kinds of emotional responses that the experiences of physical need satisfaction or frustration evoked. Just as the experience of hunger evoked subjective feelings of distress, so would the expressions of negative attitudes toward the child (harsh tones, loud voice, rough handling, turning away, saying "naughty") by the mother now evoke subjective feelings of distress *even in circumstances in which the infant was not aware of current frustration of physical needs*. Just as the experience of alleviation of hunger evoked feelings of pleasure, satisfaction, or tension release so are such feelings now evoked by expressions of positive attitudes (a soft vocal tone, a caress, drawing near, saying "good boy") by the mother toward the child, again, independently of any current experience by the infant of satisfaction of physical needs. Thus, as a result of the infant's sensitivity to the range of behaviors associated with the mother's presence (an acquired need) and of the infant's discrimination between maternal behaviors that are consistently associated with the circumstances of satisfying the infant's physical needs and the maternal behaviors that are consistently associated with the circumstances of frustrating the infant's physical needs, the expression of positive (negative) maternal attitudes has become an intrinsically gratifying (distressing) experience where formerly its gratificational relevance was in conjunction with the experience of physical need satisfaction (frustration). The infant may be said to have acquired a need to evoke positive attitudinal responses (and to avoid negative attitudinal responses) by the mother. The attitudinal responses of the mother have achieved motivational significance in that the subject will so behave as to evoke the expression of positive attitudes and to avoid the expression of negative attitudes by the mother toward himself (just as the satisfaction of physical needs present at birth and the presence of the mother, a need acquired since birth, were said to have motivational significance in that the subject behaves so as to achieve satisfaction of these needs).

The Need for Positive Self-Attitudes

It has been asserted that the child who has acquired the need to evoke positive (and to avoid negative) attitudinal responses from others in his environment would attempt to behave so far as possible in ways that would satisfy this need.

However, if this goal is to be achieved certain conditions must be fulfilled. Although, as has been stated above, the attitudinal responses to the child by adult figures may occasionally be the consequence of factors unrelated to the child's attributes, it is more often the case that expressions of positive or negative attitudes toward the child by others are consequences of the behaviors and characteristics manifested by the child. The adults' attitudinal responses represent in large measure culturally patterned expressions of their perceptions and evaluations of the degree to which the child's behaviors and attributes conform to the (again, in large measure) culturally patterned normative expectations that the adults apply to the child. To the extent that the child manifests "approved" behaviors and attributes, others will respond with expressions of positive attitudes, and to the extent that the child manifests "disapproved" behaviors and attributes, others will respond with expressions of negative attitudes.[8]

Insofar as certain of his behaviors and attributes are consistently associated with the actual occurrence of motivationally significant experiences (that is, being the object of positive or negative attitudinal responses) the subject will learn to *subjectively associate* the attitudinal responses of others on the one hand with his own attributes and behaviors on the other hand. For example, he is able to perceive that people consistently express "positive" attitudes (laugh, pay attention, say "good boy") when he behaves in certain ways (smiles, walks, plays with a ball, eats his food) and consistently expresses "negative" attitudes (frown, yell at him, say "don't") when he behaves in other ways (cries, sits passively, plays with a doll, throws his food).[9]

Because of the perceived association between the child's attributes and behaviors on the one hand and the attitudinal responses of other people on the other hand, the child becomes emotionally invested in being able to anticipate what sorts of attitudinal responses will be expressed by others toward particular subject traits and behaviors. The ability of the subject to successfully predict the attitudinal responses of others to particular subject attributes or behaviors would (within limits) permit the individual to behave in ways that would satisfy the acquired need to maximize the expression of positive (and minimize the expression of negative) attitudes by others toward the subject. That is, the subject could purposively behave in ways which would predictably evoke the desired attitudinal responses to the subject by others.

Such an ability would involve the subject in adopting the perspective of the other person and vicariously responding to himself *as if* he were the other person. That is, the subject in his own imagination would perceive, evaluate, and attitudinally respond to himself as the other person would be presumed to respond.[10] The subject could then vary his own behavior in a way that was consistent with the expectation that the other would respond with positive rather than negative attitudes.[11]

In the course of imagining how the other person responds (or would respond) to the subject attitudinally, the subject expresses an attitude toward himself that is the symbolic representation of the imagined attitudinal response of the other person and then responds to his own attitudinal expression as if the other person had actually expressed the attitude. In view of the symbolic association between the subject's own attitudinal expression and the imagined attitudinal responses of others, and in view of the subject's previously discussed acquired need to be the object of positive attitudinal responses (and to avoid being the object of negative attitudinal responses) by others, the subject would be expected to respond to his own expression of positive attitudinal responses toward himself with feelings of satisfaction, gratification, tension release, and so on, and would be expected to respond to his own negative attitudinal responses to himself with feelings of tension, subjective distress, depression, and so on. The subject's own attitudinal responses to himself thus become motivationally significant. Through their original association with the imagined attitudes of others, the subject's attitudinal expressions toward himself tend to consistently evoke relatively gratifying/distressing emotional experiences. The subject at this point may be said to have acquired the need to respond to himself in terms of positive attitudes and thereby to evoke further gratifying emotional experiences and to avoid responding to himself in terms of negative attitudes that would evoke continued experiences of subjective distress. In short, the subject is now said to have acquired the need to maximize the experience of positive self-attitudes and to minimize the experience of negative self-attitudes. Stated another way, the subject has acquired the self-esteem motive.

In summary, the self-esteem motive is seen as the normal outcome of processes that may be traced back to the infant's initial dependence upon adult figures for satisfaction of physical needs. Through the association between experiences of satisfaction of physical needs and the presence of adult figures the infant acquires a need for the physical presence of adult figures and becomes particularly sensitive to phenomena associated with the presence of adults (that is, the range of adult behaviors). The infant's perception of the actually existing association between satisfaction/frustration of the infant's physical needs and particular adult behaviors (which an observer or the adult in question might describe as expressions of positive or negative attitudes) leads to the infant's acquisition of a need to be the object of positive attitudes (and to avoid being the object of negative attitudes) expressed by significant other adults. In order to maximize the satisfaction of this acquired need, the child adopts the role of the other adults and perceives, evaluates, and expresses attitudes toward himself from their point of view in order to permit himself to behave in ways which he imagines will evoke positive attitudes from others, and the child then responds to his own expressions of attitudes toward himself as if they were in fact the expressed attitudes of others with positive or negative affect. In this way, through the symbolic association between the imagined attitudinal responses of others and his own attitudinal responses toward himself, the child acquires the need to behave in ways that will evoke positive self-attitudes and avoid negative self-attitudes — a need expressed as the self-esteem motive.[12]

By these processes the self-esteem motive might be said to develop. However, it should be emphasized that the validity of the theoretical model to be developed below does not depend upon the acceptance of all or some of the processes proposed as those leading to the development of the self-esteem motive. Rather, it depends upon acceptance of the premise that the self-esteem motive normally develops in the human being by whatever processes. The prevalence of the self-esteem motive can be argued independently of the processes by which it is said to develop.

PREVALENCE OF THE SELF-ESTEEM MOTIVE

The self-esteem motive is universally and characteristically a dominant motive; in all past and contemporary cultures it characteristically develops as a result of processes set in motion by the child's initial dependence upon others for satisfaction of basic physical needs present at birth. However, this is not to say that the development of the self-esteem motive is inevitable. Indeed, a number of circumstances might arise that could disrupt the processes such as those described above as ordinarily eventuating in an acquired self-esteem motive. For example, if the adults in the child's early experiences were either invariable (that is, uniformly positive or negative regardless of the nature of the child's behavior) or inconsistent (that is, the same behavior would sometimes evoke positive responses and at other times negative responses) the child might not learn to associate particular behaviors on his part with particular adult attitudes toward him and thus might not develop the need for positive attitudinal responses from others or the need for positive self-attitudes (which is based, presumably, on the need for positive attitudinal responses by others). However, such circumstances are regarded as rare, and the development of the self-esteem motive is viewed as a normal outcome in the psychosocial development of the human being.

If indeed the acquisition of the self-esteem motive is normal, then existing empirical data should be compatible with the inference of the prevalence of this motive. Even a brief examination of the relevant literature suggests that such an inference is warranted. The prevalence in a specified population of a motive to behave so as to maintain positive self-attitudes may be inferred from four kinds of observations: the relative frequency of positive/negative self-descriptions; the characteristic responses to self-devaluing situations and histories; the association between self-devaluating experiences and subjective distress; and the relative stability of positive/negative self-attitudes over time.

Frequency of Positive/Negative Self-Descriptions

The prevalence of the self-esteem motive could be inferred from observations that at any given time self-descriptions couched in negative terms are relatively rare, and self-descriptions in terms of qualities that are personally and/or socially desirable are relatively frequent in a specified population. This inference could be drawn whether the self-descriptions truly reflected the objective prevalence of admirable qualities, the subjects' misperceptions of their (in fact) nonadmirable qualities as if they were admirable, or the subjects' desire to avoid describing themselves in terms of their realistically perceived nonadmirable qualities. All three outcomes could be outcomes of behavior in the service of the self-esteem motive. In the first instance the subjects would have behaved to achieve admirable qualities and thus justify positive self-evaluation and consequent positive self-attitudes. In the second instance the subjects would have distorted their perceptions of reality in ways that again would permit positive self-evaluations and consequent positive self-feelings. In the third instance the subjects would have behaved to cloak their nonadmirable qualities thereby avoiding negative evaluations by others, which would have presumably influenced negative self-evaluation and consequent negative self-attitudes.

The following studies will serve to illustrate the range of investigations that provide observations of the relative frequency of favorable self-descriptions in given populations.

Chamblis (1964) presented data derived from the responses of undergraduates to adjective checklists that suggested that positive self-images are prevalent and negative self-images are relatively rare. The responses of 375 undergraduate freshmen to a 137-item adjective checklist revealed that the items most frequently used by respondents to describe themselves had highly favorable connotations while the adjectives least frequently checked were unflattering. Moreover, the responses of 140 subjects to a 30-item checklist revealed that respondents were more likely to see the positive than the negative traits as typical of them and were much more likely to see the negative traits as "never typical" of them (37 percent) than they were to thus characterize the positive traits (less than 1 percent).[13]

Wylie (1965) hypothesized and observed among 387 Air Force male subjects a tendency toward a "self-favorability bias" in ratings of evaluative traits. That is, the subjects generally rated themselves more favorably than the reality of the situation demanded. This observation was based on the results of two analyses. In the first analysis the subjects' estimates of how others in their living group would most likely rate them on five evaluative traits (friendliness, likability, generosity, intelligence, and sense of humor) were compared with the ratings actually received by the subject from his peers. The subjects significantly overestimated the ratings they would receive from their peers on the last four traits. In the second analysis a self-favorability bias was indicated by the proportion of subjects whose estimates of where their peers would rate them on the evaluative scales fell in the top half of the ratings they assigned to their group "as compared to a fifty-fifty proportion one would expect if all subjects' social self-concept ratings were accurate, or if chance alone determined their ratings" (Wylie, 1965:137). The observed proportions of subjects who placed their self-ratings in the top half were significantly higher than 50 percent once again on the last four of the five evaluative traits.

In a similar vein a self-favorability bias was apparent from the results of a study (French, 1968:114) in which ninety-two members of management offered self-evaluations of their performance relative to other men on the same unit doing the same job. Presumably if the subjects were evaluating themselves in a totally objective manner they would have been equally distributed above and below the fiftieth percentile of the scale. However it was reported in fact that only two of the subjects evaluated their performance as falling below the fiftieth percentile. In addition it was observed that "eighty-two percent of the men reported that their self-evaluation was higher than the evaluation given them by their employer."

The tendency of subjects to rate themselves positively and/or to avoid rating themselves negatively is suggested by results from a number of other studies cited by Crowne and Stephens (1961:113-117) in the course of their discussion of the possible relationship between self-evaluative responses on the one hand and phenomena variously referred to by such terms as "defensive behavior," "self-protective responses," and "social desirability" on the other hand. For example, in one investigation Cowan and Tongas (1959) reported a high (.91) correlation between ratings of social desirability and the self-concept score of the Index of Adjustment and Values. In another study Kogan and his associates (1957) found a correlation of .85 between self-description and social desirability values among a grouping of male college students.

French (1968:148) also reviewed a number of studies and tentatively concluded that these studies tended to agree in their observation of a high degree of association (r=0.85 to 0.90) between social desirability values of self-descriptive items and the mean endorsement rate of the item. He interprets these results as indicating "that there are common values in our culture and that these common values are related to the proportion of people endorsing self-descriptive statements embodying these values."

The studies cited up to this point refer to the tendency of subjects to consciously describe themselves in favorable terms. However, reports exist that suggest that a tendency toward *unconscious* favorable self-evaluating may also exist in the population. Fisher and Mirin (1966:1097) cite earlier observations by another investigator to the effect that "when persons were asked to judge representations of themselves (e.g. shadow profile) in a context where they had no reason to expect to encounter such self-representations, they showed a surprising inability to recognize them and simultaneously gave evidence of responding in an exaggeratedly favorable fashion" and presented other data compatible with these observations. Thirty-one male college students were asked to rate tachistoscopically presented shadow profiles and full-face pictures of themselves and four other people for degree of friendliness and intelligence. The pictures were obtained without the subjects' knowledge. With the exceptions of three instances of partial recognition of the full-face pictures, the subjects did not appear to recognize their pictures. Although significant differences were not observed for the full-face pictures, the subjects did tend to ascribe significantly more favorable intelligence and friendliness ratings to their own shadow profiles than to the profiles of others.

It has been argued that the several studies cited above that offer evidence of the tendency of subjects to describe themselves in overly favorable terms may be interpreted as support for the assertion that the self-esteem motive is "universal" and "characteristic" among human beings. Nevertheless, occasionally data describe a tendency among subjects in certain cultural groupings to underrate themselves on desirable traits. Such data could be interpreted as supporting the hypothesis that the self-esteem motive, rather than being universal, is variably prevalent from culture to culture. A case in point is the observation reported by Trow and Pu (1927) of the tendency, among a grouping of eighteen Chinese college students, for the subjects to underrate themselves on desirable traits, a conclusion that contradicts the results of specified self-rating studies among American subjects. However, it is argued here that such data could be accounted for by the values of the culture in question: as the authors assert, the tendency to underrate the self may be an expression of a highly valued character trait in traditional Chinese culture — the trait of humility. Thus, rather than contraindicating the existence of the self-esteem motive, the behavior of the

Chinese subjects (in underrating themselves) suggests that they are being guided by just such a motive. Self-underestimating behavior is interpretable as approximating a culturally (and presumably personally) prized value and therefore as a partial justification for self-enhancing attitudes among the Chinese student subjects. Through apparent self-depreciation the subject in fact gains self-acceptance.

Characteristic Responses to Self-Devaluation

The second kind of observation from which the prevalence of the self-esteem motive could be inferred is that relating to the ways in which the population characteristically responds to self-devaluating experiences. The prevalence could be inferred if the subjects' responses were apparently calculated to increase positive (and defend against negative) self-evaluation and, consequently, increase positive (and decrease negative) self-attitudes, whether through readjustment of their response patterns to more closely approximate positively valued goals; misperception of their attributes, behaviors, or circumstances; or a reordering of their values, and so on.

Investigations of such responses to self-devaluation may be distributed conveniently among four categories: responses to current self-devaluation; responses associated with relatively low self-esteem; responses to both current self-devaluation and to relatively low self-esteem; and self-devaluation in the service of self-esteem.

Responses to Current Self-Devaluation. The first category includes observations of the ways people respond to current self-devaluing experiences with behaviors that have self-enhancing implications. These observations generally make no assumptions regarding the subject's characteristic level of self-esteem. Among the potentially self-enhancing responses illustrated by the following studies are physical avoidance, reordering of values, devaluation of the source, and perceptual distortion.

Defensive avoidance in response to potentially devaluing circumstances was suggested by data reported by Dosey and Meisels (1969). In three experimental situations, university student subjects who were subjected to the presumed personal stress of having their physical attractiveness called into question were compared with subjects in nonstress conditions with regard to their use of personal space. The three situations in which personal space was determined called for the subjects to physically approach each other, take seats close to or far from the experimenter, and trace one silhouette in relation to another. In two of the three situations (the first and third) the subjects in the stress condition were observed to employ significantly greater spatial distances than the subjects in the nonstress condition. The results were thus interpretable as indicating that the increase of spatial distance is used by individuals to protect themselves in response to situations in which their self-esteem is threatened.

Another possible mode of response to self-devaluating circumstances would be a reordering of one's values. Such a pattern of response would decrease a subject's degree of self-rejection to the extent that he was able to decrease his valuation of qualities that he lacked and to increase his valuation of attributes that he possessed. Data reported by Ludwig and Maehr (1967) suggest that a reordering of values does take place following self-devaluing circumstances. These data concerned the relationship between the experience of approval/disapproval and changes in behavioral preference. The experimental situation called for a physical development expert to indicate either approval or disapproval of the junior high school student subjects' performance on various physical tasks. Changes in behavioral preference were determined with reference to responses to a twenty-item "Behavioral Choice Questionnaire" through which the subjects rated their preference for physical or nonphysical activity along a nine-point scale. Ten of the items were directly pertinent to the experimental evaluation situation while the other ten items referred to physical activities that were relatively unrelated to the experimental evaluation situation. The behavioral preference ratings were obtained one week before the experimental evaluation treatment, immediately following the evaluation, one week later, and three weeks later. Among the findings was the observation that the approval treatment tended to be followed by an increased preference for activities directly related to the treatment while the disapproval treatment tended to be followed by a decreased preference for such activities. Thus the results are compatible with the expectations that people would defensively respond to self-devaluing experiences by lowering the value they previously attached to associated aspects of the experiential situation.

The influence of self-devaluing circumstances in evoking self-enhancing responses is suggested by a study (Harvey, 1962) in which 188 undergraduate university student subjects were exposed to ratings of themselves that were more unfavorable than their initial self-ratings by one of five gradations. The negative ratings were apparently made by either a friend or a comparative stranger. In general, increasingly negative ratings by others tended to result in increasingly negative evaluations of the source; increasing error in recall (in a positive direction) of the ratings received up to the most extreme discrepancy; increasing judgments that the source used the scale differently from them (the subjects), was not serious in his ratings, and did not follow instructions in making the evaluations; increasing ratings of the source as careless and socially insensitive; decreasing belief that the source knew the subject well; and increasing disbelief that the source had actually made the negative ratings they saw.

Responses Associated With Low Self-Esteem. The studies in the first category were characterized by the introduction of self-devaluing experiences into the situation and the observation of subsequent responses to these experiences. Unlike these studies the second grouping of investigations contains studies in which subjects with different preexisting levels of self-esteem are compared with regard to the presence of behaviors interpretable as serving self-defensive or self-enhancing functions. In these studies a given level of self-esteem is viewed as the end product of a history of experiences that are appropriate to that level. That is, low self-esteem is said to imply a history of self-devaluing experiences. An association between low self-esteem and a potentially self-enhancing pattern thus would be congruent with the assertion that self-devaluing experiences tend to evoke self-enhancing responses, an observation from which the prevalence of the self-esteem motive is inferred. The following investigations were selected to illustrate this category of studies.

In support of the postulate that individuals tend to behave in ways that reduce the adverse impact of self-devaluing circumstances are those observations relating to the tendency of people who more frequently have such experiences (that is, people with characteristically low self-evaluation) to assume self-defensive postures. Such observations were reported in the course of a study (Washburn, 1962:85-86), the results of which will be reported in greater detail below, which offered support for the hypotheses that subjects with low self-evaluations, in comparison with subjects with high self-evaluations, were more likely to develop hostile defenses ("to be critical, suspicious, and lack identification with others") and retreating defenses ("to avoid coming to grips with problems and to deny reality").

The tendency of people to (perceptually and physically) avoid potentially self-devaluing situations is suggested by certain of Rosenberg's (1965:219, 226-227, 231) observations among a sample of high school students. He reports that subjects with lower self-esteem scores (and, therefore, those that may be presumed to be sensitive to the self-devaluation potential of certain situations) were more likely to manifest a tendency to daydream; express preferences for occupations that leave them free of supervision and involve little or no competition; and to indicate that it is relatively less important to them to get ahead in life than to subjects with higher self-esteem scores. These behaviors are all interpretable as patterns that facilitate the avoidance of situations in which they are likely to fail or the disappointment accompanying the failure.

Based on a study of some male Air Force trainees and women from an Eastern college, referred to earlier in another connection, Wylie (1965) reported that subjects with low self-regard were more likely to display the relatively specific defensive behaviors of rationalizing and projecting than subjects with high self-regard. The measures of rationalizing and projecting were based on the subject's tendency to systematically underestimate others when rating them (projection) and/or scores on a Rationalization-Projection Inventory. Self-regard was indexed by discrepancies between subject ratings of social self-concept on the one hand and the culturally stereotyped ideal self and/or personally stated self-ideal ratings on the other hand. It was expected that subjects with smaller self-ideal discrepancies would manifest less defensive behavior since they would have less need to so behave on the assumption that the smaller discrepancies indicated either realistically favorable self-concepts or the effective use of denial to alleviate anxiety.

Responses to Self-Devaluation and Low Self-Esteem. A third category of studies includes those investigations of self-enhancing responses to both current self-devaluing exeriences and characteristic level of self-esteem rather than to either of these phonomena alone. The following study will serve to illustrate this category.

The presence of the self-esteem motive might be indicated if people who frequently encounter self-devaluing circumstances (compared to people who infrequently encounter such circumstances) or people who find themselves in a particular self-devaluing situation (compared to people who are not currently experiencing self-devaluation) tended to respond with a behavior pattern that in the past has been subjectively associated with the production of self-enhancing experiences but that does not necessarily have any relevance to changing the current self-devaluing circumstances. Such a response pattern is suggested by data reported by Dittes (1959) concerning the relationship between self-esteem and a general response tendency to achieve closure defined as "the structuring of otherwise ambiguous stimuli so as to provide meaning and to end deliberation" (p. 355). The author assumed that in circumstances that threatened self-esteem the subject would become more motivated to increase his self-esteem through any of a number of means. One such method of increasing self-esteem would be through the achievement of closure on the further assumption that "such closure commonly acquires reward value as a source of self-esteem through learning experiences in which it has been associated with achievements, praise by other persons, and other fundamental sources of self-esteem . . . " (p. 355).

Based on these assumptions it was hypothesized that situationally induced threats to self-esteem would be associated with greater impulsiveness of closure. This hypothesis was supported in an experimental situation in which self-esteem was manipulated through the communication to the subjects of fictitious ratings of the subject by other group members. The data indicated that indeed the presumed threat to self-esteem of being poorly accepted was associated with significantly greater impulsiveness in closure. This relationship between situationally induced threats to self-esteem and closure was stronger for subjects with generally low self-esteem than among subjects with high self-esteem.[14] The findings then are compatible with the general postulate of a self-esteem motive in that people (particularly those with generally low self-esteem) in specific self-devaluing circumstances tend to behave in ways which will increase self-esteem. In the present case, the tendency toward impulsive closure observed among such people was interpreted as just such "a compensating source of self-esteem" (p. 354).

Self-Devaluation in the Service of the Self-Esteem Motive. All of the studies discussed above involve various methodological problems. For example, the investigations described in the second category above involve collecting data regarding self-devaluation and presumably self-enhancing responses at the same point in time, thus rendering it difficult to establish cause-effect relationships. However, studies involving one type of hypothetical self-enhancing or defensive responses pose a very special problem. The responses in question involve the expression of self-derogation as a way of reducing the degree of, or forestalling further, self-rejection. The demonstration of defensive responses involves the observation of presumably self-enhancing behaviors by self-derogating people in response to self-derogating circumstances. However, to say that self-derogating responses may also serve defensive, self-enhancing functions is to place the observer in the awkward position of hypothesizing that self-rejecting attitudes may eventuate in either self-enhancing (in the instance of effective defensive responses) *or* self-derogating (in instances where self-devaluation is said to serve a defensive function) attitudes. Thus whatever the actual result the findings may be said to support the hypothesis. In instances where negative self-attitudes are observed to be the consequence of self-devaluating experiences the resultant self-derogation may be interpreted in terms of either the absence of effective defensive responses or the use of self-derogation as a defense against the even more intense self-derogation which would occur in the absence of this response. Yet in spite of the methodological difficulties in distinguishing between self-derogation as a response to self-devaluating experiences and self-derogation as a defensive response, self-rejecting attitudes may be said to serve as an attempt to reduce the degree of, or prevent even more intense, self-derogating attitudes. Certainly the serving of such functions is consistent with a number of findings in the literature relating to self-attitudes.

Self-rejection may be thought of as an attempt to serve self-enhancing functions in either or both of two ways. First, the adoption of self-derogating attitudes may be a more or less effective attempt by the subjects to evoke positive attitudes toward themselves by significant others who in the past had held negative attitudes toward them. This would appear to be a particular instance of earning another person's approval by adopting his attitudes. Thus, paradoxically a person adopts another person's negative attitudes toward himself as a way of gaining approval from significant others and, through this approval, enhancing his self-attitudes. Congruent with this reasoning are the findings of certain studies reviewed by Wylie (1961: 153). These findings tended to support the hypothesis, based on the assumption that compliance was a defensive attempt to avoid displeasing others, that self-esteem would be inversely related to persuasibility.

The adoption of negative self-attitudes might function to prevent subsequent self-devaluation in a second way, by forestalling circumstances in which the individual would be likely to experience self-devaluation. For example, a person who defined himself as a person of low ability (a negative self-attitude) would not expect himself to perform well in a situation in which the ability in question was required. Nor, to the extent that his negative attitudes toward himself were shared by others, would others expect him to perform well. Consequently when he actually failed to perform well in future situations, he would not become the object of negative attitudes from others and negative self-attitudes. Such reasoning is compatible with the interpretation of their findings offered by Jones and Ratner (1967). Through the experimental communication of false test scores the subjects were induced to adopt low ability appraisals. The subjects then met either of two conditions. They were either given or not given the opportunity to commit themselves to the low ability appraisals by choosing a more or less difficult task to perform. The subjects then participated in a three-person social exchange situation in which they were positively evaluated by one peer and negatively evaluated by another. The results indicated that the subjects who were given the opportunity for commitment to self-appraisal more positively evaluated the peer sending positive evaluations than the peer sending negative evaluations. However, subjects who were not given the opportunity for commitment more positively evaluated the peer sending negative evaluations than the peer sending positive evaluations. The authors argued that ordinarily the acceptance of praise from others implies that the subject will participate effectively in difficult activities. However, the commitment to a low self-appraisal permits the individual to accept praise without the expectation of a high level of performance and the concomitant risk of failure. The experimental results thus were interpreted as providing support for the assertion that

> commitment to a low self-appraisal may protect a person from the undesirable implications of accepting social praise and reject-ing social censure. People appear to like praise, and they will respond favorably to it, providing that in so doing they are not also accepting its contingent responsibilities. Commitment to a low self-appraisal can effectively eliminate these respon-sibilities, and under such conditions praise can be accepted with impunity [Jones and Ratner, 1967: 445].

Self-Devaluation and Subjective Distress

If the self-esteem motive was indeed prevalent in a specified population, then by definition individuals would display negative affect, that is subjective distress, in response to negative self-perceptions and self-evaluations. Such subjective distress would be appreciably less in evidence in the absence of negative self-perceptions and self-evaluations. Thus, a third type of observation from which the prevalence of the self-esteem motive could be inferred is that relating to the affective responses of the subject to self-devaluating circumstances. The preva-lence of the self-esteem motive could be inferred if subjects were observed to more characteristically respond to negative self-evaluating experiences with negative affect and to more characteristically respond to positive self-evaluation with positive affect.

Empirical studies in fact have consistently observed significant associa-tions between chronically self-devaluating circumstances (as reflected in scores on self-esteem measures) on the one hand and such indices of subjective distress as anxiety and depressive affect on the other hand. The associations have been observed among subjects with variable characteristics (preadult as well as adult, and hospitalized as well as nonhospitalized) and over a period of time as well as at a single point in time.

Among studies of preadult populations is an investigation (Horowitz, 1962) of the relationship between anxiety and self-concept among a sample of upper elementary school children in Oregon. The investigator reported consistent negative correlations between the two variables such that high anxiety tended to be associated with a low self-concept. Rosenberg and Simmons (1971) in a study of third - to - twelfth grade pupils in Baltimore City public schools observed a tendency for pupils with low self-esteem scores to manifest high scores on a Guttman scale of depression as well as on a measure of anxiety.

In a study of subjects drawn from among New York State high school juniors and seniors, Rosenberg (1965) reported data indicating a strong association between self-esteem and measures of subjective distress including depressive affect and anxiety. Thus, on the basis of scores on a "depressive affect" scale, only 4 percent of the highest self-esteem grouping were classified as highly depressed while 80 percent of the subjects in the lowest self-esteem category were so classified. Similar results were obtained with regard to symptoms described as secondary physiological manifestations of anxiety,[15] such as hands sweating, sick headaches, nightmares, and trouble in getting to sleep and staying asleep. Considering ten such symptoms, only 19 percent of the subjects in the highest self-esteem category reported experiencing four or more of the symptoms "often" or "sometimes" while 69 percent of the lowest self-esteem subjects reported experiencing four or more of the symptoms often or sometimes.

In addition to the observations of relationships between self-esteem and self-reports of anxiety and depression, Rosenberg (1965) reported on the relationships between self-esteem and subject depression as observed by others. Among fifty young adult volunteers at the Clinical Center of the National Institutes of Health it was observed that nurses at the center were appreciably more likely to deny that subjects with high self-esteem scores, compared with subjects with low self-esteem scores, were "often gloomy" or "frequently disappointed."

Among the studies of adult populations were those reported by Kaplan and Pokorny (1969) and French (1968). Paralleling the findings of Rosenberg, Kaplan and Pokorny reported significant relationships between low self-esteem on the one hand and relatively high depressive affect and relatively frequent experiences of psychophysiological symptoms on the other hand among a sample of 500 adults. They also cited a number of other studies making similar observations. French (1968:143) referred to a study of eighty-one blue-collar workers in which a measure of self-esteem was inversely correlated at moderate levels (0.50 to 0.73) with a number of variables interpretable as indices of emotional distress, including depression, anxiety and tension, irritation, feeling burdened, and sadness.

The relationship between self-rejecting attitudes and manifestations of subjective distress were observed among psychiatric patients as well as normal subjects. For example, Harrow and his associates (1968) studying the self-perceptions of thirty-four recently hospitalized psychiatric patients, reported that depressed patients tended to have significantly lower self-images than nondepressed patients.

The studies reviewed above concerned the relationship between low self-esteem and indices of subjective distress at a single point in time. However, similar findings are apparent in investigations of changes in self-esteem over time. Thus Engel (1959), studying eight and tenth-grade pupils over a two-year period, observed that subjects who decreased in self-regard (as measured by Q sort) over the two-year period also manifested significantly higher scores on the D (depression) scale of the MMPI.

The consistent observation of significant associations between low self-evaluation and subjective distress then is congruent with the assumption of the prevalence of the self-esteem motive.

Stability of Positive/Negative Self-Attitudes

On the assumption that the avoidance of negative self-attitudes and the attainment of positive self-attitudes are indeed motives of human behavior it is to be expected that persons with initially negative self-attitudes would tend to change their attitudes in a more positive direction over time and those with initially positive self-attitudes would tend to be stable in their self-attitudes, that is, would maintain their positive self-attitudes. Observations consistent with these expectations constitute a fourth category of observations in support of the postulated prevalence of the self-esteem motive.

With regard to this fourth category of observations, individuals do appear to be more likely to change their self-attitudes over time in a positive direction than in a negative direction. Engel (1959: 214), reporting on the results of a study of the stability of the self-concept over a two-year period among public school student subjects, reported that indeed most of the change in the positive/negative quality of the self-concept occurred in the initially negative self-concept grouping:

> Ss who were classified as having negative self-concepts in 1954 more closely approached the mean by 1956. Such shift could be attributed to regression, except that no such shifting toward the mean took place in the case of Ss originally giving evidence of a positive self-concept.

The tendency of individuals to maintain this positive quality of their self-attitudes is suggested by certain of Rosenberg's (1965: 152-154) data. Adolescents with high self-esteem were observed to be appreciably more stable in their self-picture (that is, to be constant rather than changeable in the opinions or ideas they have of themselves) than adolsecents with low self-esteem.

French (1968: 149) also reports that stability of self-esteem, using the same measure of stability of self-esteem employed by Rosenberg, was positively correlated with measures of self-esteem among a sample of 188 tenth-grade boys.

Thus, this fourth grouping of studies along with those previously considered appear to be compatible with the inference of the prevalence of the self-esteem motive.[16]

SUMMARY

The emerging theoretical outline, intended to explain the adoption of deviant behavior patterns, is based upon the premise that the self-esteem motive, defined in terms of the person's need to achieve positive self-attitudes and to avoid negative self-attitudes, is universally characteristic of human beings. Self-attitudes in turn refer to the individual's emotional responses to self-perception and self-evaluation.

The self-esteem motive is said to be the normal outcome of the human infant's early dependency upon adult human needs for satisfaction of his basic biological needs. On the basis of this initial dependency the human being successively develops needs for the presence of other human beings, the expression of positive (and the avoidance of negative) attitudes toward himself by other human beings, and the experience of positive (and the avoidance of negative) self-attitudes.

In support of the assertion of the prevalence of the self-esteem motive four categories of empirical observations are discussed: the tendency of individuals to describe themselves in positive terms and to avoid negative self-descriptions; the tendency of people with low self-esteem and people in self-threatening circumstances to respond with behaviors serving self-defensive or self-enhancing functions; the tendency for people with low self-esteem to manifest subjective distress; and the tendency for subjects with positive self-attitudes to maintain this quality of their self-attitudes while people with negative self-attitudes tend to change their attitudes toward themselves in a more positive direction. These observations were interpreted as compatible with the postulate of the prevalence of the self-esteem motive in the sense that the assertion of the motive provides a parsimonious explanation of these various observations.

NOTES

[1] The proposition that the self-esteem motive is a characteristic or universal motive is implicit in the writings of a number of theorists. For example, as Becker (1962:60) states: "The child's unusually strong 'need for positive affect' is a basic human disposition. The presence of this need for positive affection is universal."

[2] The ideas presented below regarding the nature, universality, and genesis of the self-esteem motive represent a crystallization of ideas presented in, or suggested by, the writings of a number of personality theorists, including Adler (1927; Ansbacher and Ansbacher, 1956), Horney (1945, 1950), James (1890), G. H. Mead (1934), Murphy (1947), Rogers (1951a,b), Sullivan (1953), and Syngg and Combs (1949).

[3] For example, if an individual verbalizes "I am a hateful individual," he may at the same time be *perceiving* himself as a person who is hated by others in his environment, *evaluating* himself as a person who is worthy of hatred, and expressing negative *feelings* toward himself. On the other hand his behavior may be reflecting affectively neutral self-perceptions and self-evaluations. That is, he may perceive himself as an object of hatred by others and evaluate himself as worthy of hatred without experiencing concomitant negative self-feelings. It is often difficult to determine from a person's overt responses just which of these modes of response are operative.

Illustrations of the intimate interrelationship between self-perception, self-evaluation, and self-feeling may be found in the following three observations. First, it may be noted that the individual's values may well be part of his self-image. That is, he may perceive himself as a person who values intellectual pursuits, honesty, and group loyalty and who disvalues bodily pleasures, dishonesty, or individualistic pursuits. Second, an individual's specific self-evaluations may also be incorporated into the person's self-image so that he perceives himself as an individual who devalues his athletic ability or as a self-depreciating person in general. These self-perceptions may in turn become the object of self-evaluation processes. For example, a person may positively evaluate himself because of his ability to depreciate himself insofar as this self-evaluative behavior approximates other personally held values such as the ability to be "realistic" about one's limitations. Third, self-feelings may also be incorporated into the self-image and as such stimulate further self-evaluation and self-feeling. Thus a person who perceives himself as filled with self-hate may devalue himself and respond to this negative evaluation with negative self-feelings.

[4] A person's self-image may include perceptions of his physical aspects (big-boned, hook-nosed, weight 150 pounds), behavioral predispositions (aggressive, task-oriented, happy, logical), ascribed or achieved social positions (male, father, Roman Catholic, friend, businessman, motorist, middle class), characteristic role behaviors (a father who takes an interest in his children, and active member of the church, willing to do anything for a friend), specific behaviors in specific situations (someone who just told a "white" lie to his mother), and many other forms of reflexive meaning. See, for example, Gordon (1969).

[5] An individual's self-evaluations refer to the numerous judgments he makes regarding the degree to which his perceived attributes, behaviorial predispositions, and specific behaviors approximate desirable qualities or values such as beauty, utility, goodness, industriousness, and altruism. The desirable qualities or values in question may be conceptualized as continuous dimensions such that the desirable quality may be approximated in varying degrees (for example, a person may be more or less industrious, more or less beautiful) or as discrete and mutually exclusive categories (for example, a person is either good or he is bad, a person is either beautiful or not beautiful). The poles of the continuous dimensions or the discrete and mutually exclusive categories may be thought of in terms of opposite qualities, one of which is defined as desirable and the other of which is defined as undesirable (for example, beautiful vs. ugly, healthy vs. diseased, moral vs. immoral) or in terms of the presence or absence of a desirable or undesirable quality (for example, beautiful vs. nonbeautiful, healthy vs. nonhealthy, moral vs. nonmoral).

The qualities or values are "desirable" (or, in the instances of opposite poles or categories, "undesirable") in the sense that approximation to the value tends to evoke positive sanctions (rewards) and deviation from the value (or approximation of the opposite quality) tends to evoke negative sanctions (punishment). Thus an individual who is judged to be honest, industrious, efficient, or good looking compared to a person who is judged to be dishonest, less than industrious, inefficient, or not as good looking is more likely to receive expressions of approval, less likely to be shunned, more likely to be offered positions of responsibility, more likely to be invited into the company of others, and, in general, more likely to evoke behaviors defined as rewarding by his social group (and less likely to be the object of behaviors defined by his social group as punitive). To the extent that the individual accepts as his own the group's values, he will tend to apply positive and negative sanctions to himself depending upon the degree to which he perceives himself as approximating the desirable and deviating from the undesirable qualities. Generally, these sanctioning behaviors will take the form of self-approving and disapproving responses.

[6] Self-attitudes or feelings refer to any emotional responses by the individual to his self-perceptions and self-evaluations. These emotional responses to self are conceptualized as being of varying degrees of intensity and as ranging from positive (pleasurable)

to negative (distressful). The precise manner in which an individual displays and characterizes his various self-attitudes is in part a function of his sociocultural circumstances.

In describing a person's self-attitudes, one must simultaneously deal with two independent dimensions. The first dimension deals with the generality of the object of the self-attitudes. Is the person said to be emotionally responding to particular aspects of himself or to himself in general? In the latter case, the polarity (positive vs. negative) and intensity of the "global" self-attitude presumably will be affected differentially by the person's attitudes (of variable polarity and intensity) toward different aspects of himself at the time the self-attitudinal response is made. The second dimension is temporal. Does the self-attitude in question refer to the person's momentary emotional response to himself or to an aspect of himself, or to his characteristic self-attitude over a period of time? Over a specified time span, the person might express a number of self-attitudes. If it were possible to draw a representative sample of instants within that time span and then describe the polarity and intensity of the person's self-attitudes (if any) expressed at those points in time, his "characeristic self-attitude" would be said to be a function of the frequency with which the observed self-attitudes of variable polarity and intensity were expressed. Generally, "self-attitude" will refer to the person's characteristic global affective response to his self-perception and self-evaluation. Where the term is otherwise used, the meaning should be apparent from the context.

[7] "The mother" for the remainder of this explanation will be understood to refer to all motivationally significant adults, that is, to all adults whose responses are associated with the satisfaction or frustration of initially present and/or subsequently acquired needs.

[8] By virtue of the association between attitudinal responses by others and the subject's behaviors or attributes, the particular attributes or behaviors come to have an intrinsic motivational significance. That is, by association, the child's perception of the attribute or behavior in himself evokes a positive or negative affective response. This represents one of the processes, as will be suggested below, through which the attitudes of others influence self-attitudes. At the same time the child becomes aware of the system of standards by which he is judged by others — that is, that certain of his behaviors and attributes are "good" things since they evoke positive attitudinal responses and that other of his behaviors and attributes are "bad" things since they evoke negative attitudinal responses.

[9] This association between the motivationally significant attitudinal responses of others and the person's own behaviors or attributes gives impetus to the development of the self-image in two ways (in addition to being significant, as will be noted below, as a basis for the development of the self-esteem motive). First, the tendency for the person to experience particular types of responses from others in conjunction with specific subject behaviors or attributes facilitates perceptual discrimination by the subject among his various attributes and behaviors. Second, the subject is motivated to be aware of his own behaviors and attributes, since such awareness is a precondition of self-change toward the goal of influencing the motivationally significant attitudinal responses of others.

[10] The ability to adopt the perspective of the other person and thus to become an object to oneself presumes the ability to respond to and use a system of arbitrary symbols — that is, language. Through the use of such symbols (which have no necessary connection with the things they symbolize), the individual can reflect upon and otherwise respond to himself as well as imagine how others have responded, will respond, and would respond to himself under various circumstances.

[11] To the extent that this process permitted the individual to evoke positive responses by others the subject would be motivated to continue in the process by which he perceives, evaluates, and responds to his own current *and anticipated* attributes and behavior from the point of view of others. This *process* becomes motivationally significant because of its association with a personal need — successfully evoking positive (and avoiding negative) attidudinal responses by others. The need to perceive, evaluate, and attitudinally respond to oneself (regardless of the positive or negative nature of the response) is *instrumentally* valuable in predicting the probable responses of others and thus facilitating the subject's behavior modification toward the goal of evoking positive attitudinal expressions from others. As such it has an existence independent of the need, the development of which is discussed immediately below, to imagine positive attitudinal responses toward oneself from the perspective of others.

[12] In describing how the self-esteem motive develops, the process depicted recently acquired needs (the self-esteem need being the most recent) as if they derived from antecedent needs (whether acquired or present at birth). However, this is not meant to imply that the more recently acquired need displaces a previous need. With the development of the self-esteem motive, a person will still act so as to satisfy his basic physical needs and to evoke positive attitudes from significant others. Nor is this meant to imply that conflicts cannot arise between the satisfaction of the need for self-approval and other needs, whether previously acquired or present at birth. For example, it is conceivable that a person may find himself in circumstances such that he cannot survive physically without as a consequence suffering a loss of self-esteem. However, it is asserted that the self-esteem motive is based upon the need for the approval of motivationally significant others and upon the satisfaction of basic physiological needs present at birth; therefore, the conflict will be resolved (whether through perceptual distortion or otherwise) in such a way that the circumstances of the person's physical survival will appear to him to be compatible with the maintenance or enhancement of self-esteem.

[13] The author interprets these data as calling for the reevaluation of the assumption that "the 'negative' or 'unfavorable' self-image is a widespread characteristic and one which can be used to account for all kinds of behavior" (Chamblis, 1964:112). However, although the findings do appear to argue against negative self-attitudes being prevalent in a population at a given point in time, they do not offer support for the conclusion that therefore negative self-attitudes cannot justifiably be used to explain a wide variety of behaviors. Indeed, the data remain consistent with the assumptions that there exists a universal need to maintain positive self-attitudes and that human behaviors will be successfully devoted to the fulfillment of this need. Therefore (on these assumptions), it is to be expected that at any given time negative self-attitudes would be a relatively rare occurrence in the general population. A longitudinal study of self-attitudes would presumably reveal higher lifetime prevalence rates. In short, rather than offering data that negate the significance of negative self-attitudes in guiding human behavior, the data presented may be interpreted as evidence of the successful counteraction of negative self-attitudes.

[14] It was also observed that among persons experiencing a situationally induced loss of self-esteem, the persons with lower general self-esteem showed greater impulsivity toward closure than did persons with higher general self-esteem. This relationship was not significant, however, for subjects in the induced high acceptance condition.

[15] While the conceptualization of anxiety is highly variable (Ruebush, 1963), a central component of the concept is said to be the notion of a somewhat fearful, unpleasant feeling state with discernible physiological correlates (Krause, 1961).

[16] However, although the empirical literature considered above, taken as a whole, does appear to be *congruent* with the assumption of the prevalence of the self-esteem motive, it is not asserted, for any of a number of reasons, that the universality of the self-esteem motive has been *demonstrated*. Two major reasons for exercising caution in this regard are (1) the far from perfect relationships reported in these studies (whether because of psychometric deficits or for other reasons) and (2) the author's lack of awareness of similar findings in studies carried out in a wide variety of cultural contexts.

Chapter 3

Determinants of Positive/Negative Self-Attitudes

The self-esteem motive has been defined as the need of the person to maximize the experience of positive self-attitudes and to minimize the experience of negative self-attitudes. The extent to which the self-esteem motive is satisfied, however—that is, the degree to which the subject successfully develops positive self-attitudes and avoids negative self-attitudes — is a function of the complex interaction of a large number of variables. This chapter will consider groupings of particular variables that reportedly have appreciable influence upon the quality and intensity of subjects' self-attitudes.

The research literature is fairly consistent in suggesting three classes of variables that appear to have relatively direct influences upon the development of particular kinds of self-attitudes: the subject's history of self-perceptions and self-evaluations of his own attributes and behaviors; the subject's history of perceptions of being the object of particular attitudes expressed by others in his environment; and the subject's ability to respond to self-perceptions and self-evaluations and to the expressed attitudes of others in such a way that the subject will maximize the experience of positive self-feelings.[1] Each of these classes of variables will be considered in turn. With reference to each class, certain generalizations regarding the pertinent research findings will be offered and illustrative studies will be described.

32

SUBJECT ATTRIBUTES AND BEHAVIORS

The first class of determinants of an individual's self-attitudes relates to his history of self-perceptions and self-evaluations of his own attributes and behaviors. The existing literature tends to support the propositions that (1) an individual will tend to develop negative self-attitudes (feelings) to the extent that he has, in balance, a history of perceiving himself as possessing attributes and performing behaviors that, according to the criteria of *high-priority values* in his personal system of values, he evaluates negatively; and (2) an individual will tend to develop positive self-attitudes to the extent that, in balance, he has a history of perceiving himself as possessing attributes and performing behaviors that, according to the criteria of high-priority values, he evaluates positively.[2] For example, if a person has a history of perceiving himself as homely, dishonest, a member of the lower class, and unpopular, and if good looks, honesty, upper-class membership, and popularity are highly valued (by that person) attributes or behaviors, that person is more likely to develop negative self-attitudes than another person who similarly places a high value on these attributes or behaviors but who has a history of perceiving himself as approximating them (that is, as being good-looking, honest, a member of the upper class, popular).

The person's self-perceptions and self-evaluations will have less influence upon his self-attitudes if the values by which they are judged have relatively low priority in his value system. That is, a person is less likely to develop negative self-attitudes as a consequence of perceiving himself to be homely, dishonest, a member of the lower class, and unpopular if he places little value on good looks, honesty, upper-class membership, popularity than if he places a good deal of value on these attributes or behaviors.

The individual's history of perceiving and placing high negative (or positive) values on his own attributes or behaviors will in turn be the consequence of other variables, such as his objectively discernible attributes or behaviors and his personal value system. Although a person may tend to distort his self-perceptions in a direction that will raise his self-esteem, his self-perceptions will, nevertheless, be influenced by the objective state of affairs. That is, an individual is more likely to perceive himself as homely, dishonest, a member of the upper class, or popular if he *in fact* possesses those attributes or behaves accordingly than if he does not in fact possess such attributes or so behave. The value an individual places on his perceived attributes or behaviors will be influenced by his definition of the value in question and the placement of the value in the hierarchy of values. For example, the person's evaluation of his own physical appearance with regard to being good-looking will be influenced by his definition of what features constitute "good looks" and how important he thinks good looks are, whether from an absolute standpoint or relative to other values.[3]

These variables in turn are influenced by a number of factors, including cultural orientations and positions in the social system. Thus, for example, objective attributes such as the person's social class as an adult might be influenced by the social-class membership of his parents. In like manner the individual's definition of, and the priority assigned to, different values such as good looks or popularity will be, for example, a function of socialization experiences in given social classes and for particular sex roles.[4] However, the influence of these variables as indirect determinants of self-attitudes will not be considered in detail here but rather will be understood to be "givens." For present purposes, only those groups of variables that appear to have a more direct influence upon self-feelings will be considered below.

Illustrative Empirical Studies

A number of studies could be cited that report relationships between self-attitudes on the one hand and the subject's perception of possessing personally (dis-)valued attributes or behaving in (dis-)valued ways on the other hand. The relationship might be observed either in terms of changes in subject self-attitudes following experimental induction of personally (dis-)valued attributes, the association between subject self-attitudes and objective measures of past or present personally (dis-)valued attributes or behaviors, or the association between subject self-attitudes and subject self-reports of personally (dis-)valued attributes or behaviors. In these studies the subject's perception and evaluation of the attributes or behaviors in question might be either assumed or demonstrated. The subject behaviors in question might be any within a very broad range of performances. The subject's attributes might include physical characteristics, position in the social hierarchy, or psychological capabilities.

Experimental Induction of Success/Failure. The following studies serve to illustrate the range of investigations in which differences in self-attitudes are observed following experimental manipulation of the subjects' attributes and behaviors.

Diller (1954) reported on the effects of experimental induction of success and failure on an IQ test. After failure there were no changes in overt self-ratings but a significant decrease in covert self-ratings (obtained by unwitting evaluation of the subject's own handwriting) was observed. As a result of the "success" condition overt self-ratings increased.

In another study, the investigators reported results relating to the experimental induction of academic failure upon self-concept (Gibby and Gibby, 1967). The subjects consisted of sixty students "in two seventh grade classes established for bright and academically superior white children," one of which served as the experimental group and the other of which served as the control group. The failure situation focused upon the results of an English grammar test, which was said to be considered as quite important by the subjects. In the experimental condition the subjects were informed that they failed the test. The self-concept measure was determined by responses to the Gibby Intelligence Rating Schedule, the first administration of which was two days following the English grammar test and the second admininstration of which was two days later. For the experimental group the second administration followed the communication of failure on the test. The results suggested that as a result of the "failure" the experimental group subjects relative to the control group subjects came to evaluate themselves less highly and to believe that they were not as highly evaluated by other significant people in their lives.

In the studies discussed immediately above it was apparently assumed that the attributes or performances in question had high value relevance. However, other experimental studies were carried out under conditions in which the importance of the behavior or characteristics (which were experimentally manipulated) to the subjects could more easily be inferred. Thus, for example, the behavior in question could be presumed to be important to the subject if he could be said to have accepted the group's expectation of his performance and if he was highly attracted to the group by the standards of which he failed. In these connections it may be noted that experimental data reported by Festinger and his associates (1954) were interpreted as supporting the thesis that "the stronger the attraction of members to a group, the stronger will be the feelings of inadequacy on the part of those scoring less well than others and the stronger will be the feelings of adequacy on the part of those scoring as well or better than the others in the group." In like manner Stotland, *et al.* (1957), reported that under conditions in which the subject failed on a task and where he had accepted the group's expectations of him, a high group expectation was associated with low self-evaluation of task performance following failure. Under conditions of failure where the subject did not accept the group's expectation of him, the level of group expectation was not correlated with the subject's self-evaluation of his task performance in failure.

Self-Attitudes and "Objective" Measures. Another grouping of studies included observations of associations between self-attitudes and measures of presumably valued attributes or behaviors that were "objective" in the sense that they were judged to be less vulnerable to perceptual distortion by the subjects than the variables to be discussed in connection with the next grouping of studies. The following studies will serve to illustrate the range of variables that were observed to be associated with self-attitudes.

Ziller and Golding (1969) reported findings dealing with changes in self-esteem associated with winning or losing an election. A measure of self-esteem was administered to a sample of 44 political candidates at two points in time. The first administration occurred approximately six weeks prior to the general election. The second testing took place between two and four weeks after the election. The index of self-esteem was described by the authors as being

> derived from four items in which S is presented with a horizontal array of circles and a list of significant others such as doctor, father, friend, nurse, yourself, someone you know who is unsuccessful. The tasks require S to assign each person to a circle in the horizontal array. The score is the weighted position of the self. In accordance with the cultural norm, positions to the left are associated with higher scores [Ziller and Golding, 1969:441].

A comparison of winning and losing candidates revealed significant differences with regard to changes in self-esteem:

> Candidates who were elected to office tended to gain in
> self-esteem ... whereas candidates who were not elected in-
> creased in self-esteem a lower percentage of the time and de-
> creased in self-esteem a higher percentage of the time ... [Ziller
> and Golding, 1969:442].

The investigators also noted that those candidates who increased in self-esteem in spite of not being elected were all nonincumbents and suggested that the publicity associated with candidacy may have been "reinforcing."

Kaplan (1971) reporting on the conditions in which social-class position was related to self-derogation observed an inverse relationship between social class and self-derogation (low social-class position associated with relatively high self-derogation) in an adult population under circumstances that were interpretable as favoring the presence of certain general conditions: the personal and social valuation of higher social-class positions; the subject's ability to identify his relative class position; and the subject's lack of effective defenses against the negative evaluative implications of lower social-class positions.

Gunderson (1965) reported an association between body characteristics, particularly height and weight, and general self-evaluation. Among the results was the observation that among a grouping of young healthy Navy men, short-underweight and short-overweight groups tended to display the most unfavorable self-images.

Self-Reports of Attributes and Behaviors. Another grouping of studies reported associations between self-attitudes on the one hand and self-perceptions of personally valued behaviors or attributes on the other hand.

In one such study among high school senior subjects who indicated that they considered specified qualities to be essential for a young person to get ahead, low self-esteem subjects were appreciably less likely to indicate that they possessed the qualities than subjects with medium and high self-esteem (Rosenberg, 1965: 234-246). Among the qualities in question were "Ability to express yourself," "Talent, intelligence, or skill," "Ability to make a good impression," "Practical knowledge," and "Being sure of oneself."

In another study of eighty-two undergraduate student subjects Rosen and Ross (1968) reported a correlation of .52 between satisfaction with one's physical appearance and self-concept. When only those items that tended to be rated as more important by the subjects were considered, a correlation of .62 was observed in contrast to the coefficient of .28, which was obtained for items below the mean in rated importance. Thus, the observations were congruent with the hypothesis that perception of physical characteristics influences self-attitudes as well as with the expectation that the degree to which subjective perception of personal qualities is associated with self-attitudes is in part a function of the subject's evaluation of the qualities in question.

OTHERS' ATTITUDES TOWARD THE SUBJECT

The second set of determinants of an individual's self-attitudes or self-feelings relates to his history of perceiving and interpreting the behavior of more or less highly valued other people in his environment toward him as expressing more or less positive attitudes about the individual (or aspects of the individual) in question. The relevant literature is in general agreement with the proposition that an individual will tend to develop negative self-attitudes if he has, in balance, a history of perceiving and interpreting the behavior of highly valued others toward him as expressive of negative attitudes toward him in general or toward personally valued aspects of him; and the individual will tend to develop positive self-attitudes if he has, in balance, a history of perceiving and interpreting the behavior of highly valued others toward him as expressive of positive attitudes toward him in general or toward personally valued aspects of him. Thus, if a person has a history of perceiving himself as being rejected, excluded, ignored, or ridiculed by people whose good opinion he values highly (his parents, peers), he is likely to develop negative self-attitudes; and if a person has a history of perceiving himself as being sought after, listened to, admired, and loved by people whose good opinion he values he is likely to develop positive self-attitudes.

The perceived attitudes of others toward the person will have less impact on his self-attitudes if the others' good opinions of him or those aspects of him that were the objects of the others' attitudes, were not highly valued by the person than if they were highly valued by him. Thus, if a person whose opinion was not highly valued by the individual (perhaps a stranger of unprepossessing appearance) was perceived by the person as expressing negative attitudes toward an aspect of the subject that he did not value highly (perhaps his lack of skill at a recently learned sports activity) he would be unlikely to respond with negative self-attitudes. Nor would the subject be likely to develop positive self-attitudes in such circumstances if the other's attitudes were perceived as positive rather than negative. On the other hand, the person might well respond with negative self-attitudes to the perceived expression of negative attitudes by a highly valued other (for example, a respected scholar in the subject's field of professional competence) toward an aspect of the subject that was highly valued by the subject (such as his scholarly writing), as he might well respond with positive self-attitudes in such circumstances if the perceived attitudes of the other person were positive rather than negative.

The influence of the perceived attitudes of others upon the person's self-attitudes may be either direct or indirect. The perceived attitudes of others will directly influence the subject's self-attitudes to the extent that the subject adopts or identifies with the perceived attitudes of others toward him as his own attitudes. More indirectly, the perceived attitudes of others may provide cognitive cues that in turn influence self-evaluation. In this instance where the subject lacks personal standards for self-evaluation, the perceived attitudes of others toward the subject are interpreted as providing information about the value of one's attributes or the level of one's performance. Such information facilitates self-evaluation.[5]

The individual's history of perceiving attitudes toward himself by valued others will be influenced by a number of specifiable variables, including the actual attitudes of the others and the subject's past experiences with specified others. Although a person may misperceive the attitudes of others he is more likely to perceive certain attitudes toward him on the part of others if they are expressed than if they are not expressed. Moreover, a person is more likely to value the attitudes of others if the others were associated in the past with the person's need gratification (or deprivation) than if they were not.

These variables in turn are the consequences of other variables such as the individual's actual attributes and behaviors. Thus, others will express more or less positive attitudes toward the person depending upon how closely his actual behaviors and attributes are perceived (by the others) as conforming to the others' values.[6] However, detailed consideration of these variables and of the manifold sociocultural and sociopsychological variables that influence these variables are beyond the scope of the present treatment. The illustrative studies to be described below will deal primarily with the relatively direct relationship between self-attitudes and the attitudes expressed by other people toward the subject.

Illustrative Empirical Studies

Empirical studies concerning the relationship between the subject's self-attitudes and the perceived attitudes of significant others may be conveniently allocated among three categories. In each category the studies are variable, with regard to whether or not the subject's perceptions of others' attitudes toward him and/or the subject's evaluation of others are demonstrated or merely assumed. The first category includes studies characterized by observations of changes in self-attitudes following experimental induction of others' attitudinal responses toward the subject. The second category includes investigations of the concomitant variation between the subject's self-attitudes and the attitudes of others toward the subject; the others' attitudes toward the subject might have been inferred from the others' reports, the investigator's observation of the others' behaviors, or the reports of a third party regarding the others' attitudes toward the subject. The third category includes studies of the association between the subject's self-attitudes and his perception of the current or past attitudes of others toward him.

Experimental Manipulation of Others' Attitudes. The first category contains studies in which the subjects are systematically led to believe that specified others have more or less negative (positive) attitudes toward the subjects. Although a very large number of such studies could be cited, the following three investigations will serve to illustrate this category. In the first instance the influence of other people ("external authoritative sources") upon self-esteem is demonstrated in an experimental study of forty-two college students in which the experimental group was presented with fictitious research staff evaluations that consistently altered the subjects' self-ratings in a less favorable (but plausible) direction on certain items. Upon retest the experimental group (relative to the control group) showed significantly greater changes toward lower self-esteem on the altered items and also a tendency toward lower self-esteem on the unaltered items (Tippett and Silber, 1966).

The findings reported by Videbeck (1960) also illustrate experimental results regarding the hypothesized influence of others' approving/disapproving reactions upon the subjects' self-attitudes. The subjects consisted of thirty students in introductory speech classes who had been rated superior by their instructors. In the experimental session, after each subject read each of six poems a "visiting speech expert" evaluated each student's reading performance. Half the subjects received standardized approving reactions and half received disapproving reactions from the expert. The experimental conditions were such that the number of reactions by others, the consistency of the reactions within treatments, the apparent expert qualifications of the evaluator, and the subject's motivation were held constant.

Both before and after the experimental session the subject evaluated himself on twenty-four items along nine-point scales, the poles of which were "extremely adequate" and "extremely inadequate." Eight of the items constituting the "Criticized Scale" dealt with "conveying meaning and emotional tone" and "voice control in oral reading," items to which the expert reacted. Eight other items, the "Related Scale," although substantively similar to the items on the Criticized Scale, were not reacted to by the expert. Finally, the remaining eight items, constituting the "Unrelated Scale," were substantively less similar to the Criticized Scale than was the Related Scale.

The results of the study were interpreted as congruent with two hypotheses related to direction of change and spread of change between scales. The investigator concluded: "On the basis of these findings, the hypothesis that a person will rate himself closer to his ideal-self rating if he receives approval and farther away from it if he receives disapproval is considered tenable" (Videbeck, 1960: 354); and "The findings suggest that the reactions of others tend to have generalized effects upon self-ratings, but the degree of generalization diminishes as the scales become functionally dissimilar" (Videbeck, 1960: 357).

Similar results were reported by Maehr and his associates (1962) from an experimental situation in which a physical development "expert" administered either approving or disapproving ratings to the physical task performances of the male high school student subjects. The investigators reported that the expert's disapproving reactions resulted in a significant decrease in self-regard with respect to the attributes that the expert directly disapproved while the expert's approving reactions resulted in a significant increase in self-regard. As in the preceding study the investigators observed "a diminishing spread of effect to related areas of self-regard not directly approved or disapproved" (Maehr, et al., 1962:356).

Objective Measures of Others' Attitudes. Into the second category fall those studies in which the investigator demonstrates associations between the nature of self-attitudes and the "naturally occurring" (as opposed to experimentally induced) attitudes of others toward the subject. The measures of others' attitudes are objective in that they are derived independently of the subject's responses. In the first set of findings to be described below the others' responses are understood to directly indicate their attitudes toward the subject. In the second set of findings the others' attitudes are inferred from their other behaviors toward the subject (for example, choosing him as a leader). In the third set of findings, the attitudes of others toward the subject are inferred from the reports of a third party.

A study reported by Sears (1970) illustrates the category of investigations that associate independently achieved measures of subject self-evaluations and the attitudes of presumably significant others toward the subject. The investigator hypothesized that "parental attitudes toward a child which give him a feeling of being loved, wanted, accepted and respected should induce a similar attitude in him, that is, of his being worthy and successful" (Sears, 1970:269). The measures of positive/negative self-evaluations were obtained by the administration of five self-concept scales to eighty-four female and seventy-five male sixth-grade student subjects. Measures of parental attitudes were obtained from interviews with the subjects' mothers seven years earlier. The results were interpreted as indicating that maternal and paternal warmth were significant determinants of the child's self-esteem. Sears noted that his findings were congruent with those of Coopersmith (1967:164-180), who reported an association between concurrently obtained measures of maternal acceptance and self-esteem among his boy subjects.

Illustrating studies in which self-esteem is associated with the responses of others to the subject is a sociometric investigation of 272 high school seniors by Rosenberg (1965:25). The subjects were asked to nominate students in their English class whom they would be likely to choose as a leader. It was observed that self-esteem was directly related to choices received, with 47 percent of the subjects with high self-esteem scores, 32 percent with medium self-esteem scores, and only 15 percent with low self-esteem scores receiving two or more choices as a leader. Rosenberg (1965:197) also observed that with decreasing self-esteem, subjects were increasingly likely to report never having held an elected position in a club or school organization.

Reports of associations between self-attitudes and third-party reports of others' responses to the subject are also illustrated by certain of Rosenberg's findings (1965:27-28). Data were obtained from fifty normal young adult volunteers who were admitted to the Clinical Center of the National Institutes of Health to serve as subjects for approved research projects and from the reports of nursing personnel on the wards. It was observed that the nurses were appreciably more likely to deny that the low-self-esteem subject, relative to subjects with medium and high self-esteem scores, was "well thought of," "makes a good impression," was "often admired," and was "respected by others."

Subject Perceptions of Others' Attitudes. The third category of studies frequently cited in support of the proposition that self-attitudes are influenced by the attitudes of others include investigations of the association between the subject's self-attitudes and the subject's perceptions of others' attitudes toward him. The conclusions based on these studies are somewhat more tenuous than those based on the preceding two categories of studies because of two methodological limitations. First, like many of the studies in the immediately preceding category, it is difficult to establish antecedent-consequence relationships since the data relating to self-attitudes and the data relating to the perceived attitudes of others are gathered from the subjects at the same point in time. Second, it is difficult to determine whether the subject's reports of others' attitudes represent the truly preceived attitudes of others or the products of perceptual distortion in the service of self-enhancement. However, the results of these studies at least may be said to be consistent with the view that self-attitudes are influenced by others' attitudes toward the subject.

The numerous investigations in this category include reports of associations between self-attitudes and the subject's perceptions of the attitudes of generalized others, peers, parents, and so on toward the subject. Illustrative of such reports are the following.

With regard to the perception of others' attitudes in general, in a study of a sample of New York State high school juniors and seniors, as the subjects' self-esteem scores decreased they were increasingly likely to report that most people thought fairly poorly of them (Rosenberg, 1965:28). Rosenberg (1965:177) also reported that among high school juniors and seniors the subjects with decreasing levels of self-esteem were decreasingly likely to describe themselves in terms of such apparently desirable trait descriptions as "easy to get along with," "pleasant," "popular," and "well-liked by many different people."

Sherwood (1965) reported findings that bear on the association between self-evaluation and the subject's perception of how his peers evaluate him. The sixty-eight subjects were members of six training groups formed during the 1961 summer sessions of the National Training Laboratories in Human Relations Training. The groups met usually approximately twenty times for two-hour sessions during the two-week laboratory. The data were collected from questionnaire administrations. A self-identity questionnaire was administered on the second day of the laboratory. Approximately two weeks later the subjects responded to a second administration of the self-identity questionnaire as well as the objective public identity, subjective public identity, and sociometric questionnaires. With regard to self-evaluation, the data were interpreted as providing support for the hypothesis that self-evaluation is influenced by the subject's perceptions of how others evaluate him, which in turn are influenced by others' actual evaluations of the subject. The data also indicated that the extent to which others' evaluations of the subject ultimately influence self-evaluation is a function of the importance of the others to the subject, the extent to which the others' evaluations were communicated to the subject, and the extent to which group norms served as a basis for self-evaluation.

Numerous studies have considered the association between self-attitudes and the subject's perceptions of his parents' attitudes toward him. For example, Medinnus (1965:153) reported on the basis of data collected from forty-four college freshmen that "Adolescents high in self-acceptance and adjustment were likely to perceive their parents as loving but not as neglectful or rejecting." In a similar vein Rosenberg (1965:128-148) noted that, among a sample of high school juniors and seniors, subjects who indicated that their parents lacked interest in them were more likely to manifest low self-esteem than subjects who did not perceive their parents as lacking interest in them. Lack of parental interest was indicated by subject reports that their parents did not know who their friends were, were indifferent to the subject's poor grades in school, or were not interested in what the subject had to say at mealtime.

SELF-PROTECTIVE PATTERNS

Any person is likely to have some experiences in which he perceives himself as possessing disvalued attributes, as having behaved in disvalued ways, or as being the object of negative attitudes by valued others and, consequently, may experience momentary feelings of self-rejection. However, numerous studies suggest that whether or not these experiences result in relatively stable negative self-attitudes will be a function of the individual's capacity to respond in a self-protective manner.

The third class of determinants of an individual's self-attitudes thus relates to the individual's responses to self-perceptions of negatively valued attributes and behaviors; perceptions of negative attitudes toward him by valued others; or momentary negative self-feelings that may result from either or both of these sets of influences.[7] Such responses or predispositions to respond are known by any of a number of terms, including "protective attitude," which is defined as "a constellation of related ideas by means of which the individual maintains, enhances, and defends the self" (Washburn, 1962: 85), and "controls and defenses," which "refer to the individual's capacity to define an event filled with negative implications and consequences in such a way that it does not detract from his sense of worthiness, ability, or power" (Coopersmith, 1967:37).

The relevant literature[8] appears to provide support for the hypothesis that an individual will be more likely to develop negative self-attitudes if he is not characterized by the employment of protective attitudes in response to experiences of devaluation (whether by self or others) or to any consequent experiences of momentary negative self-attitudes than if he is so characterized.

Presumably the influence of protective responses may be direct or indirect. The direct influence might diminish the experience of negative self-feeling, such as by removing it from consciousness or by evoking a counterbalancing affect. The protective attitudes might more indirectly influence self-attitudes by permitting the subject to distort his perceptions of, and reevaluate, his own attributes and behaviors and/or the expressed attitudes toward him by others in his environment. Thus, an individual through the use of protective mechanisms might fail to perceive that he possesses disvalued attributes or has performed disvalued behaviors or that valued others have expressed negative attitudes toward him. Alternatively, rather than distorting his perception of reality, the subject's protective attitudes might permit him to effect changes in his evaluations such that he (1) gives higher priority to, or adopts, values that permit him to positively evaluate his existing attributes and behaviors (for example, the subject happens to be a good athlete so he defines athletic ability as a more highly valued trait, although he had not previously considered this ability to be quite so valuable); (2) gives lower priority to, or rejects, values by which he would necessarily evaluate himself negatively (for example, the subject happens to be receiving poor grades at school so he comes to value good grades less than he had previously evaluated them); (3) comes to (more) positively value than previously groups or individuals who are perceived by the subject as positively evaluating him, that is, the subject (for example, the individual comes to seek out the company of a particular clique of students whose company he did not previously value because he perceived that they admire him or probably would admire him if they became acquainted with him); and/or (4) comes to (more) negatively value than previously individuals or groups who are perceived as negatively evaluating him (for example, an individual may come to reject a group of students at school to whom he had previously been attracted because he perceives himself as being rejected by them). Any of these actions would be expected to function to enhance the subject's self-attitudes. In one sense, all protective attitudes or defenses in their more indirect influences on self-attitudes are viewed here as mediated by their influence upon perception (whether of one's own attributes and behaviors or of the attitudes toward the subject expressed by others) or evaluation (whether of one's own attributes and behaviors or of the other people who are perceived as expressing attitudes toward the subject).

The employment of defenses or protective attitudes in general or of particular kinds of protective attitudes is a function of a complex and incompletely understood system of variables that will only be referred to below in passing and for purposes of illustration. For example, the ability to employ any of several alternative protective mechanisms might be a function of such situational variables as the degree of ambiguity characterizing the situation. With reference to the selection of *specific* protective mechanisms from among those potentially available, the tendency to avoid potentially devaluing circumstances as opposed to devaluing the source of negative judgments, rationalizing one's actions, denying one's inadequacies, and so on might be a function of such variables as the defenses employed in one's membership groups and by one's role models.[9]

Illustrative Empirical Studies

The conclusion that the employment of "self-protective" patterns influences the genesis of positive self-attitudes while the failure to use such patterns increases the probability of the development of negative self-attitudes may be inferred from any of three types of findings. The first type reports that low-anxiety subjects are appreciably more likely to be characterized by the use of self-protective mechanisms than high-anxiety subjects. The second type of finding is the observation that self-rejecting subjects, in comparison with self-accepting subjects, are more vulnerable to the maleficent influences of self-devaluating circumstances and are also less likely to respond to such circumstances in ways that are calculated to increase self-acceptance. The third type of finding involves the comparison of subjects who are characterized by the employment of self-protective mechanisms with those who are not so characterized with regard to the ability to deal with self-devaluing circumstances.

High Anxiety vs. Low-Anxiety Subjects. The influence of the subject's capacity to employ self-protective attitudes upon the ultimate development of characteristic self-attitudes is strongly suggested by one of the findings resulting from

Washburn's (1962) study of the relationship between patterns of protective attitudes and differences in self-evaluation and anxiety level. The particular finding in question concerns the relationship between anxiety and the pattern of protective attitudes named "guilt deflection." Relative anxiety among a grouping of high school students was determined through identification by school counselors and confirmation by the school psychologist. Guilt deflection was said to involve

> an attempt to avoid blame and to maintain the appearance of conforming to socially approved standards of behavior. It involves such defenses as rationalization, reaction formation, and compensation. It appears to be negatively related to non-conformance [Washburn, 1962:88].

An example of the forced-choice items that constitute the measure of guilt deflection are the statements "I am usually justified in what I do even though others may misunderstand my reasons" and "I must admit there are times when I have been unfair without a good reason."

The examination of the relationship between anxiety and guilt deflection revealed that the grouping characterized by a relatively low anxiety level received significantly higher scores on the guilt deflection measure than the group characterized by a relatively high anxiety level. This finding thus supported the author's hypothesis that "Persons characteristically having more anxiety will tend to have fewer defensive attitudes justifying inacceptable behavior and avoiding blame than individuals experiencing less anxiety" (Washburn, 1962: 86). Since negative self-attitudes are defined in terms of the severe emotional distress (anxiety, depressive affects, and so on) that accompany the subject's perception of self-devaluing circumstances, this result also is compatible with the generalization that the genesis of negative self-attitudes is a function of the subject's inability to successfully employ defensive patterns in response to such self-devaluing circumstances.

Self-Rejecting vs. Self-Accepting Subjects. A number of studies compare subjects with positive and negative self-attitudes both with regard to vulnerability to self-devaluating circumstances and with regard to the employment of self-protective mechanisms in the face of such circumstances.

The influence of self-protective mechanisms upon the genesis of positive self-attitudes might be suggested by the demonstration that subjects who are vulnerable, in the sense that they lack such mechanisms, tend to have relatively low self-esteem whether the vulnerability is reflected in subjects' high scores on a "sensitivity to criticism scale" or in others' descriptions of the subjects as "touchy and easily hurt" (Rosenberg, 1965: 157-161). The inability of low-self-esteem subjects to defend themselves against potentially self-devaluing experiences is also suggested by findings reported by Leventhal and Perloe (1962) and Nisbett and Gordon (1967). In the former study it was observed that, under the condition where a communication apparently stemmed from a source who was dissimilar in personality characteristics,[10] low-self-esteem subjects were more influenced by threatening communications than by optimistic communication while high-self-esteem subjects were more influenced by optimistic communications than by threatening ones.[11] In the latter study, Nisbett and Gordon (1967:274) reported finding that "high self-esteem subjects tend to be less influencible after a failure manipulation, while low self-esteem subjects tend to be more so." This observation also would be congruent with the assumption that high-self-esteem subjects are more prone to use self-protective patterns than low-self-esteem subjects.

In contrast to those studies that demonstrate the differential vulnerability of self-accepting and self-rejecting persons to self-threatening circumstances, another group of findings concern the differential tendency of such persons to respond with relatively specific mechanisms that have self-enhancing implications. The mechanisms might operate through their influence upon the subject's evaluative or perceptual responses. The differential tendency of self-accepting and self-rejecting people to employ response patterns that influence subjects' evaluative systems is illustrated by the following set of findings.

Consistent with the view that persons with high self-esteem are better able than those with low self-esteem to protect themselves against the self-devaluing implications of an event are certain of the experimental results reported by Stotland and his associates (1957) from a laboratory study of the influence of group pressures and self-esteem upon self-evaluation. The investigators indicated that under conditions of experimentally induced failure the subjects with high self-esteem evaluated their performance as higher than those with low self-esteem, "all other variables constant" (Stotland, *et al.*, 1957:60).[12] In addition certain of the data suggested that, under nonrelevant task conditions, high-self-esteem subjects compared to low-self-esteem subjects developed concern for group expectations in a manner that was likely to facilitate positive self-evaluation of task performance. Subjects with high self-esteem expressed little concern for group expectations under conditions where they had failed and the group's expectations were high while low-self-esteem subjects under the same conditions expressed relatively great concern for the group's expectations. In contrast, under conditions where they had succeeded and the group's expectations were low, subjects with high self-esteem tended to be concerned about the group expectations while subjects with low self-esteem were little concerned.

These findings suggested then that high-self-esteem subjects reacted to the experimental situation in a way that better protected them from negative self-evaluations than did low-self-esteem subjects. Under specified conditions the high-self-esteem subjects evaluated themselves better following failure and were more concerned with group expectations when a favorable evaluation was more likely. Low-self-esteem subjects in contrast behaved in ways that might make it more difficult to improve self-esteem insofar as they responded to failure with relatively low self-evaluations and expressed greater concern with group expectations (that is, accepted the group's level of expectations) when unfavorable evaluation was most likely for them.

Under circumstances in which the self-protective mechanisms operated through their influence upon the subjects' perceptual as opposed to evaluative

processes, the self-enhancing effect might be facilitated through either perceptual avoidance, by avoiding perceptual exposure to the self-threatening
stimulus, or perceptual distortion of reality. The self-enhancing influence of
perceptual avoidance might be suggested by Silverman's (1964) observation that
college students with high self-esteem were appreciably more likely than those
with low self-esteem to have avoided participating as subjects in a psychological
experiment. On the assumption that such participation was perceived as
potentially self-threatening, this finding might suggest that individuals maintain a relatively high self-esteem partly through the perceptual avoidance of
situations with self-devaluing implications.

The efficacy of perceptual distortion through the denial of reality in influencing positive self-attitudes is suggested by a number of investigations cited
by others. Wylie (1961: 229-231) reviewed five studies (Berger, 1955; Block and
Thomas, 1955; E. Rosen, 1956a; E. Rosen, 1956b; Engel, 1959; Zuckerman and
Monashkin, 1957) that reported significant correlations between indices of
self-attitudes and scores on the K scale of the MMPI. Higher scores on this scale
are said to indicate "tendency to deny problems, worries, and feelings of inferiority; and a Pollyanna-like tendency to look at others (and at oneself) through
rose-tinted glasses . . ." (Marks and Seeman, 1963:43).

Defensive vs. Nondefensive Subjects. The findings in this category are characterized by the implication that subjects who have employed, or characteristically employ, particular self-protective mechanisms (that is, defensive subjects)
tend to be relatively successful in effecting positive self-attitudes. The following
results may be taken as illustrative of this category of findings.

Wylie (1961:255-256) discusses the results of a study by Rogers and Walsh
(1959), who interpreted their findings as indicating that a defensive group's
tendency toward self-devaluation may have been based upon feelings of self-
dissatisfaction that were denied conscious expression in order to maintain
self-esteem. In testing the hypothesis that defensiveness would influence unwitting self-evaluation, defensiveness was measured by female college students' responses to the K scale of the MMPI. In a paired-comparisons tachistoscopic procedure each subject was presented with their own photograph along
with each of four other photographs that had been judged by the experimenters
to be of average attractiveness. The subject was presumably prevented from
recognizing her own picture by the superimposition of each photograph quickly
and at a low illumination level on a neutral line drawing of a face. Defensive
subjects (as measured by K scale score) "unwittingly" evaluated their own
photographed facial expressions as less attractive than did nondefensive subjects when the latter also unwittingly evaluated their own photograph expressions although, by external judgment, the attractiveness of the photographs of
defensive and undefensive subjects was equal. The results were thus interpretable as supporting the position that defensive patterns permit an individual to
feel more positively toward himself than he otherwise would have in the
absence of such patterns (that is, unconsciously). However, this interpretation is
contingent upon the assumption, which as Wylie (1961:256) points out is not in
evidence, that subjects who score high on the measure of defensiveness also
consciously evaluate their photographed facial expressions positively.

A second set of findings involves the comparison in levels of self-esteem of individuals who appear to devalue traits and abilities in which they are deficient with those who do not. It is to be expected that subjects who evaluate themselves as "poor" in particular qualities would be less likely to devalue themselves if they were able to define these qualities as relatively unimportant than if they valued the qualities highly. Rosenberg's (1965: 246-248) findings were consistent with this expectation. Among subjects who rated themselves poor in terms of such qualities as "likable," "clear thinking, clever," "realistic, able to face facts," and "honest, law-abiding," those who indicated that they cared about the quality "somewhat, a little, or not at all" were appreciably less likely to manifest low self-esteem than those subjects who indicated that they cared "a great deal" about the quality. These findings thus suggest the efficacy of self-protective mechanisms in enhancing self-attitudes through the reevaluation of personal qualities in which the person perceives himself as deficient.

SUMMARY

An examination of the relevant literature revealed a high degree of consensus regarding three classes of influences upon the degree to which a person will approximate satisfaction of the self-esteem motive: self-perceptions of possessing positively/negatively valued attributes and/or behaving in positively/negatively valued ways; self-perceptions as the object of positive/negative attitudes by valued others; and the employment of self-protective responses. In general the findings reported in the research literature suggest these conclusions. A person will tend to develop relatively stable positive self-attitudes to the extent that he has a history of perceiving himself as possessing positively valued attributes and performing positively valued behaviors; he has a history of perceiving himself as being the object of positive attitudes by highly valued others; and he characteristically responds to perceptions of self-devaluing circumstances, and any consequent momentary self-derogation, with self-protective patterns. Conversely, a person will tend to develop relatively stable negative self-attitudes to the extent that he has a history of perceiving himself as possessing negatively valued attributes and performing negatively valued behaviors; he has a history of perceiving himself as being the object of negative attitudes by highly valued others; and he characteristically does not respond to perceptions of self-devaluing circumstances, and any consequent momentary self-rejection, with self-protective patterns.

NOTES

[1] In addition to the studies to be discussed below for purposes of illustration, a number of other studies were cited by Kaplan (1971, 1972a) concerning the relationship between self-attitudes and the categories of variables that are interpreted as determinants of self-attitudes.

[2] The group or individual will ordinarily subscribe to many different values. Certain of these values will be employed to judge particular attributes or behaviors in given situa-

tions, and other values will be used for judging other attributes and behaviors in other situations. Values of strength and beauty might be appropriate for judgments about physical characteristics, values of honesty and efficiency might be relevant for judging the performance of a political officeholder, and values of leadership potential and courage might be relevant to the evaluation of an army officer in the field. However, very often a person is placed in a situation in which he can behave in accordance with one value only at the expense of deviating from another value. In part to avoid such conflict situations, groups and individuals will order their values hierarchically such that in choice situations one value is judged to take priority over another. For example, it might be more important to act for the public good and be disloyal to a friend than to be loyal to a friend at the cost of the public good. Similarly, it might be more important to have a job that is creative but pays little rather than have one that pays well but does not permit creativity. The totality of a group's or individuals's values organized in terms of such principles as situational specificity and hierarchical priority will be referred to as a value system.

[3] The influence between actual traits and behavior on the one hand and self-perception and self-evaluation of the traits and behavior on the other hand is presumably reciprocal. The actual traits and behaviors increase the probability that the attributes and traits will be perceived and evaluated by the person. Mediated by their influence upon self-attitudes (and given the self-esteem motive), the self-perception and self-evaluation of the traits and behavior will influence the person to change (so far as possible) his traits and behavior in a direction that ultimately will raise his level of self-esteem, that is, change his self-attitudes in a positive direction.

[4] See, for example, Rosenberg (1965:254-268).

[5] Thus, the self-perception and self-evaluation of one's own traits and behaviors on the one hand and the perceived attitudes of others toward the person on the other hand may either exercise independent influences upon self-attitudes, or the influence of self-perception and of self-evaluation upon self-attitudes may be mediated by the influence of others' attitudes.

[6] It should be noted that the same variables (the person's actual attributes and behaviors) influence two partly independent sets of variables, which in turn more or less directly influence self-attitudes. In addition to the present influence, it was stated above that traits and behavior influence subject self-perception and evaluation.

It is fast becoming apparent that any model attempting to account for the formation of self-attitudes will be characterized by a high degree of complexity, involving as it does numerous reciprocal and indirect influences. For example, the person's actual traits and behaviors not only influence and are influenced by the self-perception and self-evaluation of traits and behaviors (which in turn influence self-attitudes) but also (mediated by the others' perceptions and evaluations of the person's attributes and behaviors) influence others' expressed attitudes toward him. Others' expressed attitudes influence the person's perceptions of these attitudes toward him, which in turn directly influences self-attitudes and may, at the same time, influence the person's self-perception and self-evaluation of his traits and behaviors. The latter directly influence self-attitudes and, as was stated above (given the self-esteem motive), thereby motivate the subject to change his attributes and behaviors within the limits imposed upon him.

[7] These responses exclude those patterns that involve changing behaviors and attributes so as to permit positive self-evaluations and evaluations by others. Such responses are

already implicit in the model, since the person's actual attributes and behaviors are said to exercise more or less direct influence upon both the person's perceptions of others' attitudes toward him and upon his own self-perceptions and self-evaluations. When the opportunity to do so is presented, the person apparently prefers to behave so as to change the attitudes of others toward himself in a positive direction rather than accepting the negative evaluations of others and the concomitant subjective distress. For example, Hardyck (1968) reported an experiment in which the subjects were given either a positive or a negative personality evaluation and were subsequently given a brief life-history interview by another person. Half of the subjects were informed that they could return to the first evaluator with notes made by the second interviewer. The other half of the subjects did not have this option. The data supported the predictions that among subjects who initially were provided with negative personality evaluations, those who could return to the evaluator (and presumably could influence the evaluator to change his attitudes toward the subject in a positive direction) as compared to those who could not return to the evaluator would be rated by the interviewer as trying harder to impress him and as being less depressed.

[8] It is difficult to evaluate the results of investigations dealing with the relationships between self-attitudes and defensive patterns in which the operational measures of the two sets of variables are in terms of data collected at the same point in time. In the context of the present theoretical model, temporal relationships are asserted such that (1) the antecedent failure to successfully employ defensive patterns will influence the subsequent development of negative self-attitudes, and (2) individuals with antecedent characteristic negative self-attitudes, on the assumption of the self-esteem motive, will tend to respond subsequently with defensive responses to potentially self-devaluing circumstances. The two propositions refer to different periods in the psychogenesis of the individual, periods before and after the development of characteristic negative self-attitudes. Thus, a study reporting either a positive or a negative association between self-attitudes and defensive responses at the same point in time may be interpreted as offering support for one or the other of the above assertions. An observed association between negative self-attitudes and use of defensive patterns would support the second proposition, while an observed association between negative self-attitudes and the absence of such patterns would support the first proposition. In interpreting such studies, to avoid a tendency to selectively interpret data in ways that will support the hypotheses, careful judgments must be made regarding the nature of the operational definitions of self-attitudes and defensive patterns. It must be determined whether the measure of self-attitudes appears to reflect *characteristic* affective responses to self or *momentary* emotional responses to self in the context of current circumstances. It must also be determined whether or not the measure of defensive responses refers to the more or less effective response pattern in a current situation or the *predisposition* to employ such defenses in general circumstances. Given these determinations it should be possible to offer judicious interpretations of the results as offering or denying support to the appropriate hypothesis. For example, an observed association between the predisposition to employ defenses and characteristic negative self-attitudes would be compatible with the second proposition; or an observed association between a specific self-devaluing circumstance and the failure to employ a defense mechanism would be congruent with the first proposition.

[9] See, for example, Sherwood (1967), Weinstock (1967), and Heilbrun (1972) for discussions of current situational and earlier interpersonal influences upon the development of defensive styles in general or upon the development of specific defense and coping mechanisms.

[10] See Leventhal and Perloe (1962:388) for a possible explanation of why similar findings were not observed when the communicator apparently was similar to the subject in personality characteristics.

[11] These findings were presented as relevant to the proposal that "people high in self-esteem tend to use avoidance defense mechanisms which lead them to reject threatening persuasive communications and to be receptive to optimistic messages" while people who are low in self-esteem "tend to use expressive or sensitizing defenses which lead them to reject optimistic appeals and accept the threatening ones" (Leventhal and Perloe, 1962:388).

[12] The differences were significant, however, only when the task was defined as nonrelevant to the group goal. (For possible explanations of this observation see Stotland, *et al.*, 1957:62).

Chapter 4

Self-Attitudes and Deviant Response

Up to this point it has been asserted that the need to experience positive self-attitudes and to avoid negative self-attitudes is universally and characteristically a human motive. It has been further stated that the *degree* to which a particular individual satisfies his need to attain positive and to avoid negative self-attitudes is a function of at least three broadly stated influences: the person's history of self-perceptions as possessing personally valued attributes and performing personally valued behaviors; the person's history of self-perceptions as the object of positive attitudes by personally valued others; and the person's history of responding to potentially self-devaluing experiences and to any momentary negative self-attitudes that might accompany self-devaluing experiences with self-protective patterns.

In this chapter two propositions will be presented that are based upon the preceding assertions.[1] The first proposition states that group members who, presumably as a result of the influences specified above, develop relatively stable negative self-attitudes are predisposed to adopt deviant patterns of behavior. Stated in more operational terms, persons who in the course of their group experiences have developed relatively stable negative self-attitudes are significantly more likely to adopt deviant response patterns in a specified future period than persons who in the course of their group experiences have developed relatively stable positive self-attitudes. The second proposition asserts that the adoption of deviant response patterns by previously conforming persons will

51

result in a decrease in self-rejecting, and an increase in self-accepting, attitudes. Again, stated in more operational terms, among conforming group members who at a given point in time are characterized by a similar level of self-rejecting attitudes, persons who adopt a deviant response pattern are significantly more likely in a specified future period to experience a decrease in self-rejecting attitudes (and an increase in self-accepting attitudes) than persons who do not adopt a deviant response pattern. The derivation of each of these propositions will be considered in turn. Following such consideration, empirical support for the hypotheses will be discussed.

DERIVATION OF THE HYPOTHESES

The derivations of the two hypotheses are based upon the postulated universality and characteristic nature of the self-esteem motive among human beings and the empirical findings regarding the factors that influence the development of positive/negative self-attitudes.

Self-Attitudes and Predisposition to Deviant Behavior

The first proposition states that group members who have developed relatively intense and stable negative self-attitudes, but who have not adopted deviant response patterns up to that point in time, are predisposed to adopt deviant response patterns in the future.

It was asserted above that persons with relatively intense and characteristic positive self-attitudes are likely to have had a history of (1) self-perceptions and self-evaluations of possessing highly valued attributes and performing highly valued behaviors, (2) self-perceptions of being the object of positive evaluations by highly valued others, and (3) the employment of protective attitudes to forestall or reduce the distressful effects of instances of negative self-attitudes. Conversely, individuals with intense and characteristic negative self-attitudes are likely to have frequently been unable to defend themselves against negative self-attitudes occasioned by perceptions and self-evaluation of (high-value relevant) attributes or behaviors and perceptions of being the object of negative attitudes by highly valued others.

On the assumption of the prevalence of the self-esteem motive, individuals will tend to behave in ways that will offer maximum opportunity to develop, maintain, or improve positive self-attitudes. Since it is stipulated that the individuals in question have not yet adopted deviant patterns, subjects who have developed characteristically positive self-attitudes must have done so in the course of their socialization within the normative structure.[2] It is assumed that since the development of positive self-attitudes was *in fact* associated with the kinds of experiences within the normative structure described above the individual would be likely to subjectively associate positive self-attitudes with such experiences. Such experiences (and indeed any other experiences that were apparently highly compatible with these experiences) because of their subjective association with the evocation of emotionally gratifying (positive) self-attitudes thus would come to be experienced as highly gratifying in their own right. The subject would thus be likely to continue to behave in ways that would foster these experiences. The individual would be likely to continue to perceive reality as before and to endorse the same value system as previously by the standards of which he was enabled to respond to his self-perceptions and self-evaluations with positive self-attitudes. He would continue to value the same people who in the past had expressed positive attitudes toward his behaviors and characteristics. He would be likely to continue to perform those behaviors and achieve those attributes that in the past evoked (and in the future would be likely to evoke) positive self-attitudes and expressions of positive attitudes by relevant others. Where new behaviors were adopted, the behaviors in question would be those endorsed by the individual and others in the normative environment as compatible with the individual's current positions and circumstances or as appropriate to his changing positions and circumstances. He would also be likely to continue to employ those (presumably positively sanctioned) protective mechanisms that in the past were effective in either forestalling or reducing the effects of occasional expressions of negative self-attitudes (evoked by self-perceptions and self-evaluations as possessing personally disvalued attributes and performing disvalued behaviors, or by perceptions of being the object of negative attitudes by highly valued others).

In short, the individual is motivated to behave in ways that have become intrinsically gratifying by virtue of the (actual and subjective) prior association of such normative behaviors with the genesis of positive self-attitudes. These behaviors, as they did in the past, would foster the maintenance or enhancement of positive self-attitudes. In so doing these normative responses would become more firmly associated with gratification in the individual's motivational system. By this process satisfaction of the self-esteem motive and endorsement of the normative structure would be mutually reinforcing.

As in the cases of persons who have developed characteristically positive self-attitudes, since it is stipulated that they have not yet adopted deviant patterns, persons who have developed characteristically negative self-attitudes must have done so in the course of their socialization within the normative structure. Again, as in the case of the development of characteristically positive self-attitudes, it is assumed that the kinds of experiences within the normative structure that were *in fact* associated with the development of characteristically negative self-attitudes would tend to be *subjectively* associated with negative self-attitudes by the individual. Such experiences (and any other future experiences that were apparently related to these experiences) because of their subjective association with the development of emotionally distressing (negative) self-attitudes would come to be experienced as highly distressing in their own right. The individual would thus be unlikely to voluntarily behave in ways that were likely to foster these experiences. To continue: to perceive himself as possessing (personally and socially) disvalued attributes and performing disvalued behaviors and as the object of negative attitudes by valued others; to endorse values that he cannot approximate and to value people who express negative attitudes toward him; to behave in ways that in the past were ineffective in facilitating the achievement of valued attributes and the performance of valued behaviors; to behave in ways that were ineffective in the past in forestalling or reducing the effects of expressions of negative self-attitudes would be to continue to engage in intrinsically distressing activities. The individual would thus not only be unmotivated to continue these intrinsically distressful normative activities but would be positively motivated to deviate from these intrinsically distressing normative experiences in ways that would facilitate the avoidance, destruction, or displacement of the normative experiences.

It is further argued that the subjective distress associated with those elements of the normative structure that in the past were subjectively associated with the genesis of negative self-attitudes would be generalized to other aspects of the normative structure that were not specifically associated with past experiences of negative self-attitudes but that are subjectively associated with the general normative structure. Thus, an individual who has developed characteristically negative self-attitudes in the course of his membership group experiences would not be motivated to adopt new behavior patterns (endorsed by his membership group) of which he has recently become aware because of the subjective association of these patterns with a group, past experiences in which were highly distressing. In short, the person would lack motivation to conform to and would be positively motivated to deviate from the group's normative expectations *in general*, whether or not the particular normative expectations were originally associated in the subject's mind with experience of highly distressful negative self-attitudes.

At this point the person is said to be motivated to deviate from normative patterns by virtue of their intrinsically distressing nature. Although the original negative motivational value of the normative patterns derived from their involvement in the genesis of subjectively distressful negative self-attitudes, through processes of association and generalization the normative expectations are now intrinsically disvalued. *At the same time* the person continues to experience subjectively distressful negative self-attitudes by virtue of the failure of the normative patterns to facilitate satisfaction of the self-esteem motive. Since the person remains motivated to improve his self-attitudes, he is predisposed to seek patterns of response (other than the now-disvalued normative patterns) that offer promise of satisfying the self-esteem motive. Thus, the person is predisposed to adopt deviant patterns not only because of the intrinsically distressing nature of the normative patterns (stemming from their past association with the genesis of negative self-attitudes) but also because of the fact that (given the negative hedonic value of the normative patterns) deviant patterns offer the only remaining promise for satisfying the self-esteem motive.

In discussing the predisposition or motivation of the person to adopt deviant behavior patterns (a predisposition that is traceable to the subjective association of experiences in the nomative structure with the genesis of negative self-attitudes) deviant response patterns are arbitrarily distributed among three functional categories: avoidance, attack, and substitution.[3] This typology of deviant responses appears to have some heuristic value in clarifying the functions of deviant responses not only with regard to mitigating the instrinsically distressing effects of normative patterns but also with regard to effecting changes in self-attitudes. The use of this typology does not imply that a given deviant response necessarily will fall neatly into one or the other of the categories. Indeed, a deviant response pattern is a highly complex phenomenon and may serve multiple functions. The typology is employed in order to sensitize the observer to these possible functions.

The avoidance function of the deviant pattern might be served by activities at the intrapsychic and/or interpersonal levels. In the former case the person may distort his perception of reality such that he fails to correctly perceive his disvalued attributes or performances; incorrectly perceives himself as possessing valued attributes and performing valued behaviors; fails to correctly perceive the negative attitudes expressed toward him by valued others; incorrectly perceives the expression of positive attitudes expressed toward him by valued others; or incorrectly interprets circumstances in ways that justify his possession of disvalued attributes, his performance of disvalued behaviors, and being the object of negative attitudes by valued others (or justify his failure to possess valued attributes, to perform valued behaviors, or to be the object of positive attitudes by valued others). At the interpersonal level the individual might avoid performing in normatively prescribed roles or otherwise avoid interpersonal interaction in which there appears to exist a high probability that he will fail to manifest valued attributes (or will manifest disvalued attributes); he will fail to perform valued behaviors (or will perform disvalued behaviors); or he will fail to evoke positive attitudes by valued others (or will evoke negative attitudes by valued others).

Response patterns that function to attack group members or the normative structure (as a whole or in part) may range from drastic reduction of the value placed upon previously valued people or normative standards to more overtly hostile responses by the individual, up to and including physical aggression upon the group members and material representations of the normative structure (which originally was subjectively and in fact associated with the genesis of negative self-attitudes).

Both avoidance and attack functions may be facilitated or accompanied by substitutive functions served by such deviant patterns as those involving the adoption of new group memberships and normative standards. For example, an individual may avoid participating in a group (membership in which was associated with failure to achieve value standards, negative attitudinal responses by valued others, and so on) through (or at the same time as) substituting participation in a different group that seems to be characterized by more easily attainable standards and to offer greater promise of positive attitudinal responses from other group members. Or an individual may devalue previously valued group members who respond to him with negative attitudes or previously valued standards that he had been unable to approximate through (or at the same time as) placing a higher value on other standards that the individual already approximates or on other people who express positive attitudes toward the subject.

The distinction must be drawn, however, between the form and the function of a deviant pattern. Because a deviant pattern serves one or more of the three broad self-enhancing functions it is not necessarily the case that the deviant pattern takes analogous forms. A deviant pattern may serve the function of avoidance of self-devaluating experience without the behavior taking the form of an avoidance pattern. An avoidance *function* might be served, for example, by an affiliative *pattern*. Thus, when the deviant behavior takes the form of joining a delinquent gang one of the intended or unintended functions (consequences) of the behavior might be the limitation of further experiences with the group in which negative self-attitudes developed. The avoidance function was served by an approach pattern. On the other hand, the form of the deviant pattern may very well parallel the self-enhancing function as when avoidance of self-devaluing experiences is achieved through physical withdrawal (for example, becoming a hermit).

It should also be noted that a behavior pattern is not deviant by virtue of the fact that it serves, or is intended to serve, attack, avoidance, or substitutive functions toward the goal of self-enhancement. Nor is the behavior necessarily deviant because it takes these forms. Avoidance, attack, and substitution functions conceivably may be served by normatively endorsed activities, which, indeed, may take the form of avoidance, attack, and substitution patterns. Rather, the behavior is "deviant" by virtue of its being a failure to conform to the group's normative expectations out of a lack of motivation to conform to, or a motivation to deviate from, the normative expectations. The person who is predisposed to adopt deviant behavior patterns is so disposed because these represent for him the only motivationally acceptable alternatives left to him that might effectively serve self-enhancing functions. By virtue of the person's original subjective association of the normative structure with intrinsically distressful experiences of negative self-attitudes, normatively endorsed patterns no longer have positive intrinsic or instrumental (for serving self-enhancing functions) motivational value.

The argument up to this point is to the effect that negative self-attitudes generate a predisposition or *motivation* to deviant behavior. Given the motivation to deviate, or the absence of motivation to conform, the person is more likely to seek out and find ways of satisfying his need to deviate than if he lacks the motivation to deviate or is motivated to conform. However, he will not *necessarily* adopt a deviant pattern even given the motive to do so. Certain facilitating conditions must be met. Whether the individual responds to the now intrinsically distressing normative structure (including its personal representatives) with particular kinds of deviant behaviors serving avoidance, attack, or substituting functions will depend on any number of specifiable circumstances, including early socialization patterns and visibility of these responses in the subject's contemporary environment. Some of these circumstances will become apparent in certain of the following chapters although the delineation of these circumstances will not be a major concern of this volume. However, these various circumstances may be briefly summarized as follows: Given the predisposition to adopt deviant patterns through the circumstances outlined above (namely the self-esteem motive in combination with the subjective association between self-derogation and the normative environment), the subject is likely to adopt such a deviant pattern if he (1) becomes aware of the existence of a particular pattern,[4] and (2) subjectively defines the pattern as offering a high probability of net self-enhancing experiences (probable self-enhancing consequences minus probable self-derogating consequences). However, given the initial adoption of the pattern, the further establishment of the individual in the deviant pattern will be a function of his actual experiences with the self-enhancing/self-derogating consequences of the deviant behaviors.

Deviant Behavior and Self-Enhancement

The second proposition states that persons characterized by negative self-attitudes who adopt deviant response patterns will tend to experience a reduction in self-rejecting attitudes and an increase in self-accepting attitudes.

The self-enhancing effects (whether of the nature of avoidance, attack, or substitution) of the adoption of deviant response patterns is to be expected by virtue of either or both of two outcomes of the deviant response patterns. First, the adoption of deviant patterns would be likely to reduce the occurrence of normative experiences that in fact, and in the person's mind, were associated in the past with the experience of self-rejecting attitudes. The reduction of such occurrences should then be accompanied by a reduction in experiences of self-rejecting attitudes. For example, the failure to possess attributes or to perform behaviors that are highly valued by the subject's group would be less likely to contribute to the maintenance of the person's negative self-attitudes if the subject was not motivated to accept, or rejected, the group's valuation of the behaviors and attributes in question. Nor would the adverse attitudes of group members toward the person be as likely to influence his experience of negative self-attitudes if he avoided participation in the group and thereby decreased his awareness of the group members' attitudes toward him. Second, in addition to decreasing experiences associated with self-rejecting attitudes, the response patterns adopted out of a motivation to deviate from previously held normative expectations offer the person new opportunities to experience more positive self-attitudes. For example, membership in a deviant group might offer the self-rejecting person the opportunity to achieve attributes and perform behaviors that are highly valued by the "deviant" group and to evoke positive attitudinal responses from group members. To the extent that the deviant group is highly valued by the subject his achievement of the attributes, his performance of the behaviors, and the positive attitudinal responses of the group members to him will likely eventuate in the experience of positive self-attitudes. Insofar as membership in the deviant group is associated with the gratifying decrease in normative experiences associated with the genesis of self-rejecting attitudes the subject will be likely to place such a high value on membership in the deviant group.

If the initial adoption of the deviant pattern in fact does eventuate in a decrease of experiences previously associated with the genesis of negative self-attitudes and a net increase of experiences that evoke positive self-attitudes, then the person's tendency to employ the deviant response pattern will be confirmed by virtue of its subjective association with these emotionally gratifying experiences. However, although as was suggested directly above, the probability is high that adoption of deviant patterns will have self-enhancing consequences, the adoption of a deviant pattern will not necessarily have *exclusively* beneficent consequences for a person's self-attitudes. Some of the effects of the deviant pattern might serve to exacerbate the experience of negative self-attitudes. For example, the rejection of the standards of, and membership in, one's social group in favor of the standards of, and membership in, a deviant group may have the effect of producing experiences of failure to approximate the deviant standards or being the object of negative attitudinal responses by deviant group members. These consequences might be sufficient to obviate the otherwise beneficial effects of the deviant group membership through facilitating the avoidance or destruction of aspects of the group structure that are associated with the development and maintenance of negative self-attitudes. Thus, in discussing the likelihood that a person will become confirmed in his use of the initially adopted deviant response patterns, the *net* positive effects with regard to experiences of self-attitudes must be considered. In the event that the net consequences of the deviant pattern is an increase in the experience of negative self-attitudes, the person will likely attempt an alternative deviant response since the normative structure continues to have an intrinsically aversive stimulus value by virtue of its original association with the genesis of negative self-attitudes.

EMPIRICAL SUPPORT OF THE HYPOTHESES

Without considering the empirical studies concerning specified modes of deviant behavior that will be the concern of the second part of this volume, three categories of findings may be cited in support of the two general hypotheses proposed above. The first category includes reports of the subjective association between experiences of negative self-attitudes and the normative structure. Such a subjective association is said to mediate between the actual occurrence of self-devaluing experiences in the normative environment and the predisposition to adopt deviant response patterns. The second category of empirical results concerns the relationship between self-derogation and the adoption of "deviant" patterns. The third category includes reports that appear to have implications for the hypothesized self-enhancing effects of the adoption of deviant response patterns. Illustrative findings from each of these categories will be presented in turn.

Self-Rejection and the Normative Structure

In deriving the first hypothesis it was asserted that the genesis of negative self-attitudes by a group member was influenced by his objective experiences in the group. It was further agreed that the actual association between his experiences in the normative structure and the genesis of negative self-attitudes would influence the subject to associate these two phenomena in his own mind. As a consequence of this subjective association he ultimately would be motivated to adopt a deviant response pattern.

The assertion of an association between low self-esteem and an awareness or expectation of adverse experiences in the normative structure appears warranted in the light of findings such as those reported by Korman (1967). These data indicated that among university students who "claimed to have made a definitive occupational choice" (p. 66) individuals with low self-esteem were less likely to perceive themselves as having high abilities in those areas where their chosen occupation called for high abilities than were individuals with high self-esteem. This observation is interpretable as indicating the subjective association between probable future experiences in the normative structure and a low probability of self-enhancing consequences of such experiences.

Also amenable to this interpretation are certain of the findings reported by Rosenberg (1965: 232-239) from a study of high school seniors. These findings suggest that at least in one normatively defined area — occupational achievement — subjects with negative self-attitudes are prone to anticipate adverse consequences from their future experiences in the normative occupational structure. With decreasing self-esteem, subjects were increasingly likely to indicate "average" or "below average" responses in answering the question "How successful do you expect to be in your work?" With decreasing self-esteem subjects were also increasingly likely to agree with the statements "I would like to get ahead in life, but I don't think I will ever get ahead as far as I would like," "I doubt if I will be as successful as most people seem to be," and "I doubt if I will get ahead in life as far as I would really like." Further, lower-self-esteem subjects were increasingly likely to indicate that they did not realistically think they would go into the business or profession that they would most like to enter as a life career.

Self-Rejection and the Adoption of Deviant Patterns

It was argued above that the (eventually) intrinsically distressing nature of normative experiences and the still-unsatisfied self-esteem motive would predispose the person to adopt deviant response patterns that would function to attack, avoid, and substitute for the normative structure, and that would, thereby, reduce the distress associated with the normative structure and facilitate satisfaction of the self-esteem motive. Thus, a second source of empirical support for the hypotheses is that category of findings that deal with relationship between self-rejecting attitudes or self-devaluing circumstances and the tendency to attack, avoid, or substitute for the normative structure. These empirical findings strongly suggest that experiences in any group that are associated with adverse consequences for the subject's self-attitudes will lead to the avoidance and/or rejection of the old group and attraction to substitute groups that promise to offer support for positive self-attitudes. It seems reasonable therefore to conclude that, if the former groups are socially defined as normative and the latter groups are socially defined as deviant, subjects who have experienced a history of self-devaluing experiences in their normative membership groups would avoid or reject such groups and would be attracted to deviant groups that offer promise of self-enhancing experiences.

Although as was asserted above, patterns of behavior that serve attack, avoidance, or substitutive functions (or take the *form* of attack, avoidance, or substitution responses) are not for these reasons *necessarily* deviant behaviors, they are said to be deviant insofar as the behaviors that serve these functions (or take these forms) are failures to conform to the group's normative expectations deriving from a loss of motivation to conform or the development of a motivation to deviate from the group's normative expectations. While the behaviors that are said to serve attack, avoidance, or substitutive functions (and that may take parallel forms) in the studies considered below are not clearly demonstrated to be such motivationally relevant deviations from the group's normative expectations, the contents of these studies are such as to permit the interpretation that the patterns that serve the functions (and may take the forms of) attack, avoidance, or substitution are indeed deviant behaviors in this sense of the term.

Those studies will be described in turn that appear to illustrate deviant behaviors apparently relevant to the functions, respectively, of attack, avoidance, and substitution in response to self-rejecting attitudes or self-devaluing circumstances.

Attack. The tendency of individuals to attack an environment to the extent that it is associated with self-devaluing experiences may be inferred from the results of a number of experimental situations. For example, Goldfried (1963) refers to a number of experimental studies that suggest that the induction of negative self-attitudes leads to expressions of hostility toward others. Horowitz (1958) reported a small group study in which the subjects were given the "social power" to influence the leader. The subjects' expected power or "adequacy" was manipulated by the leader's making decisions that ignored the appropriate weighting of the individuals' votes. When the leader so reduced the subjects' power the expression of hostility toward the leader increased (but not under conditions where the subject was legitimately outvoted). With restoration of power to the subjects, a reduction in hostility was observed.

In another study along the same lines, Pepitone and Wilpizeski (1960) reported that experimentally induced rejection by others (by two confederate members in three-person discussion groups) resulted in more negative attitudes toward self and toward others relative to control group members.

In apparent contradiction of these results, a study of the effects of experimentally induced success and failure on an IQ test (Diller, 1954) revealed that following failure there were no changes in overt self-ratings although there were decreases in covert self-attitudes (obtained by unwitting ratings of own handwriting). *No changes in ratings of others were noted.* However, Goldfried (1963, p. 36) suggests that lack of change in ratings of others, unlike the studies of Horowitz (1958) and Pepitone and Wilpizeski (1960) might be attributable to the fact that in the present study the others were not associated with the source of failure. After the success experience overt self-ratings and ratings of others were observed to increase.

The influence of presumably self-devaluing experiences upon the genesis of negative attitudes toward the group in which the experiences occur is apparent in results reported by Frankel (1969). The subjects were seventy-two college sophomores who were informed that they had qualified as candidates for membership in the "Student Advisory Council." The subjects were selected from the extremes of the distribution of scores on a self-esteem measure. The subjects were assigned to one of three conditions: experimentally induced success, failure, or nonparticipation on a group-relevant task. The task was said to be the next stage in the selection process and involved answering a series of multiple-choice questions. After the task administration all of the subjects rated the "Student Advisory Council" on each of four five-point scales: good-bad; effective-ineffective; capable-incapable; and want to join-don't want to join.

Among the results was the finding that on the first three scales subjects who failed gave significantly more negative ratings to the groups than those who succeeded. A similar trend was observed on the fourth scale. Apparently the effect of the success/failure condition upon attitudes toward the group was greater for the subjects with initially low self-esteem relative to those with initially high self-esteem. The investigator reported that among low-self-esteem subjects the discrepancy between the ratings of subjects who succeeded and subjects who failed on the group-relevant task was consistently greater than the discrepancy between the success and failure individuals among the high-self-esteem subjects.

It should be noted that in addition to suggesting the tendency of individuals to reject normative standards associated with self-devaluation, these data are congruent with the converse of this observation, that is, the tendency of individuals to accept group standards associated with positive self-attitudes.

A number of other studies report findings that also illustrate the association between negative self-attitudes or self-devaluing situations and the tendency to devalue or otherwise attack the apparent source of one's self-rejection.

In a study reported by Johnson (1966) the investigator systematically manipulated in a negative direction the magnitude of the discrepancy between the university student subjects' self-ratings and the ratings of the subject said to be made by another person. Among the relationships investigated was the influence of the discrepant negative ratings upon the subject's tendency to reject and devalue the source of the ratings. Rejection and devaluation were measured in terms of changes in the subject's ratings (made before and after the experimental induction of the other person's evaluations) of the source's competence (rejection) and the validity of the tests on which the source's judgments were presumably based. The results indicated that as magnitude of discrepancy increased so did the tendency to reject and devalue the source. These findings are consistent with the expectation that subjects will reject groups and devalue group standards that have self-devaluing implications and will be attracted to groups and group standards that are subjectively associated with self-enhancing experiences.

In another study (Jones, et al., 1962) the research design involved the female university students being interviewed twice under instructions either to be completely honest in presenting themselves or to impress the interviewer favorably. Following each interview the subject was told that the interviewer was favorably or unfavorably impressed. One of the major dependent variables was the subjects' impressions of the interviewer as manifested in responses on an evaluative rating scale. For present purposes, a significant finding was: "The subjects' impressions of a disapproving source were much more negative in tone than their impressions of an approving source" (Jones, *et al.*, 1962:16).

Similar conclusions may be inferred from correlational studies as well. For example, Smith and Suinn (1965:286) reported an appreciable positive correlation (r=.60) among thirty-one male subjects between a measure of self-esteem and a measure of conformity that was said to suggest that "high self-esteem scores are associated with acquiescence to conformity statements." Such a relationship would be expected if (on the assumption that the conformity statements reflect the normative structure of the subjects' membership groups) individuals in fact did accept group standards that were subjectively associated with self-enhancing experiences and did reject group standards that were subjectively associated with a history of self-devaluing experiences.

Washburn (1962) has provided one of the more obviously relevant findings concerning the relationship between self-rejecting attitudes and attack responses. One of the hypotheses tested stated: "Individuals who perceive themselves as inadequate will tend to develop more hostile defenses to be critical, suspicious, and lack identification with others than those who perceive themselves as adequate in relation to others" (p. 85).

Self-adequacy was said to be reflected by two indices. The first index was the number of adjectives checked by the subject as indicating traits he did not then have but would ideally have liked to possess (that is, "self-ideals"). Subjects who indicated greater number of self-ideals (desirable traits that he did not possess) were considered to be more self-dissatisfied than subjects who checked fewer self-ideals. By the second technique, self-devaluation was said to characterize subjects (high school students) who checked an excess of socially undesirable adjectives as applicable to themselves over those used by school counselors to rate the subjects.

Hostile defenses were measured in terms of one of three subtests interpreted as reflecting patterns of protective attitudes (defined as constellations "of related ideas by means of which the individual maintains, enhances, and defends the self"). The three sets of forced-choice items were derived from an analysis of the intercorrelations among items selected to reflect the fifteen most frequently described defenses (excluding repression) in a number of textbooks dealing with personality theory. The "Self-Other Distortion" subtest, indicating hostile defenses, was described as involving

> exaggeration of threats in the external environment and elaboration of symptoms of physical illness to excuse one's own behavior. The defenses involved include projection, displacement of hostility, substitution, and conversion or symptom formation, while this pattern tends to be negatively related to sublimation, phantasy, and identification [Washburn, 1962: 88]

Illustrative of the items included in this subtest is the forced-choice between "Most persons have a dishonest streak in them" and "Most persons are honest in most respects."

An examination of the relationship between the indices of self-devaluation and hostile defenses among the high school student subjects yielded support for the hypothesis. Students who reported more self-ideals received significantly higher scores on the Self-Other Distortion subtest than students who reported fewer self-ideals. Also, students who applied to themselves more adjectives referring to socially undesirable characteristics than were assigned them in ratings by school counselors scored significantly higher on Self-Other Distortion than a control group (Washburn, 1962:93).

These results are clearly interpretable as congruent with the expectation that individuals who developed negative self-attitudes in the course of their experiences in their membership group would be predisposed to attack the traditional normative structure that characterized the group.

Avoidance. Several findings may be cited as illustrative of the observation that negative self-attitudes are associated with the tendency to avoid experiences in the normative environment that were presumably influential in the development of the subject's negative self-attitudes. Among these findings are other results of the study described immediately above (Washburn, 1962). The investigator also hypothesized that "Persons who evaluate themselves as inadequate will tend to adopt more retreating defenses — to avoid coming to grips with problems and to deny reality — than those rating themselves adequate in relation to others" (p. 86).

The "Reality Rejection" subtest, presumably reflecting retreating defenses, was said to involve

> seeking to detach oneself from potentially threatening situations by refusing to accept and face things as they are. These defenses include suppression, regression, withdrawal, and negativism. This pattern correlates negatively with empathy [Washburn, 1962:88].

The items constituting this test may be illustrated by the forced choice between the statements "I would prbably change my job if it involved a lot of problems that worried me all the time" and "I feel a person should stick to his job no matter what problems are involved."

The results were interpreted as supporting the hypothesis. Students who received high scores on the self-devaluation indices tended to receive significantly higher scores on the Reality Rejection subtest.

Other studies that offer findings suggestive of an association between negative self-attitudes and avoidance responses are those that indicate a tendency on the part of self-rejecting subjects to become less attracted to the group, to be less likely to use the norms of the group for purposes of self-evaluation, and to be less likely to conform to normative expectations under circumstances where it was unlikely that such conformity would result in self-enhancing responses.

Some evidence of the tendency of subjects to emotionally withdraw from the group associated with self-devaluing experiences is provided by Dittes (1959b). On the assumption that subjects with low levels of self-esteem would have stronger needs to receive good evaluations from the group and to avoid negative evaluations by the group than subjects with higher levels of self-esteem, and that the former would be more rewarded by the group's favorable evaluations and more frustrated by the group's negative evaluations, it was hypothesized that the degree of satisfaction or frustration experienced as a result of the group's evaluations of the subject would be reflected in the subject's expressed attraction to the group. Dittes, in fact, reported just such a relationship between initial level of self-esteem, experimentally induced positive or negative group evaluation, and degree of attraction to the group. Among subjects whose characteristic level of self-esteem was high, the devalued and favorably evaluated subjects did not differ significantly with regard to degree of expressed attraction to the group. Among subjects whose characteristic level of self-esteem was average, there was again no significant difference between devalued and positively evaluated subjects. However, the difference was larger than it was in the case of the former subjects. Among subjects whose self-esteem was low, the devalued subjects expressed significantly less attraction to the group than was expressed by the positively evaluated subjects.

With regard to acceptance of group norms, Sherwood (1965) found that the more positively evaluated a subject was by group members who were relatively important to him, the more likely he was to be self-involved in the group, that is, to use group norms as a basis for self-evaluation. When the group did not evaluate the subject highly, he tended not to agree with the norms of the group.

The tendency of subjects to withdraw from attempts to achieve group standards in circumstances in which the attempts are not likely to result in self-enhancing responses is suggested by the results of the study reported by Hardyck (1968). In interpreting this experiment in the present context, the degree to which the subject attempted to impress the interviewer is taken to be an index of the subject's attempt to conform to group standards. The subjects were freshman girls who had previously been provided with either a positive or a negative personality evaluation. During the course of a subsequent life-history interview administered by a second person, half of the subjects were informed that they could return to the initial evaluator with the second interviewer's notes while the other half of the subjects were told they could not return to the initial evaluator. Since the former group would perceive the opportunity of improving the initial evaluator's opinion of them it was expected and observed that they would try harder than the other group to impress the interviewer and would be less depressed than the other groups. These results are interpretable as congruent with the hypothesis that motivation to conform to group expectations (here, to manifest desirable personality characteristics) is a function of the subject's association of the conforming behavior with probable increases in gratification. The subject would tend to withdraw from government by group standards where conformity to the standards was not subjectively associated with probable gratification.

A tendency to avoid participating in groups in circumstances in which the subject's experiences in the group were self-devaluing in nature is suggested also by some of the findings reported by Rasmussen and Zander (1954). Their data consisted of responses to questionnaires by eighty-five public high school teachers. Among the scores computed was the failure score, which indicated the discrepancy between the real and ideal levels of classroom performance. For present purposes one of the more relevant findings is the following. When teachers who had high failure scores were compared with those who had low failure scores, the former group was observed to be significantly less likely than the latter group to indicate that they would choose teaching if they could begin their professional career over again. That is, subjects with high failure scores were more likely to be dissatisfied with their choice of a career, an observation that is consistent with the hypothesis that attraction to a group and its standards is a function of the nature of their association with a subject's self-evaluative experiences.

Substitution. The association between self-rejecting attitudes and the tendency to substitute new patterns for those that presumably influenced the genesis of these attitudes is suggested by the following two studies.

Certain of the findings reported by Ludwig and Maehr (1967) are clearly compatible with the assertion that new activities will be substituted for old activities where the latter were associated with self-devaluation. Following the performance of simple physical tasks, the seventh- and eighth-grade male subjects received either approval or disapproval from a "physical development expert." A week in advance of the experimental treatments the subjects had responded to self-concept ratings and behavioral preference ratings. The "Behavioral Choice Questionnaire" involved the rating of one's preference for physical or nonphysical activity on a nine-point bipolar scale. One subtest contained items that related directly to the experimental evaluation situation. A comparison of the responses to this test prior to the experimental evaluations with those made following the evaluation revealed that "Whereas approval was followed by an increased preference for activities directly related to the treatment, disapproval eventuated in a decreased preference for these activities" (Ludwig and Maehr, 1967:464).

Long and her associates (1967) reported on the observed relationship between originality and self-esteem (among other variables). The subjects consisted of sixty fifth- and sixth-grade students, half of whom were selected as scoring very high and half of whom were selected as scoring very low on a measure of originality from among the 111 pupils who were administered the test. The originality score was based on the unusualness of objects drawn from thirty pairs of lines. Self-esteem was measured with reference to placement of a circle representing the self relative to other circles representing peers in a horizontal array of circles.

The investigators observed that (as hypothesized) the subjects with high originality scores tended to manifest significantly less self-esteem than the subjects with low originality scores. The relationship was interpreted in terms of the "original" child being the object of social rejection, which influences the development of a negative self-concept. However, the results are also compatible with the explanation that children with preexisting negative self-concepts behave in original ways as a manifestation of their avoidance or rejection of groups associated with their self-derogation and in order to substitute new (original) standards by which they may evaluate themselves more highly. In support of this explanation are certain of the data reported by the author that suggest that children high in originality may display a higher degree of deroga- tion for teacher or father (Long, *et al.*, 1967:54), significant figures in groups that are likely to have been associated by the subject with the genesis of relatively intense negative self-attitudes.

Deviant Patterns and Self-Enhancement

A third source of empirical support for the two hypotheses consists of studies that observed associations between behaviors apparently serving attack, avoid- ance, and/or substitution functions on the one hand and positive self-attitudes on the other. Such findings are compatible with the hypothesis that the adop- tion of deviant response patterns by self-rejecting persons will positively influ- ence changes in the person's self-attitudes on the assumption, as in the preced- ing section, that the behaviors in these studies that serve attack, avoidance, and substitution functions are in fact deviant responses (that is, failures to conform to the group's normative expectations deriving from the person's acquired lack of motivation to conform, or motivation to deviate from, the normative expec- tations).

A number of the studies indicating associations between these response patterns (serving attack, avoidance, substitution functions) and self-rejecting attitudes have been cited earlier in another connection.

With regard to "attack" responses, Stotland and his associates (1957) re- ported results that suggest the efficacy of devaluation of group standards as- sociated with failure experiences in maintaining self-esteem. In this experimen- tal study it was observed that (under "nonrelevant task conditions") subjects with high self-esteem relative to those with low self-esteem expressed little concern for group expectations under conditions where they had failed and the group's expectations were high.

The efficacy of devaluation of the normative structure in producing positive self-attitudes was also suggested by Rosenberg's (1965:246-248) findings to the effect that, among subjects who rated themselves "poor" in terms of possessing specified personal qualities, those subjects who indicated that they cared about the quality "Somewhat, a little, or not at all" were less likely to have low scores on a measure of self-esteem than subjects who indicated that they cared a great deal about the quality.

The effectiveness of avoidance responses (through perceptual distortion, and so on) in increasing self-accepting attitudes was suggested by the results of a number of studies cited by Wylie (1961:229-231) reporting significant correla- tions between positive self-attitudes and high scores on the K scale of the MMPI, which, it will be recalled, was said to indicate a "tendency to deny problems, worries, and feelings of inferiority; a Pollyanna-like tendency to look at others (and at oneself) through rose-tinted glasses . . . (Marks and Seeman, 1963:43).

The influence of substitute interpersonal affiliations whether in normative or deviant contexts upon increasing one's level of self-acceptance may be inferred from results reported by Morse and Gergen (1970). In this study the subjects were exposed to a stimulus person whose characteristics were socially either desirable or undesirable. Among the findings was the observation that, regardless of the desirability of the stimulus person's characteristics, those subjects who were rated most like the stimulus person manifested an increase in self-esteem while those who were rated unlike the stimulus person experienced a decrease in self-esteem. Thus, the presence of a person with (dis)similar characteristics apparently influences the subject's self-esteem. The authors speculate about the meaning of this relationship as follows:

> When another is seen to be similar to self, he places a stamp of legitimacy on one's conduct or appearance. Interpersonal support of this sort may be particularly important in circumstances . . . in which public appraisal is highly salient. Encountering an individual whose characteristics differ from one's own may initiate a process of self-questioning and doubt [Morse and Gergen, 1970:154].

The applicability of this finding in explanations of deviant behavior is not difficult to see. An individual who is apparently a deviant, and therefore dissimilar to others in his group, might well seek the company of other "deviants" of like characteristics toward the goal of enhancing his self-esteem. Through such a process the subject would become increasingly fixed in the deviant group since it is now gratifying in its consequences rather than disapproved as it once was from the perspective of his former interpersonal nexus: "Because another is similar, he increases one's esteem for self, and inasmuch as enhanced self-esteem is positively valued, the other may become a target of attraction" (Morse and Gergen, 1970:155).

SUMMARY

Two propositions derived concern the reciprocal relationship between self-attitudes and deviant behavior. The first asserts that individuals who have developed relatively stable negative self-attitudes are predisposed or motivated to seek out and adopt deviant patterns. Such a predisposition was said to be the result of the intrinsically distressing (for the person) nature of the normative structure stemming from its original (actual and subjective) association with the experience of negative self-attitudes, and of the person's need to seek alternatives to the intrinsically disvalued (and instrumentally ineffective) normative patterns in order to satisfy the self-esteem motive. The deviant patterns were characterized as functioning to alleviate the subjective distress associated with the normative environment and to satisfy the self-esteem motive by facilitating the avoidance of, attacks upon, and substitution for the normative environment. Given the motivation to adopt deviant responses, the subject is likely to adopt such patterns if he becomes aware of the existence of a particular deviant pattern and if he subjectively judges that the pattern will offer a high probability of net self-enhancing experiences (that is, probable self-enhancing consequences minus probable self-devaluing consequences).

The second proposition asserts that the adoption of deviant patterns by self-rejecting persons will tend to result in increased self-acceptance and decreased self-rejection. These effects are anticipated by virtue of the probable results of the adopted deviant behavior pattern in, first, reducing the occurrence of experiences in the normative structure that in the past were associated with the genesis of negative self-attitudes and, second, providing alternative opportunities for the experience of self-enhancing effects. It is recognized that the deviant pattern may actually result in an exacerbation of self-rejecting tendencies. In this event the person would be expected to attempt alternative deviant response patterns since the normative structure continues to constitute an aversive stimulus. However, to the extent that the initial deviant response pattern in fact results in self-enhancing experiences, the person will become increasingly confirmed in the employment of the deviant pattern.

Three sets of empirical findings are discussed as being compatible with, and thereby offering some support for, the two propositions. The first set of findings appears relevant to the presumed relationship between self-attitudes and the perception of the normative structure as a self-enhancing or self-devaluing influence. On the basis of this relationship the first proposition was asserted. The second set of findings suggests the tendency of persons with self-rejecting attitudes and/or in self-devaluing circumstances to employ (presumably) deviant response patterns that apparently serve attack, avoidance, or substitution functions. The third set of findings suggests the tendency of individuals who adopt such response patterns to experience an improvement in their self-attitudes.

However, these empirical findings did not deal with specific modes of socially defined deviance. It remains to be determined whether or not the literature dealing with specified modes of deviant behavior also reports results that are compatible with the emerging theoretical model, or more particularly, with the two propositions developed in this chapter that are central to the model. The consideration of such literature is the task of the second part of the volume, to which we now turn.

NOTES

[1] In deriving these propositions, certain conditions are assumed to exist. Those variables affecting the existence of these conditions will become a part of a more sophisticated statement of this emerging theoretical model. For example, the derivation of the first proposition assumes that persons who develop negative self-attitudes in the course of their group experiences subjectively associate the group experiences with their self-rejecting attitudes. It is also assumed that they do not perceive alternative conforming patterns that offer them a high probability of experiencing more positive self-attitudes. While these conditions are likely to occur, they will not necessarily do so. Thus any factors influencing the probability of the occurrence of these conditions will also influ-

ence the probability that the adoption of deviant response patterns will follow upon the development of negative self-attitudes.

Although some of these factors will be referred to in passing, they will not be considered in detail. Our purpose here is merely to present a broad outline of the emerging theoretical model.

[2] Phrases such as "the normative structure" should not obscure the fact that a person ordinarily has multiple membership groups, each of which is characterized by a set of normative expectations that may or may not conflict with the normative structures of the other membership groups. The processes to be described below should be understood to refer to the person's changing relationships to all of his membership groups considered individually and/or in total configuration.

[3] These functional categories may be thought of as having a rough correspondence with some well-known typologies. For example, all of Merton's (1957) deviant modes of adaptation to a disjunction between culturally prescribed goals and socially institutionalized means for achieving the goals are interpretable as serving some combination of avoidance, attack, and substitution functions. "Innovation" would appear to serve a predominantly *substitutive* function with some elements of *attack* and/or *avoidance* functions present. "Retreatism" would serve a predominantly *avoidance*like function with perhaps some implication of substitution. "Rebellion" would be interpretable as serving a combination of *attack* and *substitution* functions. "Ritualism" would be thought of as serving a primarily *substitutive* function (that is, accepting a new set of goals, formerly means, for a previously held set of goals) with some elements of avoidance present.

It might also be argued that the self-enhancing functions of deviant patterns under discussion roughly parallel the three types of delinquent subculture described by Cloward and Ohlin (1960): the criminal (substitution); the conflict (attack); and the retreatist (avoidance).

However, as will be indicated above the distinction is drawn between function and form of deviant response patterns. The typologies of Merton (1957) and Cloward and Ohlin (1960) would appear to refer to form while the set of categories described above are meant to indicate types of self-enhancing functions. Form may or may not parallel function.

[4] The process by which awareness of a deviant activity influences adoption of the deviant pattern is illustrated by experiments such as those cited and reported by Allen and Liebert (1969: 253) on "the influence of deviant modeling cues on adherence to previously learned rules . . ."

PART II

SELF-ATTITUDES
AND PATTERNS OF
DEVIANT RESPONSE

Part II considers the research literature concerning the relationship between self-attitudes and selected (not necessarily mutually exclusive) categories of deviant behavior. In each category of "deviant" behavior under consideration it is generally assumed rather than demonstrated that the behavior is judged to be deviant from the perspective of the subjects' predeviance membership groups. The research literature is examined with regard to the apparent compatibility between empirical findings and the outline of the theoretical model (presented in Part I), which assigns self-attitudes a central role in the process of adopting and reinforcing deviant response patterns. The following categories of deviant responses will be considered in turn: dishonesty, delinquency, and criminality (Chapter 5); drug abuse (Chapter 6); alcohol abuse (Chapter 7); aggressive behavior (Chapter 8); suicidal behavior (Chapter 9); and mental illness (Chapter 10).

Chapter 11 provides an overview of the volume in a general summary of the theoretical model of deviant behavior outlined in Part I, and of the discussion of the degree to which the bodies of literature concerning specific patterns of deviant response considered in Part II are congruent with the general theory of deviant behavior.

Chapter 5

Dishonesty, Delinquency, and Criminality

The theoretical outline developed in Part I rests upon two major assertions. First, persons characterized by negative self-attitudes are motivated to (and, given the perceived opportunity for adopting the patterns and a high subjective probability of net self-enhancing consequences of adopting the patterns, in fact would) adopt deviant response patterns that serve the functions (and may take the form) of avoiding, attacking, and substituting for aspects of the normative structure of the person's predeviance membership groups. Such motivation is said to derive from the actual and subjective association of the normative structure with the genesis of negative self-attitudes. Second, the adoption of deviant patterns in such circumstances is associated with the enhancement of self-attitudes insofar as the deviant patterns serve to decrease the significance or extent of the person's experience with self-devaluing circumstances and to increase the range of new life circumstances with self-enhancing potential. Each of the two assertions will be discussed in turn in relationship to the relevant literature dealing with dishonesty,[1] deliquency, or criminality as instances of deviant behavior.

SELF-ATTITUDES AND DELINQUENT RESPONSE

The studies relevant to the hypothesized relationship between negative self-attitudes and deviant response patterns may be distributed among five

categories according to whether variation in the adoption of the deviant response patterns is observed (1) as a consequence of experimentally induced
self-devaluation; (2) at a time subsequent to the measurement of self-esteem
levels; (3) in association with indicators of life experiences that are interpretable
as antecedent to the measurement of self-attitudes; (4) concurrently with measures of self-attitudes; or (5) as related to other variables in ways consistent with
the prediction that antecedent self-derogation will influence the adoption of
deviant patterns.

Experimental Studies

Perhaps the most acceptable support for the hypothesized influence of negative
self-attitudes upon subsequent adoption of deviant patterns is provided by the
results of experimental studies. In one such investigation Aronson and Mettee
(1968) investigated the effects of differential levels of induced self-esteem upon
cheating behavior. The subjects, forty-five female psychology students, were led
to believe that the study in which they were participating concerned the relationship between personality test scores and extrasensory perception (ESP). The
latter ability was said to be determined through the use of a modified game of
blackjack. After taking a personality test the subjects were provided with false
feedback, which was intended to temporarily induce an increase, a decrease, or
no change in self-esteem. The subjects were randomly assigned to one of the
three self-esteem conditions. During the blackjack game that followed they
were placed in situations in which they could cheat and win, on the one hand, or
not cheat and lose the game, on the other hand. The results tended to be
congruent with the hypothesis that individuals with low self-esteem are more
likely to engage in immoral behavior than individuals with high self-esteem.
People who received uncomplimentary feedback about themselves (the low-
self-esteem condition) were observed to be significantly more likely to cheat
than subjects who received more positive information about themselves.
Among the subjects in the low-self-esteem condition 87 percent cheated on at
least one occasion in contrast to the 60 percent of the subjects in the neutral
self-esteem condition and the 40 percent of the subjects in the high-self-esteem
condition who did so.

These results were paralleled by those reported by Graf (1971). As in the
preceding investigation experimental induction of self-esteem levels was attained through false feedback of personality test scores to the subjects. Dishonest behavior was determined in terms of whether or not the subject kept a dollar
bill left on the floor near the door of the testing room following completion of
the feedback of the positive, negative, or neutral personality descriptions. The
results indicated a significant relationship between low self-esteem and dishonest behavior. Some 40 percent of the low-self-esteem subjects (N=30) engaged in
dishonest behavior compared with only 17 percent of the neutral-self-esteem
subjects (N=29) and 14 percent of the high-self-esteem subjects (N=29). Thus,
in both studies the induction of low-self-esteem appeared to increase the probability of subsequent dishonest behavior.[2]

Predictive Studies

A second group of studies is also characterized by the observation of associations between antecedent self-attitudes and deviant behavior at a later point in time. However, unlike the previous group of studies, in which self-attitudes were experimentally induced, the present investigations employ indicators of what might be called "naturally occurring" self-attitudes.

The influence of negative self-attitudes upon subsequent adoption of delinquent patterns may be inferred from certain of the data from a longitudinal study of two cohorts of white sixth-grade boys from high-delinquency areas (Dinitz, Scarpitti, and Reckless, 1962). One cohort was composed of boys who were nominated by their sixth-grade teachers as being likely to stay out of trouble with the law. The other cohort consisted of boys who were nominated by their sixth-grade teachers as being headed for trouble with the law. The two cohorts were interviewed at the time of their selection and were reassessed four years later, when they were sixteen years of age. Among the findings was the observation that during the four-year interlude the nominated "bad" boys were appreciably more likely to come into frequent and serious contact with the law than the nominated "good" boys.

Unfortunately no data were reported that could be interpreted as a face valid indicator of negative self-feelings as the term is being used here. Consequently no direct test of the hypothesized temporal relationship between negative self-attitudes and subsequent deviant behavior was possible. However, the above-stated finding may be accepted as providing indirect support for the hypothesis if an assumption is made. That assumption is that the "good boy" and "bad boy" nominations reflect the characteristic positive or negative attitudes that the subjects evoke from significant others and that influence the formation of appropriate self-attitudes. On that assumption the results may be interpreted as indicating that boys who characteristically evoked negative self-attitudes from significant others were appreciably more likely to adopt delinquent patterns over the succeeding four years than boys who characteristically evoked positive self-attitudes from significant others.

In any case, not all studies of the temporal relationship between self-esteem and dishonesty indicate that antecedent self-rejecting attitudes are associated with subsequent dishonest behavior. In one study (Jacobson, Berger, and Millham, 1969) high-self-esteem subjects manifested a tendency to cheat in a task-oriented situation in which they were provided an opportunity to cheat apparently without possibility of detection. However, unlike the situation in the other studies, variable self-esteem was not experimentally induced, and the operational definition of self-esteem did not relate to global (as opposed to situationally specific) aspects of self-esteem or to apparent affectively significant bases of self-evaluation. Self-esteem was behaviorally defined in terms of the discrepancy between level of aspiration and expectancy of success on the task, — the greater the discrepancy, the lower the self-esteem. It is possible that the self-esteem index used in this study is inversely related to indices that would be based on more global and salient aspects of self-attitudes. For example, individuals may hold high expectations and high aspirations (low discrepancy —

high self-esteem) on a specific task by way of compensating for more general negative self-feelings. In such a situation the above stated result would be consistent with the findings of the experimental studies considered above. Furthermore, since the self-esteem measure was not experimentally induced, for the moment assuming the validity of the measure, it is not possible to determine the relationship between self-esteem and *prior* deviant behavior. That is, the current high self-esteem may be the consequence of the prior adoption of deviant patterns as a way of adjusting to earlier self-derogation.

Somewhat inconsistent results were reported by Mussen and his associates (1970) for preadolescent subjects. The subjects were administered a self-concept scale. Six weeks later they were given the opportunity to behave (dis)honestly in a game situation. The results tended to indicate that, for boys, low self-esteem was associated with a tendency toward honesty and, for girls, high self-esteem was associated with a tendency toward honesty. These results were discussed in terms of adequacy of socialization and sex typing of behavior. It is suggested that for children of this age independence in thought and action are appropriate masculine sex-typed characteristics while conformity and obedience are feminine characteristics. The high-self-esteem boy who cheats in the game situation may simply be reflecting appropriate sex-typed behavior in acting independently of the game rules, while the low-self-esteem boy who is honest (conforms to the rules in the face of temptation) may be reflecting inadequate sex typing in his failure to act independently of the rules without feelings of anxiety and insecurity. On the other hand, the observed tendency of high-self-esteem female subjects to conform to the rules is said to be a reflection of appropriate sex typing. If this explanation has any merit, however, it must hold for particular age groups since in a study of college-age subjects referred to above (Jacobson, Berger, and Millham, 1969) the observed tendency for high-self-esteem subjects to cheat was accounted for primarily by the female subjects. In any case the consideration of sex typing raises the question of whether or not the cheating behavior in these situations is truly deviant in the sense that such behavior by the group members (of particular sexes) is condemned by the groups in which the subjects hold membership.

The nature of the research design as well as the possible failure to take into account sex typing must again be considered as a possible explanation of the occasional observation of an inverse rather than direct relationship between self-esteem and subsequent honest behavior. In this study (Mussen, *et al.*, 1970), as in the preceding one, the self-esteem subjects might already have embarked upon deviant careers (with self-enhancing results) as an adaptation to earlier self-derogation. Thus, the dishonesty might merely reflect a continuation of earlier deviant tendencies rather than responses to particular self-esteem levels. This explanation for the apparently inconsistent results will be considered at greater length below in connection with the discussion of "concurrent variation" studies.

In short, this group of studies, perhaps more so than any of the groups of investigations to be considered, proves to be unsatisfactory for the purpose of examining the hypothesized influence of antecedent self-rejection upon deviant responses either because of the suspect nature of the measure of self-attitudes;

the absence of any clear indication that the "dishonest" or "cheating" behavior is socially defined as deviant; and/or, even given the understanding that the behavior in question was socially defined as deviant, the absence of any clear indication that the deviant pattern was not already established prior to the time when the subjects' self-attitudes were measured. Thus, these investigations provide no basis for either unequivocal support or rejection of the hypothesis.

Retrospective Reports

Unlike the next group of studies to be considered, which also consider the association between concurrent measures of self-attitudes and deviant behavior (here, dishonesty, delinquency, and criminality), the present category of investigations includes reports of associations between indicators of current contranormative behavior and concomitant self-reports of earlier experiences on the basis of which the existence of antecedent negative self-attitudes may more easily be inferred.

In one such study the data were questionnaire responses by seventh-and eighth-grade junior high school students in three Kansas communities: a middle-class suburb, a rural farm town, and a rural nonfarm community (Dentler and Monroe, 1961). Five of the items dealing with self-reports of stealing behavior (taking things from someone else's desk or locker, taking a car for a ride without the owner's knowledge, taking things of value, and so on) were said to constitute the Theft Scale. Among the findings were reports that students who reported more stealing behavior (higher scorers on the Theft Scale) were more likely to perceive their families as "essentially unloving" and were somewhat less likely to see themselves as equitably treated by their families than students who received lower Theft Scale scores. These perceptions of family suggest the kinds of childhood experiences that are likely to lead to self-devaluation. Consequently the findings lend some support to the hypothesis that antecedent self-derogation increases the probability of subsequent delinquent (in this instance, theft) behavior.

Among the earlier studies suggesting that delinquency is preceded by a history of self-devaluing experiences was that reported by Healy and Bronner (1936:122). One finding congruent with that thesis indicated that 92 percent of a delinquent sample reported feelings of being rejected by their parents in comparison with only 13 percent of their nondelinquent siblings. If it is assumed that perception of parental rejection is associated with the genesis of self-rejecting feelings then this observation may be interpreted as support for the statement that antecedent self-derogation increases the probability of subsequent adoption of delinquent patterns.

A greater tendency toward a history of self-devaluating experiences on the part of criminal offenders as opposed to nonoffenders may be inferred from data reported by Wood (1961) for Ceylon. The data to be discussed were collected by interviews with males seventeen years of age and older who had committed felonies involving personal assault or property crimes during the previous five years and with a representative sample of nonoffenders living in the same three

Sinhalese Low-County villages. Felony data were gathered from police records and local informants. A comparison of the offender and nonoffender groupings with regard to traditional or contemporary evaluative criteria revealed that the former group was significantly less advantaged. The offenders were less likely to hold title to adequate arable land, were less likely to have more prestigeful occupations, were more likely to be irregularly employed, and were less likely to have an English-language education.

In view of the observation that father and family name are significant objects of identification in Ceylon, loss of prestige relative to one's father is likely to be an influential factor in the self-evaluative process. A comparison of the respondents with their fathers in both the offender and the nonoffender samples indicates that, by the criteria of ownership of highland and paddy land, both of which are said to be necessary for a successful farming operation and occupational rank, the offender sample lost status in successive generations to a greater extent than the nonoffender sample.

Other indications of experiences that might be expected to induce self-devaluation involve the relationship between career aspirations, occupational achievement, and educational level. The offenders in comparison with the non-offenders were more likely to express career ambitions that were disproportionately higher relative to occupational achievements. Among respondents with higher levels of educational attainment, nonoffenders were more than twice as likely as offenders to enjoy higher prestige occupations. In general, the non-offenders manifested a greater consistency among occupation, educational level, and career ambition than offenders. More highly educated nonoffenders frequently enjoy the occupational success compatible with their career ambitions, and those with low educational and occupational attainments tended to have lower career ambitions. In contrast, among the offenders, higher educational attainment and career ambitions did not bring occupational success, and those with low education and occupational attainment tended to manifest fairly high levels of career ambition. As Wood (1961:747) states: "Cumulative evidence suggests a self-image of relative failure for the offender group."

In general, then, studies in this category of investigations are consistent with the hypothesis that antecedent negative self-attitudes influence the subsequent adoption of delinquent or criminal response patterns. However, it should be noted, particularly in the instances in which subject reports of prior experiences are involved, that the possibility of retrospective distortion exists.

Concurrent Variation

A fourth group of studies includes investigations of concurrent variation between indicators of delinquency or criminality, on the one hand, and measures or contemporary self-attitudes, on the other hand. These studies may be distributed among two subcategories according to whether the "delinquency" indicator referred to current delinquency status or to delinquency proneness. In the former studies the "delinquent" subjects have been formally designated as such, while in the latter study the "delinquent" subjects were designated as such by virtue of their scores on some sort of "delinquency proneness" measure.

Delinquency Proneness. In general, this category of studies tends to provide support for the hypothesized relationship between antecedent negative self-attitudes and the predisposition to adopt delinquent or criminal behavior patterns.

Reed and Cuadra (1957), for example, reported findings indicating a significant association between delinquency proneness and apparently self-derogatory attitudes. Among a group of student nurses, those who scored higher on a delinquency scale indicated their expectations of peer descriptions in terms of more unfavorable adjectives than those who scored lower on the scale. This difference was observed in spite of the fact that there were no objective differences in the adjectives actually used by the group to describe high and low scorers.

In another study of young, healthy Navy men, measures of self-evaluation were observed to be correlated with delinquency proneness (Gunderson and Johnson, 1965). Subjects who manifested more positive self-regard tended to score lower on a delinquency scale while subjects with more negative self-attitudes tended to score higher on the delinquency scale.

Also illustrative of studies that relate current self-evaluation and concurrent delinquency proneness is an investigation reported by Schwartz and Tangri (1965). The sixth-grade teachers as well as the principal and assistant principal in an all-black inner-city school in the highest delinquency area of Detroit were asked to nominate boys who they felt would never have police or court contacts ("good" boys) and boys who they felt would have such contacts ("bad" boys). When comparing the good and bad boys with regard to their scores on a semantic differential measure of self-evaluation it was observed that the bad boys had less positive self-concepts than the good boys. While this result is interpretable as providing support for the hypothesized relationship between self-rejection and adoption of delinquent patterns it should be noted that the nominations might simply reflect the attitudes toward the subjects by significant others that influence the subjects' self-evaluations. That is, the observed relationship, rather than reflecting an association between self-attitudes and delinquency proneness, might simply reflect a relationship between self-evaluation and evaluation by significant others.

Closely related findings were discussed by Schwartz and Stryker (1970). Their report was primarily based upon data collected from 398 white and black boys attending a school located in an area characterized by high social disorganization and a lower-class population in a Midwestern city. In addition data were gathered from 49 white boys attending a middle-class school. Self-concepts were measured using a semantic differential technique. Teachers in the lower-class school were asked to nominate those boys who would ("bad" boys) and those boys who would not ("good" boys) likely come into official contact with the police or juvenile courts at some future time. Consistent with the findings of the other studies in this category, the investigators reported that the black subjects who were nominated as potentially delinquent did tend to display (p<.10) more negative self-evaluations than their nondelinquent counterparts. However, also among the findings was the observation that young white bad boys did not differ significantly in level of self-evaluation from young white good boys. Whatever the explanation for this apparently inconsistent finding[3] it remains true that the general observation was congruent with the hypothesized relationship between self-rejecting attitudes and predisposition to delinquency.

Delinquency Status. Among studies of the relationship between self-attitudes and delinquency status are those that report findings that are congruent with the hypothesized relationship between self-rejection and delinquent behavior. However, more so than in the preceding subcategory, results that are apparently inconsistent with the hypothesis are also reported. In discussing these findings, it will be argued below that, although these findings might appear to be inconsistent with the particular proposition, they are congruent with the more general theoretical model. The apparent inconsistency arises from the nature of the research design, which obscures the simultaneous operation of two processes. Further, if the instances of apparent inconsistency are observed more frequently in the instances of studies of concurrent variation between self-attitudes and delinquency status than among similar studies of other forms of deviant behavior to be considered in subsequent chapters, the comparative frequency of such observations may be accounted for by the nature of the deviant patterns. It is possible that the nature of the delinquent patterns is such that the initial adoption of such patterns is difficult to determine with regard to their early or late occurrence. This situation increases the possibility of confusing the self-attitudes that influence the adoption of the deviant pattern with the self-attitudes that are the consequences of the adoption of the deviant pattern. If the point at which the deviant pattern was adopted, and therefore the period of time in which the person engaged in such behavior was distributed over a broader rather than a narrower time range in relationship to the point at which the measure of self-attitudes was administered, studies of concurrent variation would be expected to reflect the various operative processes. Thus, the group of studies as a whole would appear to offer apparently conflicting findings.

Among the studies reporting a relationship between concurrent measures of delinquency and self-devaluation is that reported by Scarpitti (1965). Inmates, all of whom had been committed for delinquency, of a boy's industrial school were compared with white ninth-grade boys from a junior high school in a lower-class area of a city and with white ninth-grade boys from a junior high school in a middle-class area of a city with regard to responses to a questionnaire. One part of the questionnaire consisted of eleven items previously developed "to assess interpersonal competence or feelings of personal worth" (p. 401). Whether considering more inclusive groupings of delinquent boys or only white ninth-grade delinquent boys, the delinquent group received the least favorable scores, the white ninth-grade lower-class boys received more favorable scores, and the white ninth-grade middle-class boys received the most favorable scores on this measure. It should be noted, however, that although this finding is consistent with the hypothesized relationship between antecedent self-rejection and the adoption of delinquent patterns other factors might also account for the relationship. For example, the fact that the delinquents were incarcerated at the time of the study might have exercised an independent unfluence upon their feelings of personal worth.

The tendency of delinquents to be more self-derogatory than nondelinquents is also suggested by data reported by Gough and Peterson (1952). Among the sixty-four items reported as having good differentiating power in distinguishing between delinquent and nondelinquent samples was a cluster of items described as "feelings of despondency and alienation, *lack of confidence in self and others*" (p. 209, italics added).

Apparently *inconsistent* results from investigations of the relationship between delinquency and self-attitudes derive, for example, from the comparison of delinquent males from a California juvenile hall with a group of nondelinquent high school students on measures of self-concept and self-rejection (Deitz, 1969). No significant tendency was noted for the delinquent subjects to rate themselves lower (using semantic differential measures) on the concept "me as I really am" than the nondelinquent subjects. However, the delinquents did tend to manifest greater self-rejection measured in terms of the discrepancy in ratings between "me as I really am" and "me as I would like to be" than the nondelinquent subjects. Since the groups did not differ in terms of the former concept, it was to be expected that the difference between the delinquents and nondelinquents in self-rejection scores would be accounted for by the greater tendency of the delinquent subjects to have higher ideal self-concept ratings.

Similarly, Cole and his associates (1967) failed to provide data in support of a relationship between negative self-attitudes and deviant responses. These investigators compared the discrepancies between the perceived self and the ideal-self of twenty-five adolescent-behavior-problem females with twelve high school female subjects comparable in age and academic records to the former group. However, the twelve girls had no records of acting-out behavior and unlike the behavior-problem subjects were not considered potential dropouts.

The behavior-problem subjects consisted of twelve delinquents who had returned to the community from juvenile homes and who were referred to a mental health center, and thirteen other subjects who were referred to a therapeutic agency. These twenty-five subjects were referred to the two agencies because of such behavioral disturbances as "sexual acting out, running away from home, and open hostility to all authority." The findings revealed no significant difference in mean self-ideal discrepancy scores between the behavior-problem subjects and the other grouping.

The inconsistent results described immediately above are perhaps to be expected in view of the nature of the research designs employed in these studies by which observations of concurrent variation between measures of deviant behavior and self-attitudes are made. Such research designs are inappropriate for testing propositions in the context of a theory in which deviant patterns are hypothesized to be both effects of, and influences upon, self-attitudes. On the one hand antecedent negative self-feelings are expected to influence the subsequent adoption of delinquent patterns. On the other hand, however, the adoption of delinquent patterns is expected to subsequently lead to a reduction in negative self-feelings. In studies investigating the relationship between concurrent self-feelings and delinquent status it would be difficult to predict whether the dominance of one or the other of the processes will produce a positive or negative relationship between the two variables, or whether the simultaneous operation of both processes will result in the observation of no significant association between indices of self-feelings and delinquent behavior.

In support of this argument are related findings from a number of studies. This explanation of the apparently inconsistent findings appears particularly appropriate when the reasoning is applied to the results of studies such as the one reported by Hall (1966). This investigator found a nonsignificant tendency for nondelinquent boys to manifest more positive levels of self-evaluation than self-reported delinquents, probationers, or institutionalized delinquents. By the argument presented above the failure to observe significant differences may have resulted from not considering the reciprocal effects of self-evaluation and delinquent behavior within a temporal framework. The hypotheses that constitute the basis for this volume assert that antecedent self-derogation increases the probability of subsequent deviant behavior and that the adoption of deviant patterns will raise the level of self-evaluation. Thus, self-evaluation and deviant behavior are hypothesized to be inversely or directly related depending upon the temporal sequence in force. However, when they are examined at the same point in time, the opposing influences of the two relationships might cancel each other out and no significant relationships between the two variables would be observed. That this is what occurred in the study under consideration is suggested by certain of the reported data. Hall divided his delinquent population according to whether they were high or low in delinquency orientation, that is, in identification with the delinquent subculture. It may be assumed that boys who commit delinquent acts and are strongly identified with the delinquent subculture are at a later stage in the delinquent career than are boys who commit delinquent acts but are not strongly identified with the delinquent subculture. [4] On this assumption, although Hall did not present the data in just this way, our treatment of Hall's data reveals just those relationships that would be expected in the light of the two hypotheses described above. Delinquents with a weaker delinquency orientation were appreciably more likely to display low self-evaluations than nondelinquents. However, delinquents with a strong delinquency orientation were as likely to display high self-evaluations as nondelinquents. This is exactly what would be expected if antecedent negative self-attitudes increased the probability of subsequently adopting delinquent patterns, and if the adoption of delinquent patterns subsequently increased the level of self-evaluation.

The simultaneous operation of both relationships (the influence of low self-esteem upon the subsequent adoption of deviant behavior, and the influence of the adoption of deviant behavior patterns upon subsequent increases in self-esteem) might also be attested to by the occasional observation of a curvilinear relationship between behavior problems and self-attitudes at a given point in time. In this regard the findings of Cole and his associates (1967) in a study discussed above are congruent with the results of earlier studies (Block and Thomas, 1955; Chodorkoff, 1954). Although the investigators observed no significant difference in mean self-ideal discrepancy scores between the behavior-problem subjects and a comparison grouping, greater variability in scores was observed for the subjects with behavior problems. Relative to the other subjects, those with behavior problems manifested both very high and very low self-ideal discrepancy scores. This relationship is, again, what one would expect if the behavior-problem grouping contained both individuals with low self-esteem who adopted deviant patterns in a provisional attempt to decrease their self-derogation, and individuals who *formerly* were characterized by low self-esteem but who had adopted delinquent patterns in successful attempts to enhance their self-attitudes, In short, the curvilinear relationship might simply reflect the inclusion in the delinquent grouping of subjects at different stages in the delinquent career.

Such a conclusion also appears warranted in the case of the somewhat inconsistent findings reported by Schwartz and Stryker (1970) described above. In view of other of their findings, one must again consider the possibility that the failure to observe consistent support for the hypothesized inverse association between level of self-evaluation and delinquency proneness is due to the nature of the research design, which forbids the clear establishment of the nature of the temporal relationship between the two variables. The observation that older bad boys had more positive self-evaluations than younger bad boys does suggest the presence of the process operative at a later stage in the delinquent career — That is, this observation suggests, on the assumption that the older boys had a longer period of time in which they could become entrenched in delinquent patterns and enjoy the self-enhancing experiences associated with such patterns, that the adoption of delinquent patterns increases the degree of self-acceptance. To the extent that this process was in fact operative, it is to be expected that unequivocal support for the association between negative self-attitudes and adoption of delinquent patterns (thought to occur at an earlier stage in the delinquent career) would not be apparent in studies of concomitant variation between self-attitudes and delinquency.

In summary, particularly with regard to studies of concurrent measures of delinquency status and self-attitudes, there is reason to believe that apparently inconsistent findings reflect the simultaneous operation of two processes, both of which are derived from the theoretical model. To the extent that this is the case, the findings are not in fact inconsistent with the theoretical model as a whole, although they may be inconsistent with one or more of the discretely considered hypotheses.

Theoretically Related Variables

Another potential source of support for the hypothesized association between negative self-attitudes and delinquent behavior is the observation of other relationships derived by the same reasoning (that is, within the context of the same theoretical model) that led to the formulation of the hypothesis under consideration. In deriving this hypothesis it was asserted that the predisposition to adopt deviant patterns stemmed from the actual and subjective association of the normative structure with past, and probable future, self-devaluing experiences. It was further proposed that the actual adoption of the deviant patterns would be associated with the subject's awareness of deviant patterns and the subject's expectation of net self-enhancing consequences (that is, the preponderance of self-enhancing consequences over self-devaluing consequences) of adopting the deviant patterns. Insofar as the hypothesized association between negative self-attitudes and the adoption of delinquent patterns was based upon these two general propositions, empirical support for these assertions would serve as indirect support for the hypothesis. Each of the two propositions will be considered in turn.

Self-Rejection and the Normative Structure. Implicit in the hypothesis that the probability of adopting delinquent patterns is greater for persons with more negative self-feelings that for persons with more positive self-feelings is the assumption that the former individuals associate past self-devaluating experiences with, and anticipate future self-devaluating experiences in, the normative environment.

Some testimony in support of the validity of this assumption is provided by data from a study on delinquency vulnerability (Dinitz, Scarpitti, and Reckless, 1962). In this investigation two cohorts of white sixth-grade boys from elementary schools in Columbus (Ohio) high-delinquency areas were tested and then reassessed four years later. One cohort consisted of boys who were nominated by their teachers as likely to stay out of trouble with the law. The other cohort consisted of boys who were nominated by their teachers as headed for trouble with the law. When those boys who could be located four years later were reexamined it was observed that the "bad" cohort was much more likely to have contained boys who had serious and frequent contact with the court during the four-year interlude than the "good" cohort.

Also reported were data bearing on the question of the relationship between the adoption of deviant patterns and perceptions of the normative environment. Among the items to which the subjects responded were "up to now do you think things have gone your way?," "do you feel that grown-ups are usually against you?," and "do you expect to get an even break from people in the future?" No appreciable change was noted in the percentage distribution of the responses of the two cohorts over the four-year period. For the "good" cohort the percentage of "favorable" responses on all three questions at age sixteen was 90. For the "bad" cohort the percentage of favorable responses to the above-listed three questions was 50, 29, and 30 respectively. Thus, the group of boys that was appreciably more likely to manifest delinquent patterns over the four-year interlude was also more likely to provide responses that were interpretable as indicating less than gratifying past experiences with, and expectations of continued negative responses from, the normative environment.

Washburn (1963) offers some data that supports the notion that the adoption of delinquent patterns involves subjective association of the normative environment with self-devaluating experiences. For present purposes, the relevant data concern the comparison of delinquent and nondelinquent subjects on one of three subtests derived from responses to a range of items said to represent self-concepts. The delinquent subjects were obtained from a juvenile hall. The nondelinquent control group consisted of counselor-selected high school students from the same community. The delinquents were matched individually with the control-group subjects on age, IQ, race, socioeconomic status, and number of siblings. The analysis was done separately for each sex. The subtest in question, *conformity*, was said to measure self-concepts "related to inner control through internalization of social norms." Subjects who scored low on this test were described in such terms, in addition to others, as being hostile toward authority, failing to relate positively to parents or teachers, and being suspicious of society. The delinquent males and females were expected, and in fact were observed, to score significantly lower than their nondelinquent counterparts on the conformity subtest. This finding is compatible with the notion that delinquents do associate the normative order with self-threatening experiences.

Further evidence of the relationship between adoption of delinquent patterns and the association of unfavorable experiences with the normative environment is provided by a comparison of delinquent boys from a juvenile hall with nondeliquent high school boys (Deitz, 1969). Although delinquent boys did not tend to perceive parental rejection of them to a greater extent than nondelinquent boys, the delinquent subjects were less likely to identify with, and to feel understood by, their parents when compared with nondelinquent subjects. Parental identification was measured as the difference in ratings between "me as I really am" and each parent "as he (she) really is" on semantic differential scales. The extent to which the subject felt understood by his parents was measured by differences between ratings of "me as I really am" and the combined concpets of "me as my father sees me" and "me as my mother sees me." These findings might be interpreted as indicating a relatively low level of expectation of future self-enhancing experiences in the normative environment on the part of the delinquent subjects.

Finally, the tendency of delinquents to associate past self-devaluing experiences with the normative environment is suggested also by data reported by Gough and Peterson (1952). In the course of constructing an assessment device for the differentiation between delinquent and nondelinquent samples, sixty-four personality test items were observed to have good differentiating power. One cluster of these items was described in terms of "resentment against family, feelings of having been victimized and exploited in childhood" (p.209), with delinquent subjects being more likely to subscribe to such sentiments than nondelinquent subjects.

Expectation of Self-Enhancing Consequences. Some evidence is also available in support of the assertion that the adoption of delinquent response patterns is associated with the awareness of self-enhancing alternatives to normative response patterns. More specifically, data offered by Short and his associates (1965) are consistent with the assumption that the adoption of delinquent patterns is associated with the perception of the absence of legitimate, and the presence of illegitimate, opportunities for self-enhancing experiences. The data were obtained from interviews with black and white lower-class delinquent gang boys, lower-class nongang boys, and middle-class nongang boys. Within each racial category, this ordering of groups was paralleled by the official delinquency rates for these groups with the lower-class gang's boys having the highest "mean number of offenses known to police, per boy" (p. 62), the lower-class nongang boys having the next lowest mean number, and the middle-class boys showing the lowest mean number of offenses.

With regard to perceptions of the legitimate opportunity structure, among the findings was the observation that, within racial categories, the highest delinquency group was least likely, and the lowest delinquency group was most likely, to perceive legitimate educational and occupational opportunities for success. The perception of legitimate educational and occupational opportunities was reflected in agreement with such items as "Most of the guys in our area will graduate from high school" and "Most of the guys in the area will probably get good paying honest jobs when they grow up," and in disagreement with such items as "In our area it's hard for a young guy to stay in school" and "In this area it's hard to make much money without doing something illegal."

With regard to perception of the illegitimate opportunity structure, within racial categories, the highest delinquency group (lower-class delinquent gang boys) was most likely to manifest perception of an illegitimate opportunity structure and the lowest delinquency group (middle-class boys) was least likely to do so. Perception of illegitimate opportunity was reflected in agreement with such items as "Some of the most respectable people in our area make their money illegally," "There are connections in this area for a guy who wants to make good money illegally," and "In this area there are some people who make their living by doing things that are against the law."

Thus, empirical support is available for propositions which form the theoretical basis for the hypothesized association between antecedent negative self-attitudes and the consequent adoption of delinquent response patterns.

DELINQUENT RESPONSES AND SELF-ENHANCEMENT

Although little direct evidence exists for the assertion that delinquent responses have self-enhancing consequences, some support for the proposition may be inferred from two types of observations. The first type of observation refers to the relationship between degree of commitment to the delinquent pattern and self-attitudes. The second type of observation concerns correlates of delinquency from which self-enhancing consequences are inferred.

Commitment to Delinquency

If the adoption of delinquent patterns does indeed have consequences for improving one's self-attitudes it is to be expected that persons who are more committed to the delinquent pattern, and/or have been fixed in the delinquent response pattern for longer periods of time, would be observed to have more self-accepting attitudes than persons who are less committed to, or established in, the delinquent response pattern. To the extent that this relationship is actually observed the assertion of a functional relationship between adoption of delinquent patterns and increased self-acceptance might more easily be accepted. Two of the studies discussed above in another connection are relevant to this issue.

Some support for the thesis that the adoption of delinquent patterns is associated with self-enhancing experiences is provided by Hall's (1966) observation that, among self-defined and adjudicated delinquents, increasing delinquency orientation is associated with increasing level of positive self-evaluation. It is argued that the delinquent subculture provides the delinquent with the opportunity to gain more positive self-attitudes by engaging in behavior that is rewarded. As an individual comes to increasingly identify with the delinquent subculture he exchanges the standards of the conventional culture that provided the basis for previously low self-evaluation for delinquent group standards of self-evaluation. To the extent that he conforms to these standards he will judge himself more positively than he did prior to identifying with the delinquent subculture. The totally committed delinquent, completely involved in only the delinquent subculture, thus would be expected to manifest a relatively high level of self-evaluation. However, the marginal delinquent has not completely detached himself from the conventional standards by which he has failed. Although he has some delinquent identity he has not yet made the delinquent group the primary reference for purposes of self-evaluation. Consequently, the marginal delinquent who has less completely identified with the delinquency subculture would be expected to manifest lower self-evaluation relative to that of the totally committed delinquent.

In testing the hypothesis that delinquency orientation is positively related to level of self-evaluation among juvenile delinquents, three categories of delinquent males were considered: The first category consisted of twenty-six self-reported delinquents from four public schools in Minneapolis. These boys admitted to having committed delinquent acts and to having friendships with delinquents. The next category consisted of thirty-nine delinquents on probation. The third grouping consisted of forty-two delinquents placed in a county institution. The selected adjudicated delinquent boys were working-class Caucasians between the ages of fourteen and sixteen who had appeared before juvenile court for theft. Delinquency identification was measured in terms of responses to questions indicating delinquent self-conceptions, negative attitudes toward parents, delinquent peer group orientation, and rejection of middle-class values and other attributes understood to be characteristic of the ideal type "totally committed delinquent." Self-evaluation was measured in terms of responses to a checklist of self-descriptive words or phrases.

As was stated above, boys who committed delinquent acts and who strongly identified with the delinquent subculture were significantly more likely to manifest more positive self-evaluations than boys who similarly committed delinquent acts but were less strongly identified with the delinquent subculture. If it is assumed that identification with the delinquent subculture represents a later stage in the delinquent's career, then the observed association is highly consistent with the view that the adoption of delinquent patterns (presumably, in part, a response to initial self-rejection) is associated with an increase in positive self-attitudes.

Data possibly indicative of a relationship between degree of fixity in a delinquent response pattern and self-acceptance are provided by a study of black and white boys attending a school in an area of the city characterized by high social disorganization and a lower-class population (Schwartz and Stryker, 1970). Among the findings was the observation that, among boys nominated by their teachers as likely to come into contact with the police or juvenile courts at some future time, older subjects (sixteen and above) were significantly more positive in self-evaluation than younger subjects (twelve to fifteen). If it is assumed that older boys are more likely than younger boys to be entrenched in, or committed to, delinquent patterns due to longer experience with these patterns, then the observation stated above may be interpreted as supporting the hypothesis that the adoption of delinquent patterns functions to increase level of self-acceptance. However, as Schwartz and Stryker (1970:79) point out, caution should be exercised in interpreting data regarding the older students in this lower-class school in view of possible circumstances attendant upon keeping them in school beyond the age of compulsory attendance.

Correlates of Delinquency

A second type of observation that provides indirect support for the hypothesis under consideration deals not with the relationship between delinquency and self-acceptance but, rather, with the relationship between delinquency and other responses from which an increase in self-acceptance is inferred.

If, as the theoretical model asserts, the genesis of self-rejecting attitudes was a consequence of the person's experiences within the normative structure of his predeviance membership groups, it is to be expected that his self-attitudes would improve to the extent that he responded in ways that would facilitate avoidance of the self-devaluing experiences in the normative structure; attack upon the normative structure (that is, upon the basis of his self-devaluation); and substitution of extranormative experiences with self-enhancing potential for the self-devaluing experiences within the normative structure. Thus, if delinquency is observed to be associated with responses appearing to serve such avoidance, attack, and substitution functions, it might be inferred that delinquency is also associated with a decrease in self-rejecting, and an increase in self-accepting, attitudes. Such observations of associations between delinquency and responses akin to those serving avoidance, attack, and substitution functions are certainly not unknown.

Avoidance. Among the observations of a relationship between delinquency and physical or perceptual avoidance of self-devaluing experiences (particularly such experiences associated with the normative structure) are those made by Shinohara and Jenkins (1967) and Washburn (1963). Shinohara and Jenkins noted the runaway delinquent as one of three types of delinquent. This type was said to respond to feelings of rejection and a relatively poor self-image with the mechanism of flight.

Observations consistent with these were reported by Washburn (1963) in the course of an investigation of protective attitudes in delinquent and non-delinquent boys and girls. Protective attitudes were said to "refer to sets of related ideas which enable the individual to maintain, enhance, and defend his system of basic self-concepts, ideals, and values" (p. 111). The test to measure protective attitudes was developed through the construction of forced-choice items related to each of fifteen commonly described defense mechanisms. A cluster analysis of the fifteen defense mechanisms (displacement, projection, rationalization, withdrawal, and so on) reflected in the test items resulted in three clusters of protective attitudes, one of which was "denial" involving detachment from potentially threatening interpersonal situations by refusing to accept and face them. It includes the mechanisms of regression, withdrawal, suppression, and negativism.

The delinquent subjects, almost entirely from lower socioeconomic strata, were obtained from a California juvenile hall. These subjects all had a record of at least two delinquent acts over the preceding three years. The nondelinquent subjects were selected from available high school subjects from the same socioeconomic strata. These control subjects had no record of delinquency or behavior problems over the same three-year period. Available records suggested that the male delinquents were members of gangs in which the delinquent acts functioned primarily as a means of achieving prestige. The delinquent acts of females, on the other hand, were far less likely to be in the context of organized group activity.

Among the findings was the observation that both male and female delinquents scored higher on *denial* than their nondelinquent counterparts, although the differences were statistically significant only for the female subjects. This finding is compatible with the association of delinquency and avoidance-type responses, which would be expected to mitigate the experience of self-devaluation.

Attack. The observation of an association between delinquent responses and attacklike functions has been made frequently by students of the problem. Delinquent groups, for example, might be said to serve as a vehicle for the rejection of the dominant middle-class values, by which standards the delinquent members have failed. The malicious, apparently nonutilitarian delinquent behavior is interpreted as a reaction formation through which the group members demonstrate their contempt for this value system (Cohen, 1966: 65-66).

The interpretation of delinquent behavior as an attack-type hostile response is compatible with Elliot's (1966) report that the rate of referral for delinquency is greater for boys while in school than out of school and with the observation that delinquents who drop out have a higher delinquency referral rate while in school than out of school. The findings are interpretable in the following terms. Lower-class delinquent behavior is associated with feelings of frustration and failure experienced in school and serves to express resentment toward the middle-class structure (and its surrogates), which provides the context for these experiences. When the individual drops out of school he effectively withdraws from competition with his middle-class peers and therefore is less stimulated to display delinquent behavior as an expression of hostility.

Data bearing on the association between delinquent behavior and rejection of, or attacks (symbolic or otherwise) upon the normative structure are offered by Scarpitti (1965) in his study of delinquent and nondelinquent perception of self, values, and legitimate opportunities. Questionnaire responses of boys (both black and white) committed for delinquency to an industrial school were compared with those of ninth-grade white boys of a junior high school in a lower-class urban area and of ninth-grade white boys of a junior high school in a middle-class area of the same city. One part of the questionnaire contained a value orientation scale and another part consisted of a measure of awareness of limited opportunity. The results provided support for the expectations that delinquents would tend to reject middle-class values more, and would perceive more limited opportunity to achieve desirable goals, than nondelinquent lower-class and middle-class subjects. The delinquent boys were most likely to reject middle-class values and to perceive limited opportunity, the nondelinquent lower-class boys were less likely to do so, and the middle-class boys were least likely to reject the middle-class values and to perceive limited opportunity.

The association of attack behavior with delinquency was also notable in the two studies discussed above in connection with denial responses. Attacklike behavior by the rejected child was apparent in one of three types of delinquent noted by Shinohara and Jenkins (1967). This type was the *unsocialized aggressive.*

Washburn (1963) also noted a relationship between delinquency and a cluster of protective attitudes that strongly suggested hostile, aggressive, or attacklike predispositions. The cluster in question, labeled *externalization,* involved exaggeration of environmental threats and suspicion and doubts concerning others. It included the defense categories of projection, substitution, conversion, and displacement of hostility. It correlated inversely with sublimation, fantasy, and identification with socially approved authority figures. It was observed that both male and female delinquents scored significantly higher on a subtest measuring externalization than their nondelinquent counterparts.

Substitution. Delinquency might potentially be associated with a third outcome that is presumed to have self-enhancing implications. This outcome involves substituting new patterns for aspects of the normative structure. The new patterns might be the adoption of a new (deviant) value system as a basis for self-approbation or new deviant routes to the same valued attributes.

Cohen (1955), for example, argues that delinquency groups provide members the opportunity to receive rewards for delinquent acts and thereby achieve status satisfaction. [5] Data reported by Washburn (1963) are consistent with the notion that, particularly for males, there is an intense need associated with delinquency to conform to a (presumably) achievable set of standards. One of three clusters of protective attitudes described by this investigator, labeled *vindication,* involved attempts to avoid blame and apparent conformity to approved social norms. It is said to include the defenses of rationalization, reaction formation, and compensation. With regard to the subtest measuring *vindication*, delinquent males were observed to score significantly higher than nondelinquent males.[6] From this observation it might be inferred that delinquency represents conformity to standards by means of which one achieves social prestige and self-approval.

Assertions to the effect that delinquency serves to substitute new deviant routes to positive self-attitudes for old normatively defined routes (which resulted in self-rejection) are suggested also by such early observations as those of Alexander and Healy (1935), who propose that stealing is a response to subjectively perceived inferiority and provides the individual with a sense of bravado and toughness. Stealing is an overcompensation for internally felt weakness.

In short, the observations noted above are generally supportive of the view that delinquency is associated with functional outcomes such as the avoidance of, attacks upon, or substitution for aspects of the normative structure. In view of the association of the normative structure with the genesis of negative self-attitudes, the improvement of self-attitudes might be expected to occur from such outcomes of delinquent response patterns.

SUMMARY

The present chapter examined literature dealing with dishonesty, delinquency, and criminality with regard to its congruence with the emerging theoretical model described in Part I. More particularly, the discussion focused upon two relationships that constitute an important part of the proposed general theory of deviant behavior.

The first relationship concerned the association between negative self-attitudes and the predisposition to subsequent adoption of deviant response patterns. The hypothesis that antecedent self-rejection increases the probability of adopting dishonest, delinquent, or criminal response patterns appears to be supported, in general, by findings from experimental studies of the relationship between induced self-attitudes and subsequent dishonest behavior; studies of the relationship between current self-attitudes and current reports of experiences that are interpretable as having occurred at an earlier period in the person's development; investigations of concomitant variation between self-attitudes and measures of delinquency proneness; and studies of relationships that form the theoretical basis of the hypothesis under consideration. The relatively few studies dealing with the relationship between antecedent measures of "naturally occurring" self-attitudes and subsequent "dishonesty, delinquency, or criminality" were judged to be unsuitable for the purpose of examining the validity of the hypothesis since these studies were characterized by such limitations as the suspect nature of the measure of self-attitudes and the absence of any clear indication that the "dishonest" or "delinquent" behavior was in fact socially defined as deviant behavior. Other findings from studies of concurrent variation between self-attitudes and delinquency status (as opposed to "proneness") suggested that the apparently conflicting findings from such studies were in fact congruent with the general theoretical model.

The second focus of the discussion was the proposed relationship between the adoption of delinquent or criminal patterns and the subsequent improvement in self-attitudes. Two areas in the literature, in the absence of direct tests of the hypothesis, were interpreted as providing indirect empirical support of the relationship. The first source of support was derived from observations of a relationship between self-attitudes and oblique indicators of commitment to, or entrenchment in, the delinquent pattern. The second source of support was derived from observations of relationships between delinquency and functional outcomes (avoidance, attack, and substitution) of response patterns from which self-enhancing consequences are inferred. The inference is permitted only by virtue of the assumption that the normative environment (which is the reference "object" of the avoidance, attack, and substitution responses) was in fact associated with the genesis of the person's negative self-attitudes.

In summary, the relevant literature dealing with dishonesty, delinquency, and criminality appears to be generally congruent with the salient features of the outline of a general theory of deviant behavior under consideration.

NOTES

[1] Dishonesty as explicitly differentiated from delinquency and criminality refers here to dishonorable behaviors that are subject only to informal sanctions, unlike the other violations that are subject to formal (legal) sanctions whether or not they are responded to with informal sanctions.

[2] The observation of a relationship between antecedent self-derogation and subsequent deviant behavior may be interpreted in any of a number of ways. For example, the observation may be explained in terms of cognitive consistency theory. That is, an individual tends to behave in ways that are consistent with his expectations of self, and deviant behavior is consistent with low self-expectations (Aronson and Mettee, 1968; Graf, 1971). However, these studies, taken together with those dealing with the influence of deviant behavior upon subsequent self-feelings, appear to be more congruent with the position that the adoption of deviant patterns serves as a more or less effective attempt to restore, maintain, or attain positive self-feelings.

[3] In this study, the explanation might be offered to the effect that the observation of the hypothesized association in the case of the black, but not the white, subjects might be accounted for by the fact that it is the black bad boys, rather than good boys, for whom teachers constitute significant others. Therefore the relatively low self-evaluations of black bad boys might be the result of incorporating the negative evaluations by significant others, as evidenced by their being nominated by their teachers as potentially delinquent, into their self-evaluations. For the white subjects, in contrast, the teachers were apparently not significant figures. Consequently their nomination as bad boys, which is presumably the expression of a negative evaluation by the teachers, would not necessarily be associated with the genesis of notably negative self-attitudes. Such an explanation might explain the failure to differentiate between good and bad white boys in terms of self-evaluation, and the success in doing so in the case of the black subjects.

[4] Again, the assumption is made that the "delinquent" behavior is socially defined as deviant by the person's predeviance membership groups.

[5] The achievement of positive self-attitudes through conformity to delinquent standards would be expected in certain circumstances whether or not the "delinquent" behavior was defined as deviant by the person's membership group. Where the situation is such that the delinquent behavior is defined as deviant by the person's predeviance membership group, the delinquent behavior could enhance self-attitude by permitting approximation to a more easily achievable set of standards (than that provided by the normative structure) as a basis for self-approval and positive self-attitudes. Where the situation is such that the "delinquent" responses are defined as normative, positive self-attitudes are contingent upon *conforming to the normative structure of the deviant subculture*, that is, being a good deviant. Here, the deviant is not adopting "antisocial" behavior patterns for the purpose of restoring or attaining positive self-attitudes. Rather, he is conforming to a set of standards (to which he has been socialized) in order to *maintain* acceptable self-attitudes.

This latter situation might fit the case of one of three delinquent types noted by Shinohara and Jenkins (1967) — *the socialized delinquent*. It was noted that most normal MMPI scores were from the socialized (rather than the *unsocialized aggressive* and *runaway* delinquents), an observation that was consistent with the hypothesis that their behavior was learned, adaptive, goal-oriented behavior. From the perspective of self-theory, these findings would support the view that the behavior of the socialized delinquent serves to maintain an acceptable self-image by conforming to internalized delinquent norms, while the behavior of the other two groups served as reactions to negative self-attitudes.

[6] Nondelinquent females were observed to score significantly higher than delinquent females on this measure. Perhaps for the female delinquent, delinquency is the vehicle for repudiation of the intense conformity that is demanded of females in our society, which these persons have been unable to achieve.

Chapter 6

Drug Addiction and Drug Abuse

This chapter considers the relationship between self-attitudes, on the one hand, and drug dependency (or addiction) and drug abuse, on the other hand. "Drug dependency," whether the dependency is psychological or physical, is taken to be a particular type of drug-abuse pattern characterized by "the compulsive, uncontrolled use of drugs beyond the period of medical need" (Pearson and Little, 1969:1167), while drug abuse more generally is taken to refer to the use of pharmacologic agents in quantities and circumstances that violate the normative expectations of the person's predeviance membership group under circumstances in which the person comes to lack motivation to conform to or becomes motivated to deviate from the normative expectations. Paralleling the organization of the previous chapter, the discussion will focus upon two relationships: the relationship between presumably antecedent self-attitudes and the subsequent adoption of drug-addition or drug-abuse patterns, and the influence of these patterns upon changes in self-attitudes.

SELF-ATTITUDES AND DRUG ABUSE

The theoretical model described in Part I leads to the expectation that, relative to persons with more positive self-attitudes, persons with negative self-attitudes are more likely to be predisposed to adopt drug-abuse patterns, particu-

94

larly under conditions where they become aware of the opportunity to adopt the patterns and anticipate self-enhancing consequences of adopting the patterns. It should be emphasized, however, that this expectation is predicated upon the assumption that the drug-abuse patterns are defined as deviant by the person's membership group(s). If the drug-abuse patterns of behavior are not defined as deviant, quite a different relationship between self-attitudes and the adoption of drug-abuse response patterns is to be expected. In order to highlight this difference drug-abuse patterns as deviant responses and as normatively appropriate responses to self-attitudes will be considered in turn.

Drug Abuse as Deviant Behavior

Although the relevant literature is not abundant such reports as exist appear to be consistent with the expectation that the adoption of a drug-abuse pattern (considered as a deviant pattern) will be associated with antecedent negative self-attitudes. It will be recalled from Part I that the predisposition to deviant behavior (in this instance, drug abuse) is said to stem from the actual and subjective association of the normative environment with the genesis of highly distressful negative self-attitudes. The available reports deal with clinical observations, findings of concomitant variations between self-attitudes (or presumed correlates of self-attitudes) and drug-abuse behavior, and/or findings of concomitant variation between drug-abuse behavior, on the one hand, and factors that are theoretically assumed to mediate between negative self-attitudes and drug-abuse response patterns, on the other hand.

Clinical Observations. The relationship between antecedent self-derogation and subsequent adoption of drug-addiction patterns has been asserted quite frequently in the clinical literature. Reports such as the following will serve as illustrative summary statements:

> The most striking clinical finding which I noted during my experience in conducting psychoanalytic psychotherapy with drug addicts is their abysmally low self-esteem. Behind the façade of their various ego defenses and their basically depressed affect, lies this low feeling of self-value which never fails to be revealed at the core of the addiction prone personality [Hoffman, 1964:265].

Congruent with this statement are some of the remarks of Pearson and Little (1969:1168-1169), who, after Rado (1957), suggested the relevancy of self-attitudes in preparing a person for addiction to the pharmacologic agent:

> Preparedness for addiction indicates that an individual is suffering from a form of psychological frustration which, if unrelieved, produces psychological pain accompanied by feelings of helplessness. Feelings of self-depreciation and depression may then

> develop. Inability to solve these problems produces tension, which contributes to a further lowering of self-esteem; thus, a condition develops which may be characterized by the term "tense depression."

Depending upon the degree of pain associated with this preaddictive state ("tense depression") the addiction will occur more or less rapidly.

> When the individual provides himself with a drug that changes his pain to pleasure and his depression is replaced by an increase in self-esteem, the first step to addiction has occurred.

Self-Attitudes and Drug Abuse. A second source of observations congruent with the hypothesized relationship between antecedent negative self-attitudes and drug-abuse response patterns is the group of studies that report associations between drug-abuse behavior and negative self-attitudes (or their presumed correlates). In these studies the data relating to both sets of variables were collected at the same point in time. The variables relating to drug abuse might refer either to past experiences with drug use or to future willingness to use the drugs. The variables relating to self-attitudes might be face-valid indicators or factors that are presumed to be closely associated with self-attitudes.

A number of findings concerning the relationship between self-derogation and the adoption of drug-abuse patterns were reported by Kaplan and Meyerowitz (1970). These investigators compared drug addicts and "normal" subjects along a variety of psychosocial dimensions. The addict subject grouping consisted of the first 300 persons with recent histories of addiction who were released into a previously defined target area in Texas by either the Texas Department of Corrections or the U.S. Public Health Service Hospital at Fort Worth. The "normal" subjects consisted of a nonrandom selection of subjects who were not excluded from consideration by virtue of being younger than seventeen years of age; having less than a fifth-grade education or more than a year of college; not being a United States citizen; having been hospitalized or treated for mental illness; having a police record for other than traffic offenses; or having ever illegally used addictive drugs. The data consisted of responses for the most part to structured and semistructured questionnaire items.

Support for the hypothesis that self-derogation is associated with the adoption of drug-abuse patterns was provided more or less directly by several discrete findings, each of which was based upon observations of the differential responses of the addict and nonaddict subjects to a series of instruments of widely differing format, all of which were manifestly related to self-evaluation. These instruments included single-item measures of self-satisfaction and self-respect, a multiple-item measure of self-estrangement, semantic differential evaluations of the concept "me," and a "What kind of person am I?" test calling for unstructured responses. On all of these tests the addict subjects were significantly more likely than the "normal" subjects to provide self-devaluing responses. These group differences could not be accounted for by observed differences in age or social class of origin between the two groups of subjects.

It should be noted, however, that these findings do not demonstrate a temporal relationship between antecedent self-derogation and subsequent adoption of drug-abuse patterns. The observation that the addict subjects were significantly more likely to manifest self-rejecting responses than the nonaddict subjects could be explained in any of a number of ways. For example, the relatively high levels of self-derogation displayed by the addict subjects could be the consequence of being deprived of the use of their preferred defense (drugs) against negative self-feelings by the circumstance of being institutionalized. Nevertheless, this possibility does not obviate the equally plausible interpretation that subjects with relatively depressed levels of self-esteem are significantly more likely to adopt drug-abuse patterns than subjects characterized by more self-accepting attitudes toward the goal of increasing their level of self-esteem.

Unlike the previous study concerning addiction, the following study relates to marijuana use. If it may be assumed that identification with worthy life goals is a reflection and or precondition of self-acceptance, then certain of the data reported by Shean and Fechtmann (1971) may be interpreted as supporting the hypothesis of an association between drug abuse and self-rejecting attitudes. Twenty-seven college undergraduate marijuana users were compared with twenty-eight control subjects who did not use drugs with regard to scores on a Purpose in Life Test. This test was said to measure the degree to which the subject "has found meaningful goals around which to integrate his life" (Shean and Fechtmann, 1971:112). The investigators reported that the drug users received significantly lower scores on the Purpose in Life Test than the nondrug users, an observation here interpreted as support for the hypothesized association between self-rejecting attitudes and drug abuse.

Data relevant to the relationship between self-attitudes and predisposition to drug abuse were reported by Brehm and Back (1968). The subjects were 333 introductory psychology students. The data consisted of responses to questionnaire items concerning attitudes toward drug use and self-image. Two of the scores resulting from the analysis were interpretable as indices of self-acceptance. The first of these indices provided scores on a factorially derived measure. The items making up this factor (labelled *insecurity* by the authors) reflected the subject's desire to change himself particularly with regard to unsatisfactory emotional states. Among these items were "If there were a drug which would make me feel less anxious, I would take it"; "Sometimes I feel I have to take something to make me less self-conscious"; and "I wish I could get some help to achieve 'the real me'." Unfortunately, for present purposes this measure is contaminated since it reflects not only feelings of inadequacy and insecurity but also a willingness to change one's emotional state through chemical means. Thus, an observed association between this measure and an index of drug use might be accounted for by this willingness to use chemical means to effect self-change as well as (or instead of) by self-rejecting attitudes. However, the availability of the second index provided an independent check on such an observed relationship.

The second index, interpreted as a measure of negative self-image, was derived from semantic differential responses to "My Ideal Self" and "My Hidden

Self." The negative self-image score was based on the discrepancies noted between self-descriptions of the "Ideal" and "Hidden" self on seven bipolar scales (calm-nervous, suspicious-trusting, and so on).

Two types of measures were available that might be interpreted as indices of predisposition to drug use. The first measure was based on responses to questions regarding the degree to which the subject, during the preceding month, felt like taking each of ten types of chemical agents. Only the factorially derived score indicating responses to hallucinogens, opiates, energizers, and tranquilizers (the "drug" factor) will be discussed below. A second type of measure is based on the degree to which the subject described himself in terms used in another study (Blum, et al., 1964) to describe LSD acceptors as opposed to those subjects who rejected its use.

In general, the results were in accord with the expectation that negative self-attitudes would be associated with predisposition to drug use: higher scores on the "insecurity" factor were significantly associated with higher scores on the "drug" factor for both males (r=.42) and females (r=.38); higher scores on the "insecurity" factor were significantly associated with ("Hidden") self-descriptions in terms used in another study to characterize drug users for both males (r=−.35) and females (r=−.34); and greater discrepancies between "Hidden" and "Ideal" self-descriptions were significantly associated with higher scores on the "drug" factor for both males (r=.28) and females (r=.19). The relationship between "Hidden" self-descriptions, on the one hand, and discrepancy between "Hidden" and "Ideal" self-descriptions, on the other hand, was discussed in terms of the observation that the hidden self was more closely related than the ideal self (for both males and females) to adjectives previously used to describe drug users. This observation was said to indicate that the type of personality described by others as associated with drug use "is devaluated relative to the image of the ideal self" (Brehm and Back, 1968:308).

Theoretically Related Variables. In addition to clinical observations and studies of the concomitant variation of self-attitudes and behaviors related to drug abuse, a third source of data bearing on the hypothesized relationship is the observation of relationships that, in the context of the theoretical model described in Part I, would be expected by the same reasoning that leads to the prediction that negative self-attitudes influence the predisposition to adopt deviant response patterns.

The hypothesized relationship between self-devaluing attitudes and drug abuse is predicated on certain assumptions. For example, it is assumed that the subject characterized by derogatory self-attitudes who adopts drug patterns anticipates that drug use will be associated with self-enhancing experiences and does not anticipate that it will be associated with self-devaluing experiences. Some support for the validity of these assumptions is provided by certain of the data resulting from a study of college students (Brehm and Back, 1968) discussed above.

Among the measures provided were scores on a "denial of effects" factor and a "fear of loss of control" factor. The former measure consisted of questionnaire items such as "People will not normally do anything they would not normally do when under the influence of drugs"; and "I would not do anything I would not normally do under the influence of drugs." The other factor consisted of such items as "I would be afraid of losing personal control under drugs"; "Even though a drug might not be physically habit-forming, I would be afraid of becoming dependent upon it psychologically"; and "I would be worried if I had to take a drug whose effects I knew little about."

Based upon the assumptions stated above it is possible to hypothesize relationships between each of these measures and a measure of predisposition to drug use. The latter, for present purposes, is indicated by scores on a "drug" factor. These scores were based on responses to a series of items indicating the degree to which, during the preceding month, the subject felt that he wanted to take opiates, hallucinogens, energizers, or tranquilizers. It was hypothesized that scores on the "drug" factor would be inversely related to scores on the "denial of effects" and "fear of loss of control" factors. These predictions were not necessarily based on the same reasoning and interpretation of the measures as that employed by Brehm and Back (1968). With reference to the theory outlined in the first part of this volume, the first hypothesis was based on the reasoning that a motive for the use of drugs is to produce self-enhancing effects. Consequently it was reasoned that subjects who anticipated that the drug would not have *any* effects would be unlikely to use the drug. The second hypothesis was based on the interpretation, here, of the "fear of loss of control" factor as reflecting negative attitudes toward presumed effects of drugs (loss of control) or toward people who espoused the use of drugs. Therefore, people who were motivated to increase their level of self-acceptance would hardly adopt drug-usage patterns as means to this end if they were contemptuous of the effects of these patterns.

In general, both hypotheses received support. For both sexes, an inverse relationship was observed between scores on the "drug" factor and scores on the "denial of effects" factor although the relationship was statistically significant only for the male subjects. In like manner, "drug" factor scores were inversely related to scores on the "fear of loss of control" factor for both sexes. In short, subjects were less likely to indicate predisposition to drug use if they anticipated that the drug would have no effects and/or that drug use would have negatively valued concomitants than under mutually exclusive conditions.

Drug "Abuse" as Normative Behavior

The present discussion provides an opportunity to illustrate an issue that has been considered at various points in this volume. It should be emphasized that this chapter (as each of the other chapters in Part II) focuses primarily upon the question of why members of a group adopt patterns of behavior that are defined as deviant by group members. In the present instance the concern is with why an individual adopts drug-abuse patterns that are condemned by the groups in which the subject holds membership. However, the same patterns of behavior may not be defined as deviant in other groups. Drug abuse, whether as an established or emerging pattern, possibly may be defined as expected behavior or at least as behavior that is acceptable or compatible with the existing system of normative standards. In such groups to ask why an individual adopts drug abuse patterns is, in effect, to ask why he conforms to, rather than deviates from, the normative standards of his group.

Nevertheless, it may also be noted that the same factors that might explain the adoption of drug-abuse patterns as *deviant* responses might be applicable also in explanations of the adoption of drug-abuse patterns as *normative* responses. That is, to explain why people deviate is to explain, by indirection, why people conform. In the preceding pages the deviant use of drugs has been discussed in terms related to the enhancement of self-attitudes. Similar terms would appear to be appropriate in discussions of normative drug-use patterns. For example, drug abuse could be interpreted (in specified social settings) as behavioral responses that in fact conform to group standards, thereby evoking positive attitudinal responses from valued group members and so facilitating positive self-evaluations and the expression of positive self-attitudes.

Certain of the observations reported by Feldman (1968) are clearly interpretable in this fashion. These observations were said to be derived from his experience as a social worker in the Lower East Side of New York City, data gathered at the drug-addiction ward of an Eastern state mental hospital, and published firsthand accounts about slum life or heroin addiction. In attempting to account for the movement of the slum youth into a pattern of drug experimentation Feldman points to the significance of the social definitions of the slum environment with regard to how prestige may be won or lost. According to the slum neighborhood ideology, high-status reputations are earned by conforming to behavior patterns that are represented in the ideal type of the "stand-up cat." In order to achieve this kind of reputation situations must arise or be sought out in which the candidate "can prove his daring, strength, predilection for excitement, and ultimate toughness" (p. 133). The introduction of drug use into the neighborhood is said to offer such an opportunity. Thus, it is asserted that in the slum environment initial experimentation with drugs is a way of achieving prestige:

> The user turns to drugs ... to capitalize on a new mode of enhancing his status and prestige within a social system where the highest prizes go to persons who demonstrate attributes of toughness, daring, and adventure. Within the life-style of the stand-up-cat, movement into heroin use is one route to becoming a "somebody" in the eyes of the important people who comprise the slum social network [Feldman, 1968:138].

In proposing this explanation the author at the same time eschews such explanations as those that view drug abuse in terms of attempted resolution of emotional problems or as a mode of retreatist adaptation to failure in the slum opportunity structures (Cloward and Ohlin, 1960). From the point of view of this volume also, such explanations would appear to be more appropriate to instances in which drug abuse constituted a clear deviation from the normative structure of the person's immediate environment than to situations in which drug-abuse patterns were compatible with the normative requirements of the social system.

DRUG ABUSE AND SELF-ENHANCEMENT

No completely satisfactory data provide direct tests of hypotheses regarding the self-enhancing effects of behaviors related to drug abuse. However, data have been reported that appear to permit inferential support for such hypotheses.

The influences of drugs upon self-attitudes may be categorized in a number of useful ways. In one such system of categories the influences of drugs may be distributed among categories that relate to properties of the pharmacologic substances themselves (particularly, effects upon the individual's affective and cognitive processes), on the one hand, and categories that relate to the circumstances associated with the use of the drugs, on the other hand. Such a system would thus yield three categories of influences upon self-attitudes. First, the pharmacologic agent may act directly upon the affect system with the effect of assuaging the feelings of subjective distress associated with negative self-attitudes. The substance may reduce the degree of anxiety or depression and/or increase euphoric feelings, emotional states more likely to be associated with self-accepting than self-rejecting attitudes.[1]

A second category of influences upon self-attitudes, which are presumed to have their origins in drug abuse or addiction, includes patterns of reality distortion. The drug is said to facilitate cognitive restructuring by the person of himself and/or of his environment. In the former instance he may perceive himself as possessed of a number of socially desirable qualities, which he might not in fact possess. In the latter case he may misperceive his environment, and particularly the nexus of interpersonal relationships within which he interacts, as more benign and less threatening to his self-esteem.

A third category of influences, rather than stemming directly from the effects of the substance upon the subject's affective and cognitive processes, is said to derive from phenomena associated with the use of the drug. Thus, if the drug abuse or addiction occurs within the context of a drug subculture social processes may be operating that have profound, if indirect, influences upon self-attitudes. Thus, the drug subculture may provide the person with a set of values more easily approximated than previously held values. As the individual approximates these newly found values his self-acceptance increases. In addition, in the contranormative subculture the person may find insulation against, and social support for the rejection of, the value system of the broader society by the standards of which he failed. By rejecting the standards by which he failed, the subject at the same time rejects the basis for his self-devaluing judgments.

Although these three categories of influence may be analytically distinguished from each other, in empirical reality they are often intertwined. Thus, for example, Hoffman (1964) points to Rado's (1956) assertion that the addict's "tense depression" is relieved by a pharmacogenic elation. This influence may be thought of as falling within the first category described above. However, in addition, it is stated that since the elation is brought about by the subject at will, the drug addict is given the feeling of all-powerful control over his mood. Such a feeling it is assumed here would enhance an individual's self-attitude. This influence of drug use would be thought of as falling within the third category described above since it does not stem from the direct effects of the substance upon the subject's affective or cognitive system but rather from a phenomenon associated with such influences — the sense of control over one's mood as opposed to the mood change itself.

Although such a system of categories might prove useful for many purposes, another system will be employed below since it appears to be applicable to the analysis of other forms of deviant behavior as well as drug abuse. These categories of self-enhancing functions of deviant responses (as described in Chapter 4) may be thought of as various ways in which the drug-use pattern permits the subject to effect self-enhancing changes in his former relationships with his environment. Three broad functional categories are suggested. The first grouping includes intrapsychic or interpersonal avoidance of, or withdrawal from, participation in the normative order that was in fact, and subjectively is, associated with the genesis of negative self-attitudes. Through denying or withdrawing from circumstances that in the past have evoked self-derogation, the individual is enabled to enhance his self-attitudes. The second category includes attacks upon aspects of the normative order that were associated with the development of negative self-attitudes. In attempting to devalue or otherwise attack the normative order the subject more or less effectively destroys the basis in reality for his own self-rejection, whether this basis is in the negative attitudinal responses of valued others or the failure to achieve normatively endorsed goals. The third category includes the substitution of new experiences that are more compatible with the development of positive self-attitudes for older social experiences that in the past were associated with the development of more negative self-attitudes. The subject, for example, might substitute new membership groups for old in the expectation that he might evoke more positive attitudinal responses toward himself than previously; he might substitute new goals for old ones in anticipation of being better able to approximate these goals and thereby evoke expressions of positive self-attitudes; or he might substitute remembered pleasurable states for current painful (self-threatening) ones.

Although, as was stated above, there appears to exist no direct test of the hypothesized relationship between the adoption of drug abuse patterns and self-enhancement, data are available that suggest that drug abuse patterns permit avoidance of, and attacks upon, the normative structure associated with the genesis of negative self-attitudes. Such responses would thus be expected to diminish negative self-feelings to the extent that the person successfully avoided or attacked (symbolically or otherwise) the normative order. Furthermore the substitution function of drug-abuse patterns is expected to increase the range of potentially self-gratifying experiences. The three categories of presumably self-enhancing influences of drug-abuse patterns will be considered briefly in turn.

Avoidance

The function of drug-abuse responses in permitting avoidance of self-devaluing experiences in the normative order is suggested by a number of clinical observations. The "avoidance" response might take the form of motivational or perceptual withdrawal.

Sharoff (1969) argues that individuals who tend to use narcotic drugs or hallucinogens try, through the use of these substances, to resolve problems related to unacceptable levels of self-esteem. Individuals who tend to use narcotic drugs whether because of objective life changes or subjective feelings of inadequacy are said to be unable to develop feelings of self-esteem. The abuse of narcotics in part depresses the intensity of the demands for achievement made by the individual's superego. The need for achievement simply seems relatively unimportant under the influence of drugs. The individual is permitted "to withdraw from his conflicts without struggle or self-condemnation" (p. 189). In addition to permitting the person to withdraw from the struggle for, and failure to gain, a sense of achievement, drug abuse bears on resolution of problems related to lack of achieving self-esteem in still other ways. To the extent that adoption of drug-abuse patterns is accompanied by rejecting attitudes on the part of society, the individual is enabled to justify his own failure by blaming it on such unfair societal attitudes toward the addict. In the face of the obstacles imposed by these attitudes, the addict can justifiably (in his own eyes) give up any further struggle for achievement. Concomitantly, the subject is said to achieve a measure of satisfaction from perceiving the trouble he has caused for the society that has rejected him.

While the narcotic drugs presumably resolve problems related to lack of self-esteem through their impact upon the subject's superego and drives, the hallucinogens tend to effect resolution of these problems through their impact upon the person's sensory and perceptual functions. The hallucinogenic substances permit the distortion of reality toward the goal of achieving self-enhancing attributes. These drugs allow the users to "feel through perceptual distortions that they have become in reality what they believe they are in imagination" (p. 192).

Attack

That drug-abuse patterns serve the function of attacking the normative order (which it is asserted was associated with the genesis of negative self-attitudes) is suggested by a number of studies.

The contranormative function of drug use is implied by certain of the data obtained by Suchman (1968) from a cross-sectional sampling survey of drug use on a college campus. Drug (predominantly marijuana) use was observed to be associated with a "hang-loose," or antiestablishment, ethic. Drug use was appreciably more likely to occur among students whose opposition to the "traditional, established order" appeared to be reflected in their self-images, attitudes or values, or behavior than among other students.

With regard to self-image Suchman (1968:151) states:

> The more the student's self-image tends to be rebellious, cynical, anti-establishment, "hippie," and apathetic, the more likely is he to smoke marijuana. Conversely, the more his self-image tends to be conformist, well-behaved, moral, and "square," the less likely is he to make use of marijuana.

With regard to attitudes or values, drug use was more likely to be observed, for example, among students who disagreed with the statement "American colleges today should place more emphasis on teaching American ideals and values" than among students who agreed with the statement; who expressed opposition to the Vietnam war and the draft than among students who did not express such opposition; who report that they get the most satisfaction out of life through leisure time recreational activities than among students who value participation in civic affairs or family relations; who feel that their parents do not respect their opinions than among students who do not feel this way.

With regard to overt behavioral manifestations of the hang-loose ethic, drug users were more likely to be observed among students who reported frequent reading of "underground" newspapers and participating in mass protests more than two times than among students who did not so report.

The possible contranormative function of drug use is suggested also by certain of the findings of a study that compared 100 illicit LSD users and 46 nonusers (similar to the users in age, sex, and father's occupation) along a number of dimensions, including MMPI profiles. The authors state:

> A fairly large percentage of the LSD user's profiles were diagnosed as "conduct disorder" and on re-examination a number of the unclassified abnormal profiles showed a pattern of three peaks, Pd, Ma, and Sc. These configurations suggest a tendency toward social nonconformity and rejection of traditional values and restrictions. To some, then, drug taking may be the chosen patterns of expressing their rejection of and deviance from the present social system [Smart and Fejer, 1969: 307].

Data reported by Kohn and Mercer (1971) are also compatible with the thesis that drug use functions to express opposition to the normative order. The responses to a questionnaire administered to 197 university students revealed significant relationships between authoritarianism-rebellion scale scores on the one hand and drug-use (and drug-use attitudes) on the other hand. The more rebellious students reported using illicit drugs (particularly marijuana and psychedelics) more often than the more authoritarian students. The more rebellious students compared to the more authoritarian students also displayed more permissive attitudes toward drug use generally in terms of an overall drug-permissiveness score and more particularly in favoring legalization of marijuana, approving use of marijuana and psychedelics, and expressing willingness to use marijuana if it were legalized.

In short, these studies are congruent with the assertion that drug use functions to enhance self-attitude by successfully attacking the normative order associated with the genesis of self-rejecting attitudes, that is, by attacking the very basis of self-rejection.

Substitution

Drug-abuse patterns may be viewed as potentially self-enhancing insofar as they facilitate the substitution of earlier gratifying experiences for current self-devaluating experiences or insofar as they permit the establishment of new, achievable, and personally valued behavioral goals.

The function of substituting earlier gratifying experiences is suggested by Hoffman's (1964) discussion. The drug addict is said to be characterized by a history of failures in interpersonal transactions that results in extremely low self-esteem. Since he has been unable to maintain an acceptable level of self-esteem through such symbolic modes of functioning as gratifying interpersonal experiences or vocational achievements he returns to a physiological mode of self-esteem maintenance. Perhaps the effectiveness of the drug in elevating self-esteem is accounted for by its ability to evoke a mood reminiscent of the euphoric mood experienced by the feeding baby:

> This stirs up unconscious memories of the warmth and security
> felt when the infant was held by its mother and attended to. It
> therefore implies being wanted, being loved, being important —
> all in relation to the crucially significant mothering figure
> [Hoffman, 1964:264].

Drug-abuse patterns may also be viewed as permitting the individual to develop and achieve new personally valued goals, and thereby gain an increased sense of self-acceptance. The need on the part of the drug user to substitute worthy and achievable goals related to the drug use for any formerly held goals (which were unachieved and/or not highly valued) is suggested by a finding reported above that drug users compared to nondrug users received significantly lower scores on a test reflecting the degree to which a person "has found meaningful goals around which to integrate his life" (Shean and Fechtmann, 1971:112). The subject might well seek to remedy this situation by seeking such goals in the individual or communal drug experience.

One way of achieving self-esteem is through the achievement of highly valued (by self and significant others) goals. To the extent that the goals are attainable with relative ease, the probability of achieving feelings of self-esteem is relatively high. It may be argued that one such relatively attainable goal is the intense experience of emotion. By making a virtue of the experience of emotion, through the use of disinhibiting pharmacologic substances the person is permitted to evaluate himself more positively upon achieving these experiences. This reasoning appears warranted in the light of the following finding.

It is sometimes observed that, particularly among subjects who have not completely excluded themselves from their normative membership groups, the adoption of deviant patterns such as drug abuse is frequently accompanied by offering justification for drug use in terms of such "lofty" motives as attaining "expansion of consciousness or more meaningful communication" (Schaps and Sanders, 1970:141). It may be argued, however, that whether or not these motives are indeed offered as implicit or explicit justification for their deviant behavior, these motives serve another function as well: they serve as achievable and laudatory *substitutes* for the legitimate motives that the persons have been unable to achieve in the course of their normative experiences. The failure to achieve these formerly valued motives occasioned negative self-attitudes. The substitution of new, personally valued motives that the individual is able to achieve permits him to enhance his self-attitudes. Enhancement of self-attitudes would also be expected to the extent that experimentation and continued use of drugs are defined as valued group activities. As such, the participant in these group activities may be expected to evoke expressions of positive attitudes toward himself by other members of the group.

SUMMARY

Although relevant empirical observations are not abundant in the literature such findings as are available appear to be congruent with the central assertions of the emerging theoretical model dealing with the adoption and stabilization of deviant behavior patterns. The conclusion that the adoption of drug-abuse patterns (as deviant responses) is influenced by antecedent negative self-attitudes is congruent with clinical observations, findings of concomitant variation between drug-abuse patterns and self-attitudes, and observations of other relationships that would be expected in the context of the theoretical model yielding the prediction of an association between antecedent self-derogation and the adoption of drug-abuse responses. However, at best the findings are compatible with, rather than direct tests of, the hypothesized relationship.

In like manner, although direct tests of the relationships are not available, a number of observations are congruent with the inference that the adoption of drug-abuse patterns has self-enhancing consequences through the mechanisms of avoidance of, and attacks upon, the normative structure associated with the genesis of self-derogation and through the stimulation of a range of substitute experiences and goals.

NOTES

[1] It might be argued in this regard that to change the mood is to change the self-perceptions and evaluations that were appropriate to the former mood state. That is, if a person who experiences a subjectively distressful affective state in response to adverse self-perceptions and self-evaluations was able to produce a euphoric affective state through the use of a drug, he would at the same time influence changes in self-

perceptions and self-evaluations that were more appropriate (less negative and more positive) to the new mood state. This reasoning implies a reciprocal relationship between self-attitudes on the one hand and self-perceptions and self-evaluations on the other hand. Just as negative self-attitudes would be a conditioned response to negative self-perceptions and self-evaluations, so could positive self-attitudes evoke positive self-perceptions and self-evaluations (when you feel good, you see yourself in a new light).

Chapter 7

Alcoholism and Alcohol Abuse

This chapter considers the literature relating to alcoholism and alcohol abuse with regard to its compatibility with the theoretical model described in Part I. As in the preceding chapters the discussion will focus upon two relationships: the association between antecedent negative self-attitudes and patterns of drinking behavior; and the influence of drinking patterns upon self-enhancement. Again, the assumption is generally made that the drinking patterns under discussion are judged to be deviant within the normative structures of the subjects' membership groups.

SELF-ATTITUDES AND ALCOHOLISM

The available literature dealing with the relationship between self-attitudes and alcoholism largely falls into three broad categories: studies of concomitant variation between experiences with alcohol consumption and self-attitudes; studies of the association between self-attitudes and retrospective reports of self-devaluing experiences; and the observation of relationships that would be expected within the context of the same theoretical model from which the proposition regarding the association between antecedent self-rejection and alcohol abuse patterns was derived.

Negative Self-Attitudes and Alcoholism

In answer to the question of whether or not alcoholics characteristically manifest more negative self-attitudes than nonalcoholics, one set of possibly relevant data is provided by comparisons between "alcohol-abuse" and "nonalcoholic abuse" subjects with regard to level of self-acceptance at a single point in time. The "alcohol-abuse" subjects may include diagnosed alcoholics or nonalcoholic subjects who display various patterns of alcohol consumption.

Alcoholic Subjects. One such study was reported by Berg (1971). The forty alcoholic male subjects were consecutive admissions to the alcoholism unit of a psychiatric hospital and were characterized by a psychiatric diagnosis of alcoholism and a history of abundant drinking, alcohol dependency, and difficulties in functioning due to alcohol use. The control group consisted of forty male employees of a penitentiary who were defined as social drinkers, that is, consumed less than the equivalent of ten ounces of absolute alcohol per week and responded in the negative to all of the items on the drinking questionnaire. The control group was so selected as to be comparable to the alcoholic subjects in age, education, and measures of neuroticism and extraversion. Self-concept was measured by self-ideal discrepancy using a Q-sort technique and by a number of scores derived from responses to the adjective check list.

On the first measure the alcoholic subjects manifested significantly greater self-ideal discrepancy scores than the control subjects. This difference was accounted for by the more derogatory self-descriptions of the alcoholic subjects relative to those of the control subjects since both groups expressed similar ideal-self descriptions. In like manner the scores derived by the second technique revealed that the alcoholic subjects were significantly more likely to endorse unfavorable adjectives as self-descriptive, were significantly less likely to endorse favorable adjectives as self-descriptive, and were significantly more likely to express "feelings of inferiority through social impotence, guilt and self-criticism" (p. 445) than the control subjects. These differences were not likely to be accounted for by variability in perceptual distortion in view of the observation that the groups did not differ significantly in scores on the "defensiveness" scale.

Although these results are consistent with the view that alcoholics are more likely than nonalcoholics to have a history of self-devaluing attitudes, the nature of the research design is such that alternative interpretations related to the circumstances of institutionalization might be offered. For example, the fact of being institutionalized for alcoholism might be taken as evidence that the alcoholic is being deprived of a favorite defense by which he was able to maintain a positive self-image, and being deprived of this defense would be expected to manifest more self-rejecting attitudes. By this line of reasoning, it might be argued that the alcoholics would have manifested self-attitudes that were quite similar to those of the control subjects if the measurement of the self-attitudes had occurred prior to institutionalization. An alternative explanation for the findings might similarly assert that the observed differences in self-attitudes between alcoholic and control subjects was accounted for by circumstances associated with institutionalization. By this argument, however, it is the alcoholic's perception of the stigma accompanying psychiatric patient status, rather than the deprivation of the alcoholic defense, that accounts for his relatively unfavorable self-feelings.

Carroll and Fuller (1969) also compared the self-attitudes, as measured by the *Standard Adjective Q Sort,* of three alcoholic groups and two groups of non-alcoholics. The alcoholic groups were drawn from a prison inmate population as was one of the nonalcoholic comparison groups. The other nonalcoholic group consisted of steadily employed men who were applying for jobs with the penitentiary service. The five groups of white male subjects were matched for age, education, Beta IQ, and occupation. The results were consistent with the expectation that negative self-attitudes are associated with the adoption of alcoholic patterns. The three groups of alcoholics displayed significantly greater self-ideal discrepancies than did the two nonalcoholic groups. However, again, due to the nature of the research design it is difficult to determine whether the observed association between negative self-attitudes and alcoholism was due to the predisposition of self-rejecting individuals to adopt alcoholic patterns or to other factors such as the experience of being deprived of a favorite self-enhancing defense (that is, the effects of alcohol) while in prison and/or under treatment.

In a third study, Tahka (1966) comparing fifty Swedish male alcoholics with a matched control group of fifty Finnish males (free of alcoholism or psychiatric disorder), reported that among the premorbid personality characteristics of alcoholics were inhibitions of aggressive and sexual impulses with a tendency toward feelings of guilt or inferiority.

Nonalcoholic Subjects. Unlike the subjects in the earlier studies, the persons who displayed alcohol-abuse patterns in the investigations now under consideration were not diagnosed alcoholics. Thus, for example, in one such study Williams (1965) reported an association between alcohol abuse and self-rejecting attitudes on the basis of an administration of two instruments to sixty-eight male college students. One instrument yielded a measure of problem drinking. The other instrument, an adjective checklist, yielded three measures of self-evaluation: a self-acceptance index; a self-criticality index; and correspondence between real-self and ideal-self. As anticipated higher scores on the index of problem drinking were observed to be significantly associated with higher scores on the self-criticality index, lower scores on the self-acceptance index, and lesser correspondence between real-self and ideal-self descriptions. To the extent that it may be assumed that problem drinkers tend to become alcoholics, these findings may be interpreted as support for the proposition that negative self-attitudes are antecedent to the development of alcoholism.

In another investigation, Maddox (1968), also observed associations between self-derogation and drinking behavior at the same point in time. In a study of male black college students it was observed that drinking behavior was related to scores on a measure of self-derogation in such a way that subjects who were categorized as abstainers were least likely to be self-derogatory (51 percent), subjects who were categorized as lighter drinkers were somewhat more likely to be self-derogatory (57 percent), and subjects who were categorized as heavier drinkers were most likely to be self-derogatory (68 percent). Maddox also reported that *changes* in drinking pattern from the freshman to sophomore year were related to changes in self-derogation. Increases in drinking were accompanied by increases in self-derogation and decreases in drinking were associated with decreased self-derogation.

The reported associations between drinking pattern and self-derogation were interpreted as suggesting that self-derogation was the result of behavior (drinking) that violated norms of respectability. This interpretation receives some support from the observation that the association between greater drinking and greater self-derogation is more likely to occur in higher social status groups, that is, in those groups that are most likely to adopt norms of middle-class respectability. However, the association between drinking pattern and self-derogation is also consistent with the view that, mainly among people of higher social status, alcohol abuse represents a deviant adaptive mode for dealing with prior feelings of self-derogation. According to such a view the adoption of alcoholic abuse patterns (that is, manifesting drinking patterns that violate any prescribed situational limits) might have been stimulated by the person's awareness of a normative drinking pattern. Possibly for persons in the other social classes similar drinking patterns might not be defined as deviant (that is, as alcohol abuse).[1]

Retrospective Reports of Self-Devaluation

As was suggested above, studies of the concurrent relationship between self-attitudes and alcohol abuse such as those described above do not permit the investigator to establish antecedent consequence relationships. This is so not only because the measure of self-attitudes is collected at the same point in time as the measure of alcohol abuse but also because the measure of self-attitudes frequently does not even *refer* to an earlier point in time. Thus, the distinction is made between indices of current self-feelings and indices of self-feelings at an earlier point in time. The reader might be more willing to interpret the observed associations between self-rejection and alcohol abuse as an antecedent consequence relationship if the index of self-rejection appeared to refer to a point in time earlier than the point at which alcoholic patterns are observed. A case in point is an investigation by Wahl (1956), which appeared to suggest that negative self-attitdes play a significant role in the genesis of alcoholism. The conclusions were based upon a study of state hospital alcoholic patients. The measure of self-attitudes was retrospective in that the self-feelings were inferred from reports of experiences that occurred earlier in the subject's lifetime. Such experiences included sibling rivalry and parental rejection. However, it must be emphasized that, although such data are consistent with the assertion that self-rejection influences the subsequent adoption of alcohol-abuse patterns, the relationship might also be accounted for by a tendency toward retrospective distortion of life experiences on the part of the alcoholic subjects.

Theoretically Related Variables

A third source of support for the hypothesized relationship between antecedent negative self-attitudes and the adoption of alcohol abuse patterns is the observation of relationships that are to be expected by the same reasoning (that is, within the context of the same theoretical model) from which the hypothesis was derived. The following two studies serve as illustrations of this source of support.

By implication, some support for the alleged association between drug abuse and negative self-attitudes may be provided by reports of significant relationships between alcohol abuse and variables known to be associated with self-attitudes. For example, it is fairly well established that measures of negative self-attitudes tend to be associated with indices of such reflections of subjective distress as anxiety or depression (Kaplan and Pokorny, 1969). Given this observation, reports of significant relationships between degree of alcohol abuse and measures of anxiety or depression are interpretable as indirect support for the hypothesis that self-rejecting attitudes are associated with alcohol abuse. By this reasoning, two variables (self-attitudes and alcohol abuse) are more likely to be in fact related to each other if each of the two variables is significantly associated with a common third variable (such as anxiety or depression) than if such associations with a common variable do not exist.

Data suggesting such a relationship between severity of alcohol abuse on the one hand and anxiety or depression on the other hand are offered by Whitelock and his associates (1971). The subjects consisted of 136 newly admitted state psychiatric hospital patients who were prescreened for at least moderate alcohol use. The subjects responded to the short-form MMPI and an alcohol-abuse questionnaire. The analysis examined the relationship between severity of alcohol abuse and MMPI profile pattern. It was observed that anxiety and depression appeared to be the predominant features of patterns associated with the highest levels of alcohol abuse.

A second study, which by implication provides support for the hypothesis that negative self-attitudes influence the adoption of alcoholic response patterns, concerns the anticipated consequences of alcohol usage. If persons in fact adopt alcohol abuse as a preferred pattern for dealing with problems related to self-devaluation, they would presumably hold expectations that an increase in self-enhancement would be associated with intoxication. That such expectations are held by alcoholics is apparent in the report of McGuire and his associates (1966). These investigators compared four chronic alcoholics with four nonalcoholic subjects regarding their attitudes and other manifest behavior before, during, and after experiences of experimentally induced intoxication. The data were gathered by interview and behavioral observation methods. The four chronic alcoholic subjects were studied on a psychiatric evaluation ward of a general hospital. The nonalcoholic subjects were studied on a correctional institution hospital ward. These subjects, unlike the alcoholic subjects, were to remain in the institution following completion of the experiment.

The data collected during the predrinking period were consistent with the view that the chronic alcoholic subjects expected, during intoxication, to achieve desirable qualities and to evoke positive evaluations by others. The alcoholics expected that they would experience, and would be so admired by others for, increased sexual potency and other masculine characteristics. They also anticipated that others would display a special curiosity about them because they were alcoholics. The alcohol itself would eliminate feelings of tightness and depression. In short, intoxication would increase self-enhancing feelings. Similar expectations were not noted for the nonalcoholic subjects.

Thus, the third category of observations as the first two categories of studies considered above, are consistent with the expectation that persons with negative self-attitudes would be predisposed to patterns of alcohol abuse and alcoholism.

ALCOHOLISM AND SELF-ENHANCEMENT

In an examination of the allegedly self-enhancing consequences of alcoholism and alcohol abuse the focus will be primarily upon studies of "problem drinking" although observations are also available concerning the self-enhancing effects of presumably social drinking. Thus, Williams (1965:592) makes reference to his earlier work, which is said to demonstrate "that alcohol consumed in all-male cocktail-party settings temporarily elevates self-evaluation."

The literature will be discussed with a view to considering two issues: the extent to which empirical observations are consistent with the general assertion regarding the self-enhancing consequences of alcohol abuse; and the conditions under which such a relationship is most likely to obtain.

Self-Enhancing Consequences

The literature relating to the alleged self-enhancing consequences of alcohol abuse will be considered in three groupings: studies that observe the "influence" of alcohol upon self-attitudes; investigations of the association between withdrawal from patterns of alcohol abuse and changes in self-attitudes; and the observation of deviant outcomes of alcohol abuse from which self-enhancing consequences might be inferred.

Effects of Alcohol Upon Self-Attitudes. In the first study to be considered, Berg (1971) investigated the effect of intoxication upon levels of self-esteem for a group of twenty male subjects who were psychiatrically diagnosed as alcoholic and were resident in the alcoholism unit of a psychiatric hospital for at least two weeks. Five days after being given the tests by which their self-attitudes were measured, the subjects submitted to the intoxication procedure during which they drank a mixture of rye whiskey and orange juice. Intoxication was defined in terms of behavioral manifestations such as slurring of speech and gross muscular incoordination and in terms of having a blood alcohol level of at least 0.11% according to a Breathalyzer test. Following the intoxication procedures the self-attitude tests, Q-sort and adjective checklist techniques, were again administered. Following this test administration Breathalyzer readings were obtained once more in order to be reasonably certain that appropriate blood alcohol levels had been maintained.

A comparison of the alcoholics' self-attitude scores in the sober and intoxicated conditions revealed that "when intoxicated the alcoholics showed more favorable and less derogatory self-concept than when sober" (p. 448). Under the intoxication condition the alcoholic subjects were significantly less likely to display self-ideal discrepancies, more likely to employ favorable self-descriptive adjectives, less likely to employ unfavorable self-descriptive adjectives, more likely to receive high self-confidence scores and less likely to receive high abasement scores than under the sober condition. Thus, this finding is supportive of the view that for alcoholics, intoxication temporarily elevates the subject's level of self-esteem, thereby reinforcing his drinking behavior.

However, the self-enhancing effects of drinking appear to hold only for those who have a history of heavy drinking and a dependency on alcohol. When essentially the same procedures were employed on a group of "social drinkers" rather than alcoholics, intoxication was observed to have an adverse effect upon self-attitudes. The twenty nonalcoholic subjects were male penitentiary employees who consumed less than the equivalent of ten ounces of absolute alcohol per week and who responded in the negative to all the items on the drinking questionnaire. These subjects were selected so as to be comparable to the twenty alcoholic subjects in the preceding study with regard to self-ideal discrepancy under the sober condition. The major difference in procedure between this study and the investigation of the alcoholic subjects related to the blood alcohol level. For this nonalcoholic grouping, the intoxication procedure brought the subjects to a minimum blood alcohol level of 0.06 percent instead of 0.11 percent due to observations in other studies that nonalcoholics manifest behavioral indices of intoxication at blood alcohol levels of 0.06 to 0.11 percent but sometimes become ill if the level is increased.

A comparison of the scores on the self-attitude tests for these nonalcoholic subjects under the sober and intoxicated conditions revealed that intoxication was related to a shift in self-attitudes in the negative direction. Under the intoxicated condition, the nonalcoholic subjects tended to display significantly greater self-ideal discrepancies, lesser employment of favorable self-descriptive adjectives, greater employment of unfavorable self-descriptive adjectives, lesser self-confidence, and greater abasement than under the sober condition.

The two sets of findings taken together are compatible with the interpretation that for alcoholic subjects intoxication represents a favored technique for enhancing self-esteem or defending against self-rejections. For nonalcoholic subjects, in contrast, intoxication does not appear to function in this way. For these subjects intoxication does not seem to be a preferred defense. Indeed, the observed decrease in self-esteem in the intoxication condition suggests that alcohol abuse either disrupts whatever favored defenses these nonalcoholic subjects characteristically employ and/or is a negatively valued activity participation that occasions self-devaluing responses.

However, it should not be inferred from the above discussion that for *alcoholic* subjects all experimental studies of the influence of alcohol upon self-attitudes have unequivocally led to the conclusion that alcohol abuse enhances one's self-attitudes. Indeed, the opposite result was observed in at least one study comparing alcoholic experimental and control groups regarding changes in self-attitudes while under the influence of alcohol (Vanderpool, 1969). Certain of the conclusions were not unlike those from other studies. Thus, the data suggested to the author that alcoholics tend to have poor self-concepts when sober. Furthermore, alcoholics are prompted to drink in order to escape from feelings of loneliness, inadequacy, and low worth and in order to gain release from psychological inhibitions toward the end of projecting a more positive self-attitude. However, unlike other studies (Berg, 1971), far from observing an improved self-concept under the influence of alcohol, the subjects tended to manifest more negative self-attitudes.

Unfortunately this study differs in many ways, and thus is not strictly comparable to, a study by Berg (1971) discussed above in which intoxication was observed to have a positive influence upon self-attitudes. Perhaps the most meaningful differences were those relating to the drinking procedure. In the present study the aim during the primary drinking session for experimental group subjects was to obtain an "optimal" drinking level so that the subject would reach a state in which he was "satisfied and able to function but not drunk." In contrast in the Berg (1971) study the alcoholic subjects continued to drink "until behavioral manifestations of intoxication such as sweating, flushing, slurring of speech, and gross muscular incoordination, were observed" (p. 447) and until the subject's blood alcohol level was at a minimum of 0.11%. The blood alcohol concentrations apparently failed to reach this level in a number of the experimental group subjects in the Vanderpool (1969) study. These differences along with other procedural variations in the drinking sessions suggest that Berg's alcoholic subjects attained a higher level of intoxication than Vanderpool's subjects. This difference might account for the observation in an increase in level of self-acceptance among the former group and a decrease in self-accepting attitudes in the latter group under drinking conditions. According to this explanation, a minimum level of intoxication must be reached before alcohol will be observed to serve self-enhancing functions.

Withdrawal From Alcohol Usage. The self-enhancing function of alcohol abuse may be inferred by noting the apparent effects of withdrawal from this pattern upon self-evaluation. Illustrative data that permit such an inference are provided by White and Gaier (1965). Among the findings reported is that result concerning the association between self-concept and interval of sobriety. The subjects were 104 male members of Alcoholics Anonymous. Self-concept was measured by scores on self-cathexis (Secord and Jourard, 1953), which required the subjects to respond to fifty-five self-concept references along a five-point scale ranging from "Have strong feelings and wish change could somehow be made" to "Consider myself fortunate." The respondents were also asked to indicate how long they had been sober at the time of taking the test. The investigators examined the group mean self-cathexis scores for subjects reporting different periods of sobriety. The results revealed a gradual decrease in self-cathexis scores ranging from a mean score of 3.54 for subjects reporting sobriety periods between 0.0 to 3.0 months to a mean score of 3.03 for subjects reporting a sobriety period of 12.1 to 36.0 months. Thereafter, self-concept scale "mean scores gradually vacillated to 3.08 for those Ss with 60 months or more of sobriety maintenance" (White and Gaier, 1965:375).

Whether or not this result is congruent with other interpretations, the reported decrease in self-satisfaction as length of sobriety increased (through the 12.1-36.0 month interval) is consistent with the following interpretation. Alcohol abuse is adopted as a pattern because it is functional in maintaining self-accepting attitudes. When an individual makes a decision to withdraw from this pattern whether because of associated self-threatening circumstances or other reasons he is deprived of a defense against self-rejection. With the passage of time, the adverse effects upon self-attitudes of being deprived of a formerly preferred defensive response become increasingly apparent until the subject has the opportunity to adopt a new pattern. The motivation to adopt a new self-enhancing pattern (perhaps through identification with Alcoholics Anonymous as a worthy cause) is stimulated by the increase in subjectively experienced self-rejecting attitudes.

White and Porter (1966) also report data that are similarly interpretable as supporting the view that when alcoholics enter into periods of sobriety they deprive themselves (or are deprived) of previously preferred mechanisms for maintaining acceptable levels of self-esteem. The subjects for this study were thirty-five hospitalized male alcoholics who were actively participating in the Alcoholics Anonymous program at a state hospital. The subjects' sobriety intervals ranged from eight to ninety-four days. Self-concept data were derived from responses to the McKinney Sentence Completion Blank. The investigators reported a negative correlation between length of time sober and what was taken to be an index of favorability of self-concept, and a positive correlation between sobriety interval and responses interpreted as indicating self-defeat, guilt, and fear. The authors concluded:

> Although the correlations are low, there is some suggestion that the longer the alcoholic remained in the hospital and abstained from alcohol, the less favorable self-concept he reported, the more guilt feelings he expressed and the less ego strength he exhibited in facing up to crises [White and Porter, 1966:354].

These findings may be accounted for in any of a number of ways. For example, the increased negativity toward self with increased intervals of sobriety might be explained in terms of group (Alcoholics Anonymous) pressure on the subject to admit personal weakness and culpability with regard to his craving for alcohol. However, again, the finding is also consistent with the position that alcoholism constitutes a preferred defense against self-rejecting attitudes, and deprivation of this defensive pattern increases the probability of developing increasingly negative self-attitudes.

Deviant Outcomes and Self-Enhancement. As part of the theoretical model developed earlier it was asserted that, due to the association of the normative environment with the genesis of negative self-attitudes, persons would be predisposed to adopt deviant patterns, including alcohol abuse. It was further asserted that the adoption of these patterns would serve self-enhancing functions insofar as the adopted deviant patterns increased the probability that the person could avoid the self-devaluating experiences associated with the normative environment, attack the normative environment and thereby attack the basis of his self-derogation, and substitute for his self-devaluing experiences in the normative environment a new range of experiences with self-enhancing potential. If the avoidance, attack, and substituting functions do increase the probability of self-enhancing experiences, then the observation that alcohol abuse is associated with these deviant outcomes (that is, avoiding, attacking, and substituting for the normative environment) might be interpreted as indirect support for the assertion that alcohol abuse serves self-enhancing functions.

A number of observations in the literature suggest that alcoholism and alcohol abuse do indeed facilitate avoidance of, attacks upon, and substitution for aspects of the normative environment. The following reports will serve to illustrate such observations. Although the functions are frequently described in different terms, they are easily translatable into avoidance, attack, and substitution mechanisms.

In view of the findings of other investigators, Mogar and his associates (1970) concluded that alcoholism was likely related to many different personal meanings and motives. They anticipated that distinctive personality subtypes would be discernible in a population of alcoholics. Indeed, based upon their scores on the thirteen standard clinical scales of the MMPI, these researchers were able to identify four model profiles among 101 male subjects and five personality types among 100 female subjects all of whom were alcoholic patients admitted to a state hospital. Depending upon the sex and personality type in question alcoholism was interpreted as being involved with attempted resolution of any of an array of problems through any of a number of different mechanisms related to alcohol abuse. Problems involving feelings of self-derogation or personal insecurity were specifically cited in connection with the normal-manic, hysterical, and passive-aggressive personality types among the female subjects. Such problem areas were associated specifically with the depressive-compulsive and schizoid-prepsychotic personality types among the male alcoholic subjects. However, even among the remaining personality types of the male and female alcoholic subjects, problems related to self-rejecting attitudes are discernible.

Alcohol abuse may be thought of as functioning in any of a number of ways to resolve these problems more or less directly related to self-rejecting attitudes. Thus, these investigators note that among female subjects drinking may function to deal with feelings of insecurity about their personal female identity (normal-manic personality); to reduce anxiety and sexual inhibitions, and to facilitate interpersonal (particularly male-female) interaction (normal-depressive personality); to evoke sympathy and facilitate interpersonal manipulation, methods stemming partly from a deep lack of self-respect (hysterical personality); to compete with men (psychopathic personality); and, as a tranquilizer, to alleviate anxiety and to inhibit feelings of self-contempt (passive-aggressive personality). Among the male patients, alcohol may function to escape recognizing personal weakness and failure (passive-aggressive personality); to relieve guilt feelings generated by an excessively punitive conscience (depressive-compulsive personality); to relieve the loneliness resulting from the fear of interpersonal closeness associated with a history of emotional rejection and deprivation (schizoid-prepsychotic personality); and as a passive way to express aggression or as a way to attract attention, in either case allowing the subject to assert himself in closer approximation to the masculine social sterotype (passive-dependent personality).

To summarize, although Mogar and his associates did not *necessarily* discuss the functions of excessive drinking directly in relationship to problems associated with feelings of self-rejection, the remarks made above are interpretable as indicating that the apparently diverse functions of alcohol abuse are directly *or indirectly* related to dealing with the fundamental problem of coping with such self-rejecting attitudes.

The second report under consideration also suggests that alcohol abuse may be adopted as a response pattern for any of a number of reasons, all of which are interpretable as serving the function of increasing self-esteem. Thus, intoxication might be sought in order "to facilitate fantasy fulfillment, to enhance arbitrary interpretations of reality and to eliminate sober realizations" (McGuire, *et al.*, 1966:22). Alcoholism may also be adopted as a way of gaining self-esteem because of its implications for participation in a particular interpersonal milieu. This route to self-acceptance is suggested by such studies as that of McGuire and his associates (1966) in which four chronic alcoholics and four nonalcoholics were compared with regard to their behavior before, during, and after experimentally induced ethanol intoxication. For the alcoholic subjects the fraternity of alcoholics appeared to take on many of the characteristics of a secret society.Intoxication was one way of maintaining membership in the subcultural group. This group had implications for increasing one's level of self-acceptance insofar as membership and participation in the society of alcoholics was perceived as conferring upon the subjects manly characteristics that were admired by others. Other people in their environment, including staff members and other patients, were believed to admire the alcoholics' ability to drink great quantities of alcohol and to be otherwise fascinated by alcoholism.

The group aspects of alcoholism may be said to be relevant to increased levels of self-esteem in yet another way. The alcoholic subculture apparently had its own value system and set of rules. Conformity to this value system presumably evokes positive responses from other alcoholics who share the subculture. Such rules and values would concern the amount and kind of alcohol ingested, the ways in which alcohol was obtained from others, helping relationships within the community of alcoholics, the method of drinking, commitment to drinking, and achievements during drinking periods. By evoking positive responses from other group members through conformity to the rules and approximation of consensual values, the alcoholic achieves more positive self-feelings.

Thus, identification with and participation in the alcoholic subculture is said to increase level of self-acceptance in at least two ways: by permitting the subject to perceive positive evaluations of him by others who do not participate in the subculture; and by conformity to subcultural values through which the subject presumably earns the positive evaluations of other chronic alcoholics who share the subculture.

Conditions for Self-Enhancing Consequences

In Chapter 4 it was asserted that the adoption of deviant patterns (including alcohol abuse) would increase the *probability* of experiencing self-enhancing attitudes since the deviant pattern increased the probability of the self-derogating person being able to avoid the self-devaluating experiences associated with the normative structure; to attack the experiential basis (that is, the normative environment) of his self-devaluation; and to substitute for aspects of the normative structure a new range of (deviant) experiences that have self-enhancing potential. The literature discussed above suggests that the probability of such outcomes, and, therefore, of self-enhancing experiences, is indeed increased. However, the experience of self-enhancement is anticipated in terms of probability, not in terms of absolute necessity. Whether or not the adoption of the deviant (here, alcohol-abuse) pattern in fact eventuates in self-enhancing experiences depends upon certain conditions — the consequences of adopting the deviant pattern. Depending upon these conditions is the degree to which the individual will experience self-enhancement; and depending upon the experience of self-enhancement is the probability that the person will remain fixed in the deviant response pattern. A number of discussions appearing in the alcoholism literature appear to support these theoretical assertions.

To the extent that alcohol abuse is functional in enhancing one's self-attitudes it is to be expected that persons who have adopted alcohol abuse patterns would manifest an increase in self-acceptance relative to their prealcoholic state and indeed might well be undifferentiated in this regard from a nonalcoholic population. However, this expectation is based on the assumption that the adoption of this pattern, as a provisional attempt to deal with preexisting self-rejecting attitudes, does not evoke new experiences that would exacerbate negative self-attitudes. To the extent that such experiences are evoked, alcoholism should not be expected to result in improved self-attitudes and, to the contrary, might be associated with increased self-rejection.

Congruent with the above reasoning are certain of the findings reported by Nocks and Bradley (1959). These results were based on data collected in the course of interviews with male patients admitted to the acute alcoholic wards of a state hospital. Among the results was the observation that those patients who denied having a drinking problem received significantly higher scores on a measure of self-esteem than the other patients. It should be noted that all of the patients included in this study had been diagnosed as alcoholics. This finding is interpretable in a number of ways. For example, the denial of a drinking problem might reflect the continuity of relatively intact defenses that serve to shield the subject from self-rejecting attitudes. On the other hand, and not inconsistent with the previous interpretation, admission to a drinking problem might reflect the occurrence of a number of self-devaluing experiences consequent upon adoption of the drinking pattern such as being the object of rejecting attitudes by one's family, friends, and employer. Such experiences might not only have neutralized what otherwise might have been a self-enhancing effect of alcohol abuse but might even have intensified self-rejecting attitudes. In short, the above observation is congruent with, but does not demonstrate, the position that alcohol abuse is functional in increasing self-acceptance under conditions in which this pattern does not induce new self-devaluing experiences. Admission to a drinking problem might be interpreted as an indication that such experiences have arisen. Denial of a drinking problem might be interpreted as a sign that the alcoholic has successfully shielded himself from the negative responses of significant others to his excessive drinking.

To review this line of reasoning, alcohol abuse and alcoholism are thought to fall along a range of deviant patterns that could be adopted as a way of increasing one's level of self-acceptance. The efficacy of the pattern in actually increasing the level of self-esteem would depend upon a number of circumstances. Thus, if alcohol abuse evokes negative responses from significant others, if the validity of this pattern is called into question, then it might be expected that alcohol abuse would be less effective in enhancing self-attitudes than it might otherwise have been. Also consistent with this expectation are certain of the findings resulting from a comparison of three categories of nonpsychotic patients committed to either of two state hospitals for treatment of alcoholism (Mindlin, 1964). One category consisted of patients who previously had psychotherapy (five or more sessions). A second category consisted of patients who had previous experience (ten or more meetings) with Alcoholics Anonymous but had never been in psychotherapy. A third category of patients (the "no-help" group) consisted of patients who had not reported previous therapy for alcoholism or Alcoholics Anonymous experience. Among the findings was the observation that self-esteem was highest in the no-help group and lowest in the therapy group. Although alternative interpretations would be permitted by the data, this finding also suggests that the nature of the processes characteristic of therapy and the Alcoholics Anonymous experience might serve to call into question the acceptability of the alcohol-abuse pattern, thus, to a degree, negating what might otherwise have been the self-enhancing effects of alcoholism.

That the experience of self-enhancing attitudes as a consequence of adopting deviant response patterns is a conditional event is an observation that has important implications for the continuity of the deviant pattern. Just as self-enhancing consequences of the alcohol-abuse pattern would be expected to confirm this mode of response, so would self-devaluating consequences be expected to have adverse effects upon continuity of the pattern. If at the same time that the person experienced self-devaluing attitudes associated with the deviant patttern he had reason to anticipate self-enhancing experiences as a result of discontinuing the pattern, that person would be even more likely to discontinue the behavior in question.

To expand upon this theme, one of the implications of the theoretical model is that for an individual to currently reject a deviant pattern such as alcoholism that previously might have served self-enhancing functions, either or both of two conditions must be met. The first condition is that the deviant pattern has come to be associated with experiences that are so self-devaluing in nature that they counteract any previously self-enhancing functions of alcohol abuse. For example, as a result of excessive drinking the individual may become incapable of performing well in personally valued occupational, familial, and other interpersonal roles. He may no longer be capable of rationalizing his drinking behavior. He may be unable to reject the validity of the reproving attitudes of significant others. He may no longer be (or perhaps never have been) able to isolate himself from perception of such negative attitudes by insulating himself from the normative environment and immersing himself in a deviant subculture. Given such outcomes, the subject would be unlikely to maintain an alcohol-abuse pattern that previously had been functional in attaining, maintaining, or restoring self-accepting attitudes.

The second condition for dropping a previously self-enhancing deviant pattern is the subject's acceptance of a new pattern that had fewer implications for self-devaluation and greater potential for self-enhancement. Thus, for example an alcoholic might cease drinking and join Alcoholics Anonymous in the process perceiving that membership in this organization appeared to carry with it approving responses from other members for giving up drinking and the opportunity to engage in the important work of helping other alcoholics. Thus, the member conceivably could gain self-respect both by identifying with worthy values and by evoking positive responses from presumably significant others. In addition, membership in this organization might imply perpetuation of the sick role, which carries with it freedom from the obligation to resume one's normal social roles (Lovald and Neuwirth, 1968). This circumstance would be particularly meaningful for increasing the level of self-esteem to the extent that inadequate performance in normal social roles was associated with prior self-derogation.

SUMMARY

Although few direct tests of the theoretical propositions are available, and important empirical exceptions are noted, the literature on alcoholism and drug abuse appears to be consistent with the central elements of the emerging theory of deviant behavior. That antecedent negative self-attitudes increase the probability of adopting alcohol-abuse response patterns is supported by observations of concomitant variation between alcohol abuse and self-rejecting attitudes; association between retrospective reports of experiences suggesting self-derogation and alcoholism; and the existence of other relationships that are theoretically consistent with the hypothesized association between negative self-attitudes and alcoholism.

The self-enhancing consequences of alcoholism are suggested by observations of the effects of induced intoxication upon self-attitudes (although inconsistencies in findings, possibly associated with methodological variability, are noted); associations between negative self-attitudes and withdrawal from alcohol-abuse patterns; and outcomes (avoidance of, attacks upon, and substitution for aspects of the normative structure) of the drinking patterns from which the probability of increased self-enhancement is inferred.

However, it is also noted that observations in the relevant literature are consistent with the theoretical assertion that the stabilization of the deviant pattern is conditional upon the absence of self-devaluing consequences of the alcohol-abuse pattern that might counterbalance the otherwise self-enhancing effects of alcohol abuse. The implication is that, given such self-devaluing consequences along with subjective anticipation of self-enhancing consequences of alternative patterns, the probability that the alcohol-abuse pattern will be discontinued is greatly increased.

NOTES

[1] The "respectability" factor might also account in part for the apparent failure of drinking patterns to reduce feelings of self-rejection, which is also to be expected in the context of the theoretical structure under consideration. Perhaps one reason for failure to observe less self-rejection on the part of more confirmed drinkers is the continuing commitment of the person to the norms of middle-class respectability in conjunction with the circumstances of being unable to hide his drinking pattern, thereby evoking negative responses from significant others in his environment, which in turn influence negative self-attitudes. In short, the data reported by Maddox (1968) are consistent with the view that drinking was an attempted deviant mode of adaptation to self-derogation but an unsuccessful one by virtue of the person's inability to isolate himself from partial commitment to the normative structure or from the adverse responses to his drinking by significant others in his environment.

Chapter 8

Aggressive Behavior

The present chapter considers the literature dealing with aggressive behavior, hostility, and (in its extreme manifestation) violence, with regard to its relevance to the emerging general theory of deviant behavior. As in the preceding chapters in Part II, the discussion is organized around two basic relationships: the association between antecedent negative self-attitudes and aggressive response patterns; and the influence of aggressive response patterns upon self-enhancement. Each of these relationships is reviewed in turn.

NEGATIVE SELF-ATTITUDES AND AGGRESSIVE BEHAVIOR

When the outline of the theoretical model developed in Part I is applied to aggressive behavior, it is assumed that such behavior is one of several categories of responses that are defined as deviant by the person's predeviance membership groups.

As a result of their experiences within their significant membership groups, it is argued, certain of the group members will develop relatively stable negative self-attitudes. In view of the actual association between self-devaluing experiences and the genesis of negative self-attitudes, the probability is increased that these persons will subjectively associate the group experiences with the genesis of negative self-attitudes. On the postulate of the self-esteem motive, such negative self-attitudes are emotionally painful states. Since the group experiences are associated in the person's mind with affectively painful experiences, he is predisposed or motivated to deviate from the group's normative structure with the effects of avoiding or attacking the group or of substituting contranormative experiences with greater self-enhancing potential.

Aggressive behavior is one of several potential deviant response patterns through which the person might avoid or attack his membership group or that might afford the opportunity for substitute self-enhancing experiences. Therefore, persons who have developed negative self-attitudes in the course of their membership group experiences would be predisposed to adopt aggressive response patterns (as well as other deviant response patterns) and, given certain facilitative conditions, in fact would adopt such patterns. The extent to which this expectation is warranted will be examined in the present section with reference to two types of literature: observations of the association between aggressive behavior and self-rejecting attitudes, and observations of the association between aggressive behavior and other conditions that appear to facilitate the adoption of such response patterns.

Self-Rejection and Aggressive Responses

Many of the studies related to the apparent role of prior self-derogation in the genesis of aggressive behavior patterns have been reviewed elsewhere (Kaplan, 1972a). The following studies illustrate those that lead to the conclusion that individuals who have adopted aggressive (more particularly, personal assault) response patterns have histories compatible with the genesis of pervasive self-rejection.

The significance of self-derogation as an antecedent of aggressive behavior is apparent in Leon's (1969) discussion of the characteristics of criminals who committed "atrocious crimes" (those crimes characterized by an "excess of aggression and cruelty") during the period known as "La Violencia" in the recent history of Colombia. The author argued "that the most ferocious of these criminals are probably individuals overwhelmed by fear and guilt, who perceive themselves as weak and worthless and hate themselves and their environment for that" (p. 1573).

Among the characteristics of the bandits suggested by published biographical data, some interviews, and recorded transcripts of certain of the confessions are those interpretable as indicating a strong vulnerability to self-devaluating attitudes. An underlying self-derogation is suggested both by the bandits' contemporary defensive postures and their earlier socialization experiences. They are described as boastful about their aggressive and sexual abilities, easily flattered and at the same time as quick to react to provocation, suspicious, impulsive, and unpredictable. Negative self-attitudes might also be expected on the basis of characterizations of the bandits' early cultural and familial settings. Their early broad environment is said to have imposed a variety of social, economic, religious, and cultural restrictions that did not permit the children "to channel their impulses and biological needs so as to achieve self-expression and self-realization" (Leon, 1969:1571). Within the family, the child is unable to establish a satisfactory self-image in the face of a brutal father who attempts to impose rigid moral demands on his son at the same time he violates the code. The repressive attempts by the father are said to have been particularly heavy in the areas of aggression and sexuality. Thus, the repressive behavior ultimately led to "feelings of inadequacy, impotence, bitterness, helplessness, and worthlessness" (Leon, 1969:1571).

Other family characteristics would also be seen as contributing to the genesis of self-rejecting attitudes. Thus, the size of the family was such that the child could not easily receive individual attention and satisfaction of his need for affection.

An association between self-rejecting attitudes and aggressive behavior is suggested also by a study of fifty-three homicide offenders (Tanay, 1969). On the basis of interview and history data, the investigator reported that 68 percent of the offenders could be classified as having a severe superego. Self-punishment was said to be easily seen in these individuals "in the nature of interpersonal relations and self-abusive behavior." However, only 7 percent of the homicide offenders could be described as having a supportive superego as indicated by a positive self-image and the absence of self-punitive behavior.

Consistent with these findings is the report by Miller (1968) that a grouping of wife murderers as well as a grouping of attempted suicides, when statistical controls were introduced, differed from a presumably normal control group in being more self-derogating and scoring higher on a self-estrangement measure as well as in a number of other respects such as scoring lower on an ego-strength scale and manifesting less closeness in interpersonal relationships.

Finally, a study (Wood, 1961) cited elsewhere in this volume is also relevant here insofar as it concerns the apparent relationship between felonies involving personal assault as well as those involving property crimes, on the one hand, and self-attitudes, on the other. Data were collected by personal interview with two groupings of subjects. One grouping consisted of males, seventeen years of age or older, who had committed personal assault or property felonies during the preceding five years. The second grouping consisted of a representative sample of nonoffenders who were living in the same three Sinhalese Low-Country villages. Data concerning the felonies were collected from police records and local informants. A comparison of the offender and nonoffender groupings suggested that, with reference to evaluative standards that appeared to be meaningful in that particular cultural context, the offenders were appreciably more likely to have had the kinds of experiences that were compatible with receiving negative evaluations from others and evoking self-rejecting attitudes.

Relative to the nonoffenders, the offenders were less likely to be regularly employed, have an English-language education, or hold a relatively prestigeful occupational position. When the subjects were compared with their fathers regarding land ownership and occupational rank, the offenders were more likely than the nonoffenders to have lost status in successive generations. The offenders were also less likely to manifest consistency between career aspiration, occupational achievement, and educational level than the nonoffenders. Wood (1961:748) summarized the situation as follows: "Cumulative evidence suggests a self-image of relative failure for the offender group."

In sum, such observations as those made in the four reports discussed above appear to be consistent with the expectation that persons who develop negative self-attitudes in the course of their membership group experiences will be predisposed to adopt deviant aggressive response patterns.

Facilitating Conditions

It is hypothesized that to the extent that a person through a long history of self-devaluing experiences in his group develops characteristic self-rejecting attitudes, the probability is greatly increased that he would adopt some mode of deviant response. If this were in fact the case, the question would arise as to why the person would adopt aggressive responses to the exclusion of other possible deviant responses to the actual and subjective association of his experiences within the normative structure with the genesis of his self-rejecting attitudes. Indeed, it was suggested in the earlier chapters of Part II that negative self-attitudes predispose individuals to adopt other specified modes of deviant response.

In attempting to account for the adoption of aggressive response patterns rather than, or in addition to, other deviant response patterns, Kaplan (1972a) offered a series of propositions based upon a review of the relevant literature. Among the factors said to influence the adoption of aggressive patterns were cultural setting, the subject's social positions, and the social relationships constituting the context of the subject's behavior. It was hypothesized that aggressive response patterns were more likely to occur if the subject was raised in cultural or subcultural settings in which the overt expression of aggression was permitted or encouraged, if the subject occupied social positions the roles of which endorsed aggressive responses, and if the subject perceived aggressive behavior as appropriate within the context of the social relationships in which he was participating.

It might be argued that such a series of propositions was not relevant in explaining why aggressive response patterns were adopted as one of a range of *deviant* patterns since to say that the expression of aggressive behavior is approved as part of a social role in a specific relational and cultural context is to say, by definition, that aggressive behavior under these conditions is *not* deviant. However, there are circumstances in which these propositions could be considered relevant explanations of why an individual adopts aggressive responses from among a range of possible deviant response patterns. Although aggressive behavior might be an acceptable pattern of behavior (that is, not at all deviant) in particular subcultures or for particular social positions or relational contexts within the subculture, it may be argued that the adoption of aggressive patterns of behavior that *in their extreme* are judged to be deviant in that cultural context is a consequence of the awareness of positive sanctioning of less extreme instances of the aggressive patterns. Thus, the degree of legitimacy attached to aggression and the visibility of aggression as a response to stress remain relevant variables in accounting for why aggression *as a deviant pattern* is adopted from among a range of available deviant patterns in response to prior self-devaluation. In effect it is suggested that prior self-derogation will increase the probability of adoption of specified modes of deviance if those deviant modes *in more moderate degrees* are regarded as prevalent and acceptable responses in the subject's cultural context and more immediate interpersonal circumstances.

The idea that modes of deviant response patterns are exaggerations of "normal" response styles is apparent, for example, in the research on Boston State Hospital schizophrenics carried on by Breen (1968). The investigator hypothesized and observed that blacks were more likely to be diagnosed as paranoid schizophrenic while Jewish patients were more likely to be diagnosed as simple, hebephrenic, or catatonic schizophrenic. It was argued that the particular schizophrenic symptomatology could be seen as an exaggeration of the normal culturally defined coping styles. The black subculture was characterized in part as encouraging aggressive assertion and independence while the Jewish subculture was characterized in such terms as dependence on the family for the satisfaction of affectional and other needs. Thus, in the event of a schizophrenic break, the black would be more likely to fight. He would more likely be diagnosed as paranoid since "in his deterioration, the fear of assault that he has always lived with" (p. 284) would be exaggerated. In contrast, the Jewish subject in the event of a schizophrenic break would be more likely to cling than to fight. Thus, he would more likely be diagnosed as simple, hebephrenic, or catatonic schizophrenic, each of which is regarded as a form of *dependency* schizophrenia since such patients are said to be in greater need of care and direction by the hospital staff than the more intact and independent paranoid schizophrenic.

Such variables as the person's cultural setting, social positions and roles, and relational contexts are viewed as exerting two relatively direct sets of influences leading to the adoption of aggressive response patterns (which are manifested to such a degree and in such circumstances that they are judged to be deviant). The first set relates to their effects upon a person's awareness of the behavior pattern in question. A second set concerns effects upon the person's anticipation of net self-enhancing consequences.

Awareness of Aggressive Response Patterns. Under the predisposing circumstances outlined above, it is argued, variables that increase the probability of a person's becoming aware of the availability of the aggressive response pattern will thereby increase the probability that the person will subsequently adopt the pattern. Such a formulation appears to be implicit in the observations of Lachman and Cravens (1969:11) regarding homicidal patients previously cited by Kaplan (1972a:607): ". . an unstable individual brought up in an environment in which violent behavior is the most typical response to stress, with weapons at his disposal, is more likely to commit homicide than an unstable individual unfamiliar with weapons, reared in a more restrained environment."

One of the results reported by Anderson (1969) also suggests the impact upon a person's awareness of aggressive response patterns of such variables as child-rearing experiences in which significant others were observed by the subject to engage in the behavior under consideration. This investigator compared the MMPI responses of parents of neurotic, aggressive, and normal boys. Among the fndings was the observation that the fathers of the aggressive boys manifested higher scores on the Pd scale, which was said to indicate difficulty with control of overt aggression. This result was congruent with a view that the child's aggressiveness was influenced by his persistent exposure to the pattern during his early socialization experiences.

Other variables that apparently influence the subject's awareness, and hence his adoption, of aggressive response patterns includes the presence of symbolic cues that are traditionally associated with aggressive behavior. Berkowitz (1970), in this connection, cites several studies that suggest that such cues as painful sounds, a prize fight film, or weapons serve to increase the probability of eliciting aggressive behavior.

Anticipation of Self-Enhancement. Given the predisposition to adopt some form of deviant behavior, the actual adoption of aggressive response patterns will be influenced by the scale of the person's anticipation of net self-gratifying consequences (probable self-enhancing consequences minus probable self-devaluing consequences) subjectively associated with the aggressive behavior. Variables increasing the subjective probability of self-enhancing consequences and decreasing the subjective probability of self-devaluing consequences associated with aggressive behavior will thereby increase the probability that the person will adopt an aggressive response pattern.

Included among such variables are circumstances influencing the subject's evaluation of aggressive behavior *per se,* as well as variables that influence other more or less self-enhancing outcomes. To the extent that a person disapproves of violent behavior, he would be likely to disapprove of himself for displaying such behavior; and to the extent that such behavior appears morally justified, he would be likely to approve of himself (or at least would be unlikely to disapprove of himself) for displaying such behavior. The person would be less likely to adopt aggressive behavior patterns as preferred deviant responses in the former than the latter circumstances. A number of investigations are consistent with the view that the probability of adopting aggressive response patterns is a function of the degree to which the aggressive behavior occasions self-accepting versus self-rejecting responses in the subject. Berkowitz (1970) cites several studies carried out in his own laboratory that appear to be relevant to this thesis. In one series of investigations the subjects (college students) viewed a filmed prize fight in which the protagonist was apparently badly beaten. The introduction to the film was said to have led the audience in some instances to regard the beating as ethically unjustified and in other instances to regard the beating as justified. Subsequently when the male subjects were given an opportunity to attack a person who had angered them, they were more likely to display the strongest aggression under the "justified" condition. As Berkowitz (1970:3) stated: "It is as if the justified aggression on the screen made their own aggression seem morally proper, thereby temporarily lessening their inhibitions against aggression." The same investigator (Berkowitz, 1970:4-5), noting that under certain conditions aggressive behavior by a subject seems to lead to even stronger aggressive behavior by the same subject "as if the first attack had introduced additional aggression-evoking stimuli," speculates that in some instances " . . . self-justification, or dissonance reduction, may be at work; people who voluntarily attack or derogate someone else often seek to justify their initial hostility by expressing further criticism of their victim, presumably when the initial hostility is inconsistent with the values they hold for themselves and they cannot compensate the victim . . ."

In addition to anticipated self-approval or self-disapproval contingent upon the adoption of aggressive response patterns, other outcomes might be relevant to the person's expectation of improved self-attitudes. Such outcomes might include perceptions of an increase in relative power. Kaplan (1972a:610-611) cites a number of studies that are congruent with the conclusion that a person is more likely to adopt aggressive response patterns if he has a basis in past experience for believing that such response patterns will eventuate in an increase (presumably self-enhancing) in relative personal power.

In short, a number of investigations suggest that a seond set of variables that might affect a person's adoption of deviant aggressive patterns (given a predisposition to deviance) includes any influences upon his subjective anticipation that the net consequences of such behavior would be an increased/decreased level of self-acceptance, either because of the intrinsically worthy/unworthy aspects of the behavior or because the behavior was likely to lead to essentially self-enhancing/devaluing experiences. These variables (in affecting the anticipation of positive/negative self-attitudes) influence the emotional tone subjectively associated with the aggressive behavior, unlike the first set of variables (which have consequences for the individual's awareness of the existence and availability of the aggressive response patterns).

AGGRESSIVE BEHAVIOR AND SELF-ENHANCEMENT

In the application of the general theory of deviant behavior to aggressive response patterns up to this point it has been asserted (1) as a result of the actual and subjective association of past experiences in the normative environment with the genesis of negative self-attitudes, the individual will be predisposed to adopt deviant behavior patterns that in effect serve to avoid or attack the normative structure and to substitute alternative experiences with greater (relative to experiences in the normative structure) self-enhancing potential; and (2) the subject will adopt the specific response patterns of aggressive behaviors to the extent that he becomes aware of the existence and availability of these patterns and anticipates that these patterns will eventuate in net self-enhancing consequences.

To continue the application of the general model to aggressive behavior, insofar as aggressive behavior facilitates the successful avoidance of, attacks upon, and provision of substitute opportunities for self-enhancement, the adoption of aggressive response patterns would be expected to result in increasingly positive and decreasingly negative self-attitudes. Through the experience of such personally gratifying outcomes, the use of aggressive response patterns would receive positive reinforcement. The available literature on aggressive behavior relevant to this part of the theoretical model appears to fall into two categories. The first grouping of reports concerns the observed associations between aggressive behavior and self-enhancing attitudes. The second set of observations concerns the functions of aggressive behavior in permitting avoidance of, attacks upon, and substitution of new experiences for the normative environment. Self-enhancing outcomes of the adoption of aggressive response patterns are inferred from the observation of such functions. Each set of reports will be considered in turn.

Aggressive Behavior and Self-Attitudes

The beneficent effects of adopting aggressive response patterns upon improved self-attitudes is suggested by observations among violent offenders, the results of experimental studies, and observed relationships between self-attitudes and degree of fixity in aggressive response patterns.

Violent Offenders. Toch's (1969) findings from a study of sixty-nine violent offenders tend to support the view that violent response patterns are vehicles, the purpose and/or effect of which is to generate, defend, or maintain positive self-attitudes. Toch typed the offenders by "primary theme" and reported that 28 percent could be classified as "Self-image promoting," 13 percent could be classified as "Self-image defending," and 14 percent could be typed as "Rep defending." This last theme appeared to imply the maintenance of self-esteem through conformity to role obligations, including expressions of violent behavior. In addition to the 55 percent of the violent offenders who fell into the above three categories, an additional 22 percent (for a cumulative total of 77 percent) were said to fall into thematic categories within the general grouping "encompassing essentially self-preserving strategies, with violence used to bolster and enhance the person's ego in the eyes of himself and of others" (p. 135).

Experimental Studies. The results of a number of experimental studies are consistent with the view that aggressive behavior functions to reduce the subject's level of self-rejection. Although these studies do not directly demonstrate a decrease in negative (or an increase in positive) self-attitudes subsequent to the subject's aggressive behavior, they do indicate that indices of tension associated with prior self-devaluing experience are lowered following aggressive behavior. Berkowitz (1970:5-6) cites a number of studies by Hokanson and his students (Hokanson and Burgess, 1962; Hokanson, Burgess, and Cohen, 1963; Hokanson and Edelman, 1966) in which the college student subjects manifested an appreciable increase in systolic blood pressure after being insulted by the experimenter (a circumstance here interpreted as a self-devaluing experience). Following the condition in which the subjects were provided the opportunity to behave aggressively toward the experimenter (by giving the latter personal electric shocks), the subjects displayed a quick reduction in systolic blood pressure. For the physiological tension reduction to occur it was apparently necessary that the target of the aggressive behavior be the person associated with the self-devaluing experience. Thus, although a rapid reduction of the subject's systolic blood pressure followed the opportunity of giving electric shocks to the person who insulted him, there was a much slower decline in blood pressure when the subject attacked some other person.

Pattern Fixity. If it is assumed that aggressive behavior is functionally related to the reduction of self-rejecting feelings, then it should follow that greater degrees of commitment to, or fixity in, aggressive behavior patterns should be associated with more positive self-attitudes than lesser degrees of commitment to such patterns. Operationally "degree of fixity in the pattern" might be indicated by perceived probability that the subject will change his pattern of aggressive behavior. Data interpretable as supporting this train of thought were provided by Schwartz, Fearn, and Stryker (1966). These authors studied seventy-eight children who were being treated as inpatients in two Canadian psychiatric institutions. The children were all said to be engaged in highly aggressive "acting-out" behavior. Apparently none of the subjects was seriously psychotic or autistic. The children were administered a semantic differential instrument by which they rated "How you feel about yourself" (as well as other stimuli) on an evaluative index consisting of polar adjective scales such as bad-good, clean-dirty, stupid-smart.

The children, whose average age was 12.5 years, were distributed by the therapists among four prognostic categories: very good, good, poor, and very poor. The various groupings were quite similar in terms of a number of variables, including length of time in therapy, age, and sex. An examination of the results revealed that the children in the "poor" and "very poor" categories rated thmselves appreciably higher and were less variable in their self-rating than the children in the "good" or "very good" prognosis categories. That is, children who were (according to their therapists) least likely to recover were most likely to offer consistent and positive self-evaluations.

Although alternative interpretations are possible, these observations are also consistent with the view that the adoption of patterns of aggressive behavior is functionally related to the reduction of self-rejecting feelings. The observed association between poor prognosis and positive self-evaluation might reflect either or both of two processes that would necessarily be operative in the establishment of such a functional relationship. First, the observed association might reflect the process by which the adoption of aggressive behavior patterns leads to more positive self-feelings. Second, the observed association might reflect the process by which those children (from among a more inclusive grouping of children who tentatively perform aggressive acting-out behavior) who experience aggressive behavior as self-enhancing and anxiety-reducing become confirmed in the aggressive acting-out behavior pattern. In the former case, the aggressive behavior pattern is understood to be temporally prior to change in self-attitudes. In the latter case, the establishment of the aggressive behavior pattern is understood to be a consequence of the prior experience of improved self-attitudes as a concomitant of experimentation with aggressive behavior. It must be emphasized, however, that in either case, the explanation rests upon the interpretation of therapists' prognostic evaluations as an index of pattern fixity.

In summary, the studies reviewed above are judged to be consistent with the expectation that the adoption of aggressive response patterns would be associated with consequent improvement in self-attitudes and that the subjective gratification associated with this outcome would serve to positively reinforce the employment of aggressive response patterns. However, it must be noted here, as in the preceding chapter, that to the extent that aggressive responses also become the occasion for increased self-devaluation, the subject would be somewhat less likely to become fixed in aggressive response patterns. Increased self-devaluation might result, for example, if aggressive behavior contravened internalized normative patterns that deplore overt aggressive responses in certain circumstances, such as the apparent suffering of the victim. In such circumstances, the person who might otherwise have been inclined to display aggression would be expected to inhibit its expression.

Consistent with this expectation are the results of an experiment reported by Geen (1970) in which forty-eight subjects were placed in a situation in which they were either attacked or not attacked (that is, given shock in criticism of the subject's opinion) by an experimental confederate posing as another subject. The subject was later given the opportunity to apparently shock the confederate, who either expressed or did not express suffering upon receiving the shocks. The results indicated that the subjects tended to give significantly milder shocks under the condition in which the confederate expressed suffering than under the condition in which he did not. Under the assumption that causing suffering to another person is culturally and personally deplored, then, these results lend support to the thesis that aggressive behavior tends to be inhibited in circumstances whereby such behavior would be the occasion for self-devaluation.

Nevertheless, insofar as the self-enhancing effects of avoiding, attacking, or substituting experiences with self-enhancing potential for the normative structure outweigh such self-devaluing effects, the adoption of aggressive response patterns will be reinforced.

Self-Enhancing Function

Aggressive behavior may be thought of as serving self-enhancing functions in any number of ways. Throughout this volume it has been convenient to classify the mechanisms through which self-enhancement is achieved into three categories: (1) intrapsychic or interpersonal avoidance of those aspects of the normative structure that are subjectively associated with the genesis of negative self-attitudes; (2) symbolic or physical attacks upon the normative structure, its representations, or its representatives; (3) substitution of new experiences with self-enhancing potential for experiences within the normative structure.

With regard to avoidance functions, the adoption of socially disvalued aggressive behavior patterns might serve to assert the person's separation from a world in which he is not valued. Alternatively, hostile behavior might permit an individual to avoid recognizing his own objectionable characteristics or self-devaluing experiences. In order to assure himself that a potentially self-devaluing experience such as rejection by another person is not a result of his own "badness," the subject must ascribe this "badness" to, and therefore feel hostile toward, the other person. Thus, hostility may be regarded as a defense against lowered self-esteem (Hoffman, 1964:265-266).

With regard to the "attack" functions of aggressive response patterns, successful aggression against a target who (which) is associated with prior self-devaluing experiences might serve to symbolically diminish the significance of the target and therefore the role of the target in creating self-rejecting attitudes. Thus, if the attitudes of "society" (or parents, peers, particular social institutions, and so on) toward the subject are perceived by the subject as derogatory and at the root of his own self-rejection, then successful aggression against society (or parents, peers, social institutions) might serve as symbolic rejection of the standards associated with these targets by which the subject has come to devalue himself. By attacking and perhaps "destroying" these standards the person attacks the basis of his own self-devaluation.

In addition to permitting the person to avoid or attack the normative structure associated with the genesis of self-rejecting attitudes (and thereby to reduce the person's level of self-rejection), the aggressive response patterns might provide substitute self-enhancing experiences in any of a number of ways. First, aggressive behavior might signify to the person the presence in him of other personally valued traits. Thus, successful aggression might symbolize not only the nullification of the standards by which the person has failed but at the same time his own supremacy over those standards. Not only does the subject destroy the basis for his self-devaluation, but he provides evidence of his own potency that belies his previously felt impotence. Second, the aggressive behavior might evoke responses from others that indirectly permit him to reevaluate his own worth. Thus, the value of the aggressive responses for the person's self-attitudes might rest in the fact that it invites punishment. To the extent that the subject is indeed punished, he may relieve himself of severe feelings of guilt associated with a pervasive sense of worthlessness. By being punished for a disvalued activity (aggression), the subject relieves himself of felt guilt for having possessed certain characteristics or performed certain behaviors in the past that are subjectively even more significant in evoking self-rejecting attitudes. Third, violence might be self-enhancing through its employment in the service of ideally desirable goals. To the extent that the person identifies with "worthy" values or causes — the true religion, justice for all, peace in our time — and employs violence toward the goals of realizing these values, he might perceive himself as more worthy by virtue of his aggressive pursuit of worthy goals. Fourth, aggressive response patterns might enhance an individual's self-attitudes in other ways quite independent of the nature of the target of the aggression or the goals in the service of which aggression is employed. These ways relate to the valuation of aggression itself. An individual frequently highly values and identifies with groups in which he is not yet a member but in which he desires membership. To the extent that such groups are perceived as valuing aggressive behavior for its own sake, the person might adopt such behavior as a personally valued behavior or in the expectation of evoking positive responses from the members of these reference groups. In either case his self-attitudes might be enhanced.

A number of observations suggest that aggressive responses function to reduce self-rejection through facilitating avoidance of, or attacks upon, the normative structure and to enhance self-attitudes through the provision of substitute experiences. Such observations have been made with reference to both criminal violence and social protest.

With regard to the former category of behavior, Leon (1969), discussing excessively cruel crimes, suggests that the person perceives aggressive behavior as a vehicle for self-enhancement and indeed, through aggressive behavior, may evoke self-gratifying responses from others. In this connection he notes that the criminals were frequently boastful about their aggressive ability and occasionally enjoyed great prestige. Thus, Leon (1969:1572) states that among the possible factors that may bring about the appearance of the criminal atrocities under consideration is the pressure generated by continued feelings of inadequacy and worthlessness "toward the commission of atrocious acts as a form of self-assertion and achieving distinction. The criminal in this way gains notoriety and steps out of the limbo of mediocrity and anonymity in which he feels immersed. This amounts to achieving self-assertion through outdoing others in cruelty."

Expressions of positive attitudes toward those committing violent acts were also apparent in a study of a riot in a maximum security federal reformatory in Oklahoma (Skelton, 1969). Although Indians accounted for less than 5 percent of the general population, they constituted over 35 percent of the inmates who assaulted officers and were not represented at all among the inmates who defended the officers during the course of the riot. After the riot, interviews held with Indians who did not participate in the riot revealed that most of them felt pride upon considering the large number of Indians who did participate in it.

The function of aggression in enhancing self-attitudes would appear to some to be relevant also in considerations of civil disorders that are in part characterized by violence against person or property. It has been suggested, for example, that civil disorder or urban revolt is one of many forms of acting-out behavior (other forms including hippiedom, civil rights actions, and fanatical patriotism) that for many people constitute ways of maintaining "psychological equilibrium" (Usdin, 1969:92). Many of the people who engage in civil disorder in the name of a moral cause are said to do so to satisfy any of a variety of psychodynamic frustrations: "Their needs may be to destroy, to rebel, to get caught and punished, to be one of the group, to secure attention, or to be martyred by injury or imprisonment" (Usdin, 1969:92).

The satisfaction of such needs are clearly interpretable as fulfilling self-enhancing functions: By being punished, the subject may relieve himself of guilt regarding a more profound basis of self-rejection; by "destroying" or rebelling against society, the person destroys or denies the relevance of the source of his self-rejection; the gaining of a group identity and attention attests to the subject's becoming a person of note; by being "martyred" the person evidences his strong identification with a highly worthy cause, thus demonstrating his own worth as well. This last presumed influence of acting-out behavior on

behalf of a "worthy" cause is perhaps the one potentially beneficent
for enhancing self-attitudes that is not activated by antisocial acting-out behavior. Such an outcome might account for the observation by some that an
increase in "prosocial" acting out leads to a decrease in antisocial acting-out
behavior. Thus, Solomon and his associates (1965) offer data suggesting an
association between organized civil rights activity and the reduction of crimes
of violence by blacks in three cities. The authors argue that a long-term effect of
racial segregation has been the blocking of avenues of self-assertion through
which blacks might openly express felt resentment against their second-class
status. Because they lack alternative channels, violent crimes (predominantly
directed toward other blacks) are utilized as a more easily available way to
express aggression. Organized civil rights activity, however, offers an alternative that may have more beneficent effects upon the blacks' self-attitude since
it is perceived as for the "good of society." "Prosocial acting out" thus is seen as
an alternative to antisocial acting out: "When he becomes aggressive *against
segregation*, the Negro's sense of personal and group identity is altered; race
pride partially replaces self-hatred, and aggression need not be directed so
destructively at the self or the community" (Solomon, *et al.*, 1965:234).

Also illustrative of the hypothesized self-gratifying outcomes of aggressive
social protest activity are the results of a survey of black residents in a Detroit
neighborhood following the 1967 riots (Hahn, 1969). Substantial portions of the
sample provided responses to items that indicated that as a consequence of the
riots they perceived a greater probability that they would have more to say about
what should be done in the neighborhood, receive more attention from city
officials, and have more power.

In short, available observations suggest that aggressive response patterns
frequently have outcomes (comprising avoidance of and attacks upon the normative structure and the substitution of new experiences) from which the
reduction of self-rejecting attitudes and an increase in self-accepting attitudes
may be inferred.

SUMMARY

A consideration of the literature dealing with aggressive behavior leads to
conclusions that are compatible with the general theory of deviant behavior
outlined in Part I. Although the literature does not contain direct tests of the
major hypotheses constituting the theory, the reported findings do suggest that
(1) persons who are characterized by negative self-attitudes are predisposed to
adopt deviant aggressive response patterns; (2) persons who are predisposed to
adopt such patterns, under conditions facilitating awareness of the pattern and a
subjective expectancy of net self-enhancing outcomes, in fact will tend to adopt
such patterns; and (3) persons who adopt such patterns will tend to experience
outcomes that will function to reduce self-rejecting, and increase self-accepting,
attitudes.

Chapter 9

Suicidal Behavior

This chapter considers the applicability of the general theory of deviant behavior to suicidal responses, particularly with reference to the hypothesized reciprocal relationship between self-attitudes and suicidal behavior. The particular questions to be answered are: (1) Does the presence of relatively stable negative self-attitudes predispose a person to suicidal responses? (2) Does suicidal behavior by intent or (in the instances of *uncompleted* suicides) effect function to reduce self-rejecting, and increase self-accepting, attitudes?

SELF-DEROGATION AND SUICIDAL BEHAVIOR

Perhaps more so in the case of suicidal behavior than for any other form of deviant response, explanations of the behavior under consideration have relied heavily upon the significance of self-rejecting attitudes. One of the clearest statements currently available concerning the relevance of self-evaluation to the suicide process has been provided by Warren Breed (1968). This author outlined a social-psychological theory of suicide that was based for the most part on his study in which the survivors of 264 completed suicides in New Orleans were interviewed. He focused upon what he called "failure suicides," thus excluding from consideration those suicides who were very sick, aged, psychotic, or characterized by "extraordinary and chaotic life histories." "Failure suicides" were those whose suicidal behavior appeared to be related to inadequate performance in major life roles such as those based on occupational, marital, or parental position. Breed estimated that at least one-half of the more than 20,000 suicides each year in the United States were "failure suicides."

Breed addressed himself to the question of what characterizes the failure suicide in contrast to those who fail but do not suicide. The model presented, which was said to be only partly confirmed by the evidence, was based upon the assertion of four characteristics of failure suicides. First, failure suicides in contrast to failure nonsuicides were characterized as having internalized cultural norms of success to such an extreme that failure battered their self-conceptions, and they thus experienced severe pain and discomfort. Second, failure suicides were said to be extremely sensitive to failure in that they "had a high capacity to feel shame, and a small capacity to overcome it" (p. 287). The third characteristic, which appears to greatly overlap the second, relates to the rigidity or inflexibility of the personality. Failure suicides characteristically were unable to shift goals and roles so as to increase the probability of success. Nor did they appear to be able to employ defense mechanisms that might serve self-protecting functions in the face of failure. Finally, the failure suicide, because he anticipates rejection by significant others and/or in reality becomes the object of negative evaluations by the significant others, was said to suffer in his ability to sustain satisfying social relationships. Thus, he was deprived of social support and restraints upon his behavior.

The above model of the suicide was stated in the context of "self" theory in which the self is conceived of as having three components: the self-image, the self-demands, and the self-judgments, which are a function of the relationship between the first two components. The person is conceived of as being motivated to so act as to enhance his self-judgment through the reduction of the disparity between his self-image and his self-demands.

Also illustrative of formulations concerning the genesis of suicidal behavior in which the self-esteem motive occupies a central position is the statement by Gould (1965:236). This observer notes that the common factor underlying the wide variety of events that appear to precipitate suicide attempts in children and adolescents is (fear of) rejection and deprivation that is the consequence of loss of love and support. This experience is seen as having a profound influence upon the person's feelings of self-acceptance:

> The feeling of being abandoned and rejected means he must be a bad human being and this is his punishment. There follows a decrease in self-esteem and a sense of worthlessness. This is intolerable, and the resulting state of mind of the youngster depends on a variety of factors operant for the individual. Depression in some form seems an invariable accompaniment of a feeling of decreased self-esteem, worthlessness, and loneliness. Frustration, anger, guilt, exaggerated needs for love, attention, and support, the desire to punish, be punished, or both, are felt in varying degrees and may result in suicidal behavior.

Both of these formulations are compatible with the outline of the theoretical model proposed in Part I insofar as self-rejecting feelings are conceived of as the outgrowth of experiences in the person's membership groups, and suicidal behavior is conceived of as a possible outcome. The outline asserts that as a result of the person's subjective association of the normative environment with the development of his emotionally distressing self-rejecting attitudes, he is predisposed to adopt any of a range of deviant responses, including suicidal behaviors, which might function to facilitate avoidance of or attacks upon the normative environment and the provision of substitute experiences with self-enhancing potential. Which, if any, of the available deviant patterns are in fact adopted is a function of a number of facilitating conditions.

The available literature, although it does not permit an intensive examination of these aspects of the theoretical model, does provide some reports relating to the association between self-derogating attitudes and suicidal behavior, self-rejecting attitudes as a predisposing factor in multiple forms of deviance, and variables associated with the adoption of suicidal response patterns to the exclusion of other deviant patterns. Each of these aspects will be considered in turn.

Negative Self-Attitudes and Suicidal Behavior

Available studies of the relationship between negative self-attitudes and suicidal behavior may be distributed among two categories. The first category includes investigations of common characteristics of suicidal subjects. The second category includes studies comparing suicidal with nonsuicidal subjects.

Observations of Suicidal Subjects. A number of studies of people who have displayed suicidal behavior report the presence of self-rejecting attitudes or behaviors by the subject and significant others that might be expected to eventuate in negative self-attitudes. For example, Glaser (1965:225) in a report based on the study of fifteen children and adolescents who made suicide threats or attempts and were subsequently referred for psychiatric evaluations and/or treatment asserted: "Low self-esteem and a feeling of being unwanted was a common characteristic."

Other studies report interpersonal events such as loss of significant others or interpersonal hostility, which, as was indicated in Part I, might be expected to lead to self-rejecting attitudes. In one study, cited above (Gould, 1965:236), the observer noted: "Although the conscious reason for the suicide attempt seems to be that it is an escape from a situation too difficult to face, the common theme underlying the myriad precipitating events is rejection and deprivation, or fear of rejection and deprivation, which results from the loss of love and support." Another report suggests that the expression of hostility and death wishes for the subject by members of his family and other significant persons in his life seems to play an important role in the genesis of suicidal behavior (Rosenbaum and Richman, 1970).

Suicidal vs. Nonsuicidal Subjects. A number of studies are available comparing suicidal and nonsuicidal persons with regard to the nature of their self-attitudes. Hattem (1964), for example, reported that in comparison with the responses of their spouses suicidal individuals manifested a greater discrepancy between their self and ideal-self on the dominance scale of the Leary Interpersonal Adjective Check List. Among the author's conclusions was the assertion that the suicidal subject tended to be characterized by feelings of weakness, dependency, and inferiority. In a similar vein, Braaten and Darling (1962) having compared suicidal college students with a nonsuicidal group suggested that the suicidal subjects were characterized by self-hate as well as a number of other traits, including anger, hostility, and dependency. Miller (1968), also, contrasted the self-attitudes of attempted suicides with those of a group of suicide prevention workers. The author in addition to reporting that attempted suicides and wife murderers were alike in a number of respects indicated that these individuals differed from a normal comparison group along several specified dimensions. Among the differences noted were the greater tendencies on the part of the suicidal subjects and wife murderers to be more self-derogating, to score higher on a self-estrangement measure, and to score lower on an ego-strength scale.

In the course of investigating the effectiveness of self-concept measurement in the prediction of suicidal behavior, Wilson and his associates (1971) provided data relevant to the relationship between self-derogation and serious suicidal behavior. The subjects consisted of twenty-two suicide attempters, twenty-two psychiatric controls, and twenty-two normal controls. The suicide attempters were matched with the control subjects for sex, age, education, and (for the psychiatric controls only) diagnosis. The subjects were administered the Miskimins Self-Goal-Other Discrepancy Scale. Among the scores derived from this scale was the "plus Self-Other discrepancy" factor. A high score on this factor (which is highly correlated with depression) was said to be indicative of self-derogation. A comparison of the scores of the suicide attempters on this factor with those of the psychiatric and normal controls revealed that the suicide attempters tended to receive significantly higher scores than either of the two control groups. Thus, the investigators observed that the suicide attempter "apparently values himself considerably less than he feels others value him and is not able to relieve this discrepancy" (p. 309).

Although the results are not perfectly consistent with regard to self-attitudes, certain of the findings of yet another study are suggestive of a process whereby self-rejecting attitudes predispose a person to adopt suicidal response patterns. In this investigation Kamano and Crawford (1966) compared three groups of white, female, adult mental hospital patients with regard to measures of self-abasement and self-satisfaction. The suicidal attempt grouping consisted of eighteen patients who were said to have made serious attempts at self-destruction. The "suicidal gesture" grouping consisted of twenty-eight patients "who had made impulsive or premeditated acts judged as not serious attempts at self-destruction" (p. 278). The control group consisted of fifty-six presumably nonsuicidal patients. The authors reported no significant differences on the semantic differential measure of self-satisfaction between the three groups of subjects. However, consistent with the hypothesis under consideration in the present discussion is the observation that the two suicidal groups did not differ from each other with regard to self-abasement scores but did manifest significantly higher self-abasement scores than the control group subjects. Since the self-abasement measure is said to involve in part the felt "need for punishment for wrongdoing" this finding leads one to speculate that those individuals who engage in suicidal behaviors may be motivated to expiate their guilt through the self-injurious behavior and, thereby, to raise their level of self-acceptance higher than it might have been in the absence of the suicidal behavior.

In addition to citing investigations such as those considered immediately above that compare suicidal and nonsuicidal subjects with regard to relatively direct indices of self-attitudes, general reviews of the suicide literature (Farberow and Shneidman, 1961; Lester, 1970) cite a number of other studies that are interpretable as offering empirical support for the hypothesis that self-derogating individuals are more likely to engage in suicidal behavior than self-accepting individuals. This grouping of investigations includes those studies that, although they do not directly demonstrate relationships between suicidal behavior and negative self-attitudes, do report associations between suicidal behavior on the one hand and variables *that other studies have shown to be related to negative self-attitudes* on the other hand. Such variables include the tendency to reject other people, being the object of negative attitudes by significant others, and the experience during childhood of parental remarriage, each of which has been reported to be associated with suicidal behavior (Margolin and Teicher, 1968; Tucker and Reinhardt, 1966; Jacobs, 1967; Hattem, 1964; Fawcett, *et al.*, 1969; Kumler, 1964; Tabachnick, *et al.*, 1966; Ganzler, 1967; Jacobs and Teicher, 1967). However, whether these reports may properly be taken as support for the hypothesized relationship between suicidal behavior and negative self-attitudes is somewhat problematic since such an interpretation must assume that the correlations between self-attitudes and these variables are sufficiently high so that an association between suicidal behavior and one of the variables necessarily implies a significant association between suicidal behavior and negative self-attitudes. Nevertheless, the bulk of the available literature is sufficiently consistent to offer the conclusion that self-rejecting attitudes are associated with suicidal behaviors.

Predispositions to Deviant Patterns

The outline of the general theory of deviant behavior under consideration asserts that the person's history of self-devaluing experiences in and his subjective association of this history with the normative structure of his membership groups predispose him to adopt any of a range of deviant response patterns, among which are suicidal behaviors. In view of this assertion it is to be expected that suicidal persons would not differ from individuals who were predisposed to adopt other modes of structured psychosocial deviance with regard to level of self-esteem (or with regard to known correlates of self-acceptance) although subjects in both deviant groupings would be expected to be more self-derogatory than non-deviant subjects. These expectations appear to be warranted particularly in the comparison of suicidal subjects with psychiatric and normal controls. Thus, Tucker and Reinhardt (1966) reported that among male military subjects, attempted suicides were more likely to have had parents who fought and who were not kind and loving than presumably well-adjusted controls. However, the attempted suicides did not differ from psychiatric controls in these regards. Ganzler (1967) reported that suicidal subjects did not differ from psychiatric controls but did differ from well-adjusted controls in more negative ratings of their significant others. Nor did the suicidal subjects differ from the psychiatrically disturbed controls in the extent to which they felt that life events were controlled by forces external to them and beyond their control although they did feel less powerful than the well-adjusted controls. In addition, on social contact and interpersonal satisfaction scales there were no appreciable differences between the suicidal subjects and disturbed control subjects although both groups were less social and less satisfied than the well-adjusted controls.

Also consistent with the findings of the above-mentioned studies are the results reported by Farberow (1950) and Kamano and Crawford (1966), which indicated no significant differences in characteristic level of self-esteem or self-satisfaction between suicidal and nonsuicidal mental hospital patients. Thus, an ample number of observations have been made that are congruent with the conclusion that suicidal behavior and other forms of mental illness are alternative responses to self-rejecting attitudes although some reports do cite differences in level of self-esteem between suicidal and nonsuicidal psychiatrically disturbed subjects (for example, Wilson, et al., 1971; Farnham-Diggory, 1964).

Another variety of investigations has yielded results that are congruent with the thesis that suicide is one of a range of deviant responses to self-derogation. These studies in varying degrees suggest the increased probability that suicidal as opposed to nonsuicidal subjects will have displayed other forms of deviant response such as mental illness and alcoholism. These studies are conveniently reviewed by Lester (1970:117-123, 134-135). It should be noted, however, that the observed association between various forms of deviant behavior are also compatible with other explanations. For example, it might be asserted that suicidal behavior is a response to the negative consequences of prior performance of other deviant acts. Nevertheless, in spite of the possible alternative explanations and the few contradictory reports, the bulk of relevant findings appear to be congruent with the proposition that suicidal patterns are among a range of deviant responses to which the self-rejecting person is predisposed.

Suicidal Response Patterns

The theoretical model under consideration hypothesizes that a history of self-rejecting experiences subjectively associated with the normative environment predisposes an individual to adopt any of a range of deviant response patterns, including suicidal behaviors. The actual adoption of suicidal response patterns to the exclusion of other deviant patterns is said to be a function of a number of

facilitating conditions. The detailed specification of the conditions that facilitate the adoption of each deviant pattern is not necessary in the context of a
general theory of deviant behavior, although such specification is appropriate in
the development of any special theory (such as a theory of suicide, delinquency,
or alcoholism). However, even a general theory of deviant behavior should
describe the broad facilitating conditions that bridge the behavioral gap between
predisposition to deviant responses and the *adoption* of deviant responses.

Although the available literature on suicide does not permit an organized
exposition of the conditions facilitating the performance of suicidal behaviors
by persons who are predisposed to adopt some form of deviant response, the total
body of literature does offer some clues in this regard. The most useful literature
for the purpose is derived from investigations comparing suicidal subjects with
other deviant groupings. Frequently, variables that differentiate between these
groupings suggest conditions associated with the adoption of one rather than
another of the deviant response patterns.

In previous chapters it was convenient to distribute variables that reflected
hypothetical facilitating conditions among two categories: variables that influence subjective awareness of the deviant pattern in question; and variables that
influence the subjective probability of net self-enhancing consequences of the
anticipated deviant behavior. Another way of expressing these two categories of
variables might be in terms of the cognitive and affective stimulus value of the
situation involving adoption of the deviant (here, suicidal) response patterns. In
either case an inspection of the relevant literature dealing with suicidal behavior suggests that these categories would be useful organizing devices in the
present context as well.

Awareness of Suicidal Alternatives. Among the conditions that would facilitate the adoption of suicidal response patterns by people who are predisposed to
deviant response patterns are those that evoke awareness of the suicidal response patterns and exclude from awareness the consideration of alternative
deviant patterns. With regard to the former conditions, a history of frequent
experience with violent responses, for example, might make a person more
aware of self-injurious patterns. In this connection, Farberow and his associates
(1966) compared male psychiatric patients who completed suicides with nonsuicidal psychiatric patients with regard to their history of behavior on the ward
and found that those who went on to complete suicide were more violent
(needed restraints, engaged in fistfights, and so on) than the nonsuicidal patients. By way of further illustration, Whitlock and Broadhurst (1969), comparing attempted suicides and nonsuicidal psychiatric patients, reported that the
former subjects had more violent experiences such as accidents in general, road
mishaps, and fights and brawls during their lifetime.

Other variables such as social isolation and psychological inflexibility
might influence the exclusion from awareness of a range of deviant response
patterns. Thus, Ganzler (1967) reported that current social isolation was more
characteristic of suicidal subjects than of the disturbed or well-adjusted control
subjects. Neuringer (1964) reported that suicidal patients scored higher on tests
intended to indicate rigid thinking than psychosomatic patients and "normal"

patients. Presumably, the rigid person would be less able to find and use new solutions to crises.

Anticipated Self-Enhancement. The second category of conditions for the adoption of suicidal patterns would concern the expectation of self-enhancing/self-devaluing experiences contingent upon anticipated suicidal as opposed to alternative responses. In this connection certain findings suggest that suicidal options are selected by persons whose conception of future events is such that a state of nonbeing appears to be more self-enhancing (or less self-devaluing) than a state of being. Ganzler (1967), for example, reported that suicidal subjects viewed their present and future life in more negative terms than psychiatric controls.

Whether or not such reports are interpreted as indicating that a state of nonbeing appears to be self-gratifying, other reports suggest that the probability of self-injurious responses is increased when alternative deviant responses appear to have self-devaluing implications. Thus, Teele (1965) studying white psychotics aged twenty to twenty-six, compared subjects who were suicidal with those who were assaultive. He reported that the degree of social participation of the mother of the patients was related to the choice of suicidal behavior by the patients. Teele argued that social participation implies a greater normative orientation, which in turn implies greater acceptance of the rights of others. Such respect for others serves to inhibit expression of aggressive impulses toward outgroup individuals and thus influences the turning inward of aggression.

SUICIDAL BEHAVIOR AND SELF-ENHANCEMENT

In applying the theoretical model to suicidal behavior, the distinction must be drawn between completed suicides and other modes of suicidal response such as suicide attempts. With regard to completed suicide, one can only speculate as to whether or not the suicide was to avoid further severe emotional distress associated with self-derogating attitudes.

With regard to all other suicidal behaviors it is more meaningul to ask if subjects who have engaged in (uncompleted) suicidal behaviors manifest improved self-attitudes and, if such improved self-attitudes have been demonstrated in fact, through what mechanism the increase in self-acceptance (or decrease in self-rejection) has been accomplished. For example, does the suicidal behavior represent an *attack* upon others by evoking feelings of guilt or causing them inconvenience? Does the suicidal behavior represent a sincere attempt to *avoid* continuing stress associated with self-devaluing experiences in the normative environment? Or does suicidal behavior permit the individual to *substitute* for former self-devaluing experiences new outcomes with greater self-enhancing potential? For example, in this connection, do individuals who have attempted suicide evoke positive sympathetic responses from significant others that in turn influence more favorable self-evaluations? Alternatively does the act of attempted suicide permit the person to purge himself of a sense of worthlessness by feeling that the self-injurious behavior has in some way atoned for his previous reprehensible behavior? Although the relevant literature does not permit the reader to draw a definitive conclusion, a small number of studies do suggest that suicidal behavior may have some such self-enhancing outcomes.

Farnham-Diggory (1964) compared three groups of psychotic males with regard to level of self-evaluation. One group consisted of twenty-one "overt suicidals" who had made an attempt to kill themselves as evidenced by scars or witnesses. The second group consisted of twenty-two "covert suicidals" who talked about suicide but who were not known to have made an attempt to kill themselves. The third group consisted of fifty-three "nonsuicidal" patients in whose records no indication appeared that they had ever been considered suicidal by anyone at any time. The three groups were comparable on a number of characteristics including race, education, marital status, religion, father's occupation, diagnosis, number of hospitalizations, and length of current hospitalization. The author reported that the nonsuicidal subjects tended to display most positive self-evaluations, followed closely by the overt suicidal subjects. The covert suicidal subjects were least positive in their self-evaluations. The differences in self-evaluation between the nonsuicidal and overt suicidal subjects was not significant. However, the difference in level of self-evaluations between the covert suicidals and nonsuicidal subjects was statistically significant at the .05 level. That is, the self-evaluations of the overt suicidals more closely approximated the relatively positive self-evaluations of the nonsuicidal patients than did the self-evaluations of the coverts. Thus, although the data do not permit determination of whether or not the attempted suicide evoked positive environmental responses and/or was in some measure cathartic, the results are consonant with the thesis that the active attempt to suicide exerted a self-enhancing influence on the subjects' self-attitudes.

Also consistent with this thesis is the report by Farberow (1950) that subjects who *threatened* suicides manifested significantly more negative feelings on the Hildreth Feeling and Attitude Scale than did *attempted* suicides and nonsuicidal patients, a result that would be expected if active suicidal behavior was indeed functional in increasing one's level of self-acceptance.

Based upon data collected from and about females who have engaged in suicidal behavior Maris (1971) offered arguments that are compatible with the point of view of the present volume — that deviant behaviors, including attempted suicide, frequently by intent and/or effect are modes of adaptation to self-rejecting attitudes. Maris' conclusions are based on the observations of the positive intercorrelations of a cluster of variables and the positive correlations of these variables with suicide attempts, and the further observations of negative correlations between this cluster of variables and attempted suicide on the one hand and completed suicide on the other hand.

> To sum up, the argument is that female suicide attempts (and antecedent behavior) are most appropriately conceived of as partial self-destruction to the end of making life possible — not ending it. The majority of self-destructive women are engaging in

forms of ego-defensive risk-taking, which *may* prove fatal but are intended to be problem-solving ... These women's persistent self-destructive coping assumes the character of "lifeworks," or "achievement in a vocation." The "job" is to stay alive through a kind of psychic surgery: cutting themselves off from pathological families of origin, evolving a narcissistic personality to fend off labels of "worthless" and "inadequate," deviating from prescribed sexual behavior in a manner to find warmth and affection, withdrawing from time to time into a subcommunity of drug users, even attempting suicide — a dramatic *communiqué* and plea to a public that has stigmatized and ostracized them. Although this is not the best of all possible worlds, it seems to work [Maris, 1971:123].

In short, the few studies briefly reviewed immediately above are congruent with the assertion that overt suicidal behavior is functional in decreasing the person's degree of self-rejection.

SUMMARY

A review of the relevant literature dealing with suicidal behavior appears to suggest conclusions that are not inconsistent with the emerging general theory of deviant behavior under consideration. Observations of suicidal persons and comparisons of suicidal with nonsuicidal subjects do suggest that suicidal individuals are characterized by histories that lead to pervasive self-rejecting attitudes. Although suicidal individuals are not unlike other categories of deviant responders in this regard, pervasive self-rejecting attitudes in combination with specifiable facilitating conditions appear to lead to the adoption of suicidal response patterns in particular. The suicide literature suggests that, given self-rejecting attitudes, the adoption of suicidal response patterns is more likely to occur under conditions that facilitate awareness of self-injurious response patterns and preclude awareness of alternative response patterns and that offer the promise that a decrease in intolerable self-rejecting feelings will be a concomitant of suicidal behavior, and that an increase in self-devaluing responses will not be a concomitant of suicidal responses.

Although the findings in the relatively few relevant studies are far from conclusive, these observations suggest that (uncompleted) suicidal behavior may be functional in decreasing self-rejecting and increasing self-accepting attitudes whether through avoidance of continued self-devaluing experiences, attacks upon elements of the person's membership group that are subjectively associated with the person's self-rejection, or substitution of self-enhancing experiences that are (presumably) concomitants of suicidal behavior for former self-devaluing experiences.

Chapter 10

Mental Illness

The literature dealing with the relationship between mental illness[1] and self-attitudes will be examined here to determine the applicability of the general theory of deviant behavior outlined in Part I as an explanation of this category of behavioral patterns. This task will be attempted in two stages. First, observations of the self-attitudes of persons described as mentally ill and the results of comparisons of various categories of "mentally ill" individuals with "normal" persons will be presented. Second, these observations and findings will be considered with regard to their congruence with the general theory of deviant behavior.

With reference to the second stage, it should be recalled that the theory is intended as an explanation of voluntary, motivationally relevant, deviant behavior, that is, as an explanation of why persons who have not previously done so behave in ways that fail to conform to the normative expectations of the person's membership groups as a result of either lack of motivation to conform or a motivation (conscious or unconscious) to deviate. Thus, any discussion of the compatibility of research findings with the theoretical model must distinguish between voluntary, motivationally relevant behavior and the mutually exclusive category of behavior that is *not* voluntary, motivationally relevant, and must exclude from consideration this latter category of behavior. By this criterion, patterns of mental illness thought to be organically caused would be excluded from the discussion.

146

However, even within the category of nonorganic patterns a number of other patterns of mental illness by the above criterion will be considered irrelevant within the context of the proposed general theory of deviant behavior. A number of discernible patterns of behavior exist that by the standards of the psychiatric community and/or the lay public fall within the "mental disorder" category. Some of these patterns are characterized primarily by the experience and expression of severe subjective distress and, perhaps, by behavioral dysfunction (including tissue damage) that may be the consequence of the severe subjective distress. By one criterion these patterns may be deviant behaviors insofar as they are instances of failure to conform to normative expectations of the person's membership group (normative expectations relating to the proper intensity and manifestations of subjective distress and to standards of behavioral functioning). However, by the other defining criterion described in Chapter 1 these patterns do not constitute deviant behavior. The patterns are not generally said to arise out of a loss of motivation to conform to or a newly developed motivation to deviate from the normative expectations in question. In this sense the deviant behavior is involuntary. For example, a severely anxious person is not said to develop his anxiety or any consequent tissue damage out of a loss of motivation to remain free of anxiety or tissue damage or out of a motivation to become anxious and have consequent tissue damage (whether because these states are intrinsically desirable or because they are instrumental to the achievement of some desirable end). Since they do not conform to the definition of mental illness presented above, such patterns of behavior are not judged to be explicable within the context of the theoretical structure presently under consideration. These patterns of mental disorder that are said to be characterized in terms of the experience and expression of severe subjective distress as well as by any behavioral dysfunction consequent upon the subjective distress, and that thereby[2] (although perhaps constituting deviations from normative expectations) are not said to arise from the loss of motivation to conform to or the acquisition of motivation to deviate from the normative expectations will be termed *predominantly expressive* mental disorders.[3]

However, there also exist a number of other discernible nonorganic patterns that by the standards of the psychiatric community and/or the lay public do fall within the "mental disorder" category. These disorders, whether or not they are also characterized by various degrees of manifestations of subjective distress, are primarily characterized by any of a number of sets of behavioral responses, including internally consistent sets of beliefs, patterned modes of perception, affective responses to self and others, and modes of establishing, maintaining, or discontinuing relationships with other persons and groups. As is the case with predominantly expressive disorders, by one criterion these disorders may be said to be deviant behaviors insofar as they constitute deviations from any of a number of normative expectations, including those governing appropriate patterns of cognition, affect expression, and interpersonal discourse. However, unlike the predominantly expressive disorders, the consideration of the literature dealing with the etiology of such disorders suggests that these deviant patterns are interpretable as deriving from a loss of motivation to conform to subjectively distressful normative patterns or from the acquisition of a motive to deviate from distressful normative patterns in ways (consciously or unconsciously) calculated to reduce the distressful effects of the prior normative patterns. The patterns of mental disorder that are said to fall within the residual category of nonorganic, nonexpressive mental disorders will be termed *predominantly instrumental* disorders in order to emphasize the presumed motivational relevance of these response patterns for reducing the intensity and number of subjectively distressful experiences.[4]

The general theory of deviant behavior developed in the first part of this volume is only applicable to the explanation of those deviant patterns of mental disorder that may be said to properly fall within this residual category of (presumably instrumental) nonorganic, nonexpressive mental disorders since, according to the proposed defining criteria of deviant behavior, any behavior is said to be deviant not only by virtue of its failure to conform to the normative expectations of the person's membership group but also because the failure to conform is voluntary (in the sense that it derives from a loss of motivation to conform to, or the acquisition of the conscious or unconscious motivation to deviate from, the normative expectations). Thus, within the context of the theoretical model under consideration, the predominantly instrumental mental disorders will be explained with reference to their origins in self-rejecting attitudes and their consequences for enhancing self-attitudes. However, neither the origins nor the consequences of the organic or nonorganic expressive[5] disorders will be explained in these terms since these behaviors, although perhaps constituting failures to conform to normative expectations, are said to be instances of *involuntary* failures to conform.

Although the literature dealing with the relationship between (nonorganic) mental illness[6] and self-attitudes generally does not explicitly characterize the instances of mental disorder in terms of their predominantly expressive and/or instrumental nature, the description of the subjects frequently permits such a judgment to be made with some feeling of confidence. In the course of considering this literature, therefore, the attempt will be made to determine which of the studies apparently deal with predominantly expressive mental disorders and which the predominantly instrumental disorders. Following such determinations, that portion of the literature concerning apparently instrumental patterns of mental disorder will be considered with regard to the compatibility of these findings with the proposed general theory of deviant behavior.

SELF-ATTITUDES AND MENTAL ILLNESS

The literature concerning the relationship between self-attitudes and mental illness may be divided conveniently into two categories depending upon the nature of the observed relationship. Into the first category fall a number of studies showing an association between self-rejecting attitudes and psychiatric disorder. The second category includes studies suggesting the existence of self-enhancing effects of specified patterns of mental illness. Although the assumption is made that the patterns of mental illness are in fact deviations from the normative expectations of the person's membership group(s), "mental illness" tends to be operationally defined in terms of *psychiatric* diagnosis in both groupings of studies. The observations in the first category tend to be made for diagnosed neurotic or mixed patient groups while the second category of studies tend to focus upon psychotic (generally schizophrenic) patterns or personality disorders.

Mental Illness and Self-Rejection

Wylie (1961:205-218) has cited several studies in which neurotic subjects and/or mixed psychiatric patient groups were compared with presumably normal control subjects on some measure of self-regard. In general, the neurotic and/or psychiatric patient subjects displayed significantly lower levels of self-acceptance than the normal controls. For example, Sarbin and Rosenberg (1955) reported that student subjects who were diagnosed as neurotic and were recommended for psychotherapy tended to be significantly less self-accepting and more self-critical than normal volunteer student subjects. In another study (Rogers and Dymond, 1954) a comparison of applicants for psychotherapy with volunteer control subjects matched for age revealed a significantly higher average self-ideal correlation for the volunteer control subjects.

Wahler (1958) reported correlations across items between a group's average self-rating on each item and independently obtained social desirability ratings for each item. The correlation for nonpsychotic outpatient male veterans receiving psychotherapy (.37) was significantly lower than that for male applicants for admission to the same outpatient psychiatric clinic (.66), male medical (exclusive of neurological or psychiatric disorders) outpatient veterans (.75), or male university students (.76). The significantly higher correlation for the applicants in comparison to the psychotherapy patients was presumably due to the greater defensiveness on the part of the applicants.

In like manner Hillson and Worchel (1957) reported that neurotic subjects who were comparable to a grouping of normal subjects with regard to educational level, age, and sex were significantly more unfavorable in their self-ratings and manifested larger self-other discrepancy scores than the normal subjects. Friedman (1955) reported that neurotic male subjects manifested significantly lower self-ideal correlations than normal male subjects who were roughly comparable to the neurotic subjects with regard to age and education. Chase (1957) also reported a significantly higher self-ideal correlation for nonpsychiatric subjects in comparison with a group of neurotic subjects not significantly different from the normal subjects in terms of marital status or average age and education.

A number of other studies in addition to those cited by Wylie (1961) reported that mixed psychiatric patient groupings tend to display relatively higher levels of self-rejection than nonpsychiatric groupings. For example, when the self-ratings of thirty-four adolescent and young adult psychiatric patients were compared with those of twenty "normal" control subjects of similar age and educational level it was observed that the self-ratings of the patients were significantly poorer than those of the comparison group (Harrow, *et al.*, 1968).

The patient grouping was mixed, consisting of fifteen schizophrenics, seven depressives, six character disorders, and six of varied diagnoses. However, sixteen of the thirty-four cases had either a primary or a secondary diagnosis of depression.

Data regarding the differential self-attitudes of normal subjects and of apparently variously diagnosed psychiatric patients were also provided by Wilson and his associates (1971). Although the investigators were primarily interested in suicide attempters they administered the Miskimins Self-Goal-Other Discrepancy Scale to psychiatric controls and normals as well. These groups were matched for sex, age, and education. Among the scores derived from responses to the scale was the "self-other plus discrepancy." This factor, which is highly correlated with depression, was said to reflect self-derogation. In addition to manifesting higher scores than the normals on other of the derived factors, the psychiatric patients showed higher self-other plus discrepancy. Thus, relative to the normal controls, the psychiatric patients apparently valued themselves less than they felt others valued them.

Depression has long been regarded as a response to lowered self-esteem. The relationship between severe clinical depression and extremely low levels of self-esteem has been associated with a loss of meaning in the external world. As Hoffman (1964:265), citing Becker (1962), asserts:

> When a locus of meaning is lost, as for example, by the death of an important figure in our interpersonal world, this implies that the external world contains that much less that serves to signal our importance, to remind us of our significance in it. This means that our sense of self-value, based as it is to a very great degree, even in adults, on the reflected value which others place upon us, is lessened. This "void in meaning" means there is less in reality that interests us, that holds our attention, that inspires action. We feel that something is missing — we feel depressed.

Finally, Long and her associates (1970) cited an earlier study in which male adult patients in a neuropsychiatric ward of a veteran's hospital displayed lower self-esteem than normal controls and also reported similar results in a comparison of institutionalized adolescents with a control group. The institutionalized grouping consisted of fifty-eight adolescents in a state residential treatment center. The classifications of the adolescents by the staff psychiatrists were said to range from mildly neurotic to psychotic (childhood schizophrenia). The control subjects consisted of "a random selection of public school students from a nearby community of the same age and sex as the institutionalized group" (p. 44). Among the findings was the observation that the mean value on a measure of self-esteem was significantly lower for the institutionalized grouping relative to the control grouping. The authors speculated that this finding might be accounted for by the stigma associated with institutionalization as well as by differences in socioeconomic background between the two subject groupings.

The observed relationship between diagnosed neuroticism and self-rejecting attitudes might be accounted for in any of a number of ways, including explanations related to the frequent circumstance of the subjects' occupying the status of patient. In accepting the status of patient it may be presumed that the subjects in effect have recognized their personal inadequacies in dealing with their problems. That is, by voluntarily undergoing psychiatric treatment they may be expressing self-rejecting attitudes. Consequently, the relationship between neuroticism and self-derogation may be the result of the investigators' focus upon a biased sample of neurotics — those who feel inadequate and express their inadequacy by seeking professional help. The presumption is that if a *representative* sample of the neurotic population had been tested, the results with regard to characteristic level of self-acceptance might have been quite different.

A possible alternative explanation, not necessarily exclusive of the preceding one, might account for the relatively high level of self-derogation observed among diagnosed neurotics. This explanation asserts that by entering into a relationship with a mental health professional the subject thereby occupies the stigmatized status of "mentally ill" and evokes negative attitudinal responses from significant others. These responses by others in turn influence feelings of self-derogation. Data reported by Hartlage and Hale (1968) tend to support the view that, at least in the case of neurotic patients, mental hospitalization does have an adverse effect upon self-attitudes. A semantic differential scale consisting of twenty pairs of self-evaluation items was employed to measure self-concept. The scale was administered to twenty-four subjects who were entering a mental hospital for the first time and was readministered twice at two-week intervals. The same scale was administered at similar intervals to twenty-four outpatients, who were paired with the inpatients by age, sex, and diagnosis. The authors reported a significant decline in self-concept over the testing period for the inpatients but did not observe changes in self-concept for the outpatient grouping. Thus, hospitalization did appear to be associated with increasing self-rejection. However, the data did not permit conclusions regarding whether or not the apparent increase in self-derogation was a consequence of the stigma associated with mental hospitalization, the breakdown of self-enhancing defenses in the course of psychotherapy, or any of a number of other possible factors.

In both of the explanations presented above, the association between self-derogation and neurosis is accounted for by factors (preselection or occupancy of a stigmatized status) associated with entering into the treatment situation. However, if these hypotheses are appropriate it is difficult to account for the failure to observe similar results for other categories of psychiatric patients, particularly diagnosed psychotics.

In any case, alternative explanations might account for the observation of negative self-attitudes among neurotic and mixed patient groups. For example, the findings in the studies cited above could be interpreted as indications that negative self-attitudes are predisposing factors in the adoption of defensive patterns that are judged to be pathological and that therefore result in referral for psychiatric treatment. The positive association between self-rejection and psychatric patient status according to this interpretation would reflect either the ineffectiveness of the pathological mechanisms in reducing self-derogation or an early stage in the process that would (at a later stage) eventuate in the enhancement of self-attitudes.

Finally, the observation of self-rejecting attitudes among neurotic patients and persons in mixed patient groupings might be accounted for in terms of the nature of the psychiatric disorders. By this explanation the patients in these groupings are said to have mental illnesses of the kind characterized by severe subjective distress (and any concomitant behavioral disorganization) that *expresses* the emotionally significant failure to achieve the self-esteem motive. That is, the severe subjective distress is a reflection of the self-rejecting attitudes. The nature of the research designs does not permit a definitive interpretation in each individual study of the observed association between psychiatric patient status and negative self-attitudes. Nevertheless, when the mental disorders represented in most of these studies are considered against the background observations in the following section, this last explanation appears to be among the more plausible interpretations, a point of view that will be developed at greater length below.

Mental Illness and Self-Enhancement

Unlike the observations of self-derogation among neurotic and mixed patient groups reported above, a number of clinical formulations and empirical comparisons suggest that particular patterns of mental illness may be associated with self-enhancing functions.

Clinical Formulations. Several clinical formulations lend support to the view that particular forms of mental disorder arise in response to prior histories of self-rejecting attitudes and function to reduce the person's level of self-derogation. In a relatively general statement, for example, Arieti (1967:732) asserts that many psychologic defenses are ways of protecting the self and provides several examples.

> The detached or schizoid person decreases his emotional or actual participation in life in order not to feel inadequate and injure his self-image. The hypochondriacal protects his self by blaming only his body for his difficulties. A woman leads a promiscuous life; she feels she is unacceptable as a person, but as a sexual partner she feels appreciated . . . In typical psychoneuroses, such as phobic conditions and obsessive-compulsive syndromes, the self is protected by a partial return to primary cognition . . . In the schizophrenic psychosis the self is defended by a much more extensive return of cognitive cognition.

Arieti (1967:734) thus interprets an appreciable part of psychopathology "as connected to secondary cognition — that is, as related to the evolving of the self and to ways to build, preserve or defend an acceptable or less unacceptable self-image."

Similar formulations concern particular patterns of mental illness. With regard to paranoid patterns, Becker (1962:149) states:

> Paranoid hostility is basically an infusion of meaning into the environment, by an ego that feels its fundamental weakness and helplessness in the face of the achievements of others. By holding others responsible for one's fate and accusing them of plotting and hatred, the paranoiac salvages a sense of self-value. He is at least *worth hating*, and his life takes on positive meaning, if only in relation to the malevolence of others.

Eisenman (1965) discusses the utility of Adler's concepts of inferiority and life style with regard to treating the schizophrenic in group therapy. The orientation is toward the patient's early feelings of inferiority and failures, and toward his unrealistic rigid goals and generally constricted self-defeating life style, which is adopted as a means of threat avoidance.

The functional role of psychopathic behavior with regard to coping with negative self-attitudes is also suggested. Thus, La Barba (1965) argues that the psychopath does experience anxiety, contrary to popular belief and the lack of manifest anxiety during the clinical interview. This anxiety is said to derive from the psychopath's feelings of inadequacy and inferiority. By focusing upon emotionally neutral and externalized aspects of behavior during the interview, by admitting to and describing his socially undesirable behavior, he is enabled to maintain his distorted sense of superiority and keep any felt anxiety covert.

In like manner, homosexual behavior has been interpreted in terms of attempts to enhance devalued self-images (E. A. Kpalan, 1967). A central feature of the relationship is said to be the search for an ego ideal. In brief, admiration for individuals who have highly valued characteristics may be sexualized and immediate identification vicariously achieved in the context of the homosexual relationship.

Finally, the self-protective function of obsessions and phobias is asserted by others. Salzman (1965), for example, interprets these conditions as avoidance methods that arise by way of defending against threats of self-esteem.

This association of self-enhancing functions with particular patterns of mental illness asserted in the clinical formulations reviewed above is apparent also in empirical comparisons of the self-attitudes of psychiatric patients and "normal" subjects.

Empirical Comparisons. In contrast to those studies consistently reporting that neurotic subjects or mixed patient groups are significantly more self-devaluing than are normal subjects is that category of investigations comparing the self-attitudes of psychotic patients with those of normal or (nonpsychiatric) medical patient control subjects. Although there are exceptions to this generalization, these studies tend to report either that schizophrenic subjects (generally) are not significantly different from nonpsychiatric controls or that schizophrenic patients are *less* self-rejecting than normal controls. Several relevant studies are cited by Wylie (1961:209-215).

In one study (Rogers, 1958) self-ideal congruence was measured in terms of centimeters of overlap between two four-inch squares of translucent glass: a red square of glass representing "self" and a blue square of glass representing "ideal-self." The investigator reported that thirty paranoid schizophrenic patients manifested significantly greater average overlap — *that is displayed a higher degree of self-ideal congruence* — than did thirty psychiatric aides working at the hospital from which the patient subjects were drawn.

Several other studies failed to observe any significant differences in self-attitudes between diagnosed psychotic subjects and presumably normal controls. For example, Epstein (1955) compared the "conscious" and "unconscious" self-evaluations of schizophrenic patients with those of normal medical patients who were matched with the schizophrenics on education, age, sex, veteran status, and institutionalization. The "conscious" self-evaluations were established by the subjects' ratings of their own attitudes toward their voices, handwriting, names, and selves relative to other samples. The "unconscious" self-evaluations were measured by the subjects' ratings of their own disguised voice and handwriting relative to other samples and in terms of speed of tachistoscopic recognition of their own names. The investigator concluded that with regard to central tendency, the evaluations of the schizophrenic patients were not significantly different from those of the normal medical patient subjects on a conscious measure of self-judgement. In like manner on each measure of unconscious self-evaluation the observed difference between normal control subjects and schizophrenic subjects was not significant. However, on all such measures the schizophrenics tended to receive more favorable values than did the normal medical patients.

Similarly, Hillson and Worchel (1957) reported that schizophrenic subjects and normal subjects, comparable in sex, age, and level of education, tended to obtain similar self-scores and self-ideal discrepancy scores. Consistent with these findings was the observation (Friedman, 1955) of no significant differences in self-ideal correlations between normal and paranoid schizophrenic subjects. Ibelle (1961) also reported results supporting the hypothesis that discrepancies between self-concept and ideal self-concept among paranoid schizophrenics would be similar to the discrepancies manifested by normal subjects. Finally, Havener and Izard (1962) reported that paranoid schizophrenics manifested smaller self-ideal discrepancies relative to other schizophrenics but were not different from normals in magnitude of self-ideal discrepancy. The authors also reported that the paranoid schizophrenics tend to be less accepting of others compared to either the normals or the other schizophrenics. These data are compatible with the interpretation that the paranoid schizophrenic style effectively enhances phenomenal self-esteem by utilization of a mechanism by which one rejects others.

Although the general evidence up to this point appears to support the conclusion that psychotics (particularly schizophrenics) are not more self-rejecting than (or, are as self-accepting as) presumably normal subjects, exceptions to this finding have been noted. These exceptions include the report of Tamkin (1957) that nonpatient subjects had significantly higher self-acceptance scores than schizophrenic subjects, and Chase's (1957) observation that nonpsychiatric patients manifested significantly greater self-ideal congruence than did any of the groups of psychiatric patients (one category of which consisted of psychotics) tested. While evidence is not available that might permit an explanation of these findings, the clinical formulations reviewed above do suggest a possible explanation, since within these formulations it is proposed that selected patterns of mental illness serve self-protective functions. Given this assertion, the above exceptions to the general rule might be accounted for by the variability in circumstances that to differing degrees permit maintenance of the deviant patterns. The mental illness should be expected to enhance self-attitudes only insofar as the defensive structure is not threatened. If it is argued that chronic schizophrenia is functional in enhancing self-attitudes, then it is to be expected that the functional value of the illness will be decreased if the setting in which the subject operates provides him with devaluing experiences, for example, by reminding him of his inadequacy through the imposition upon him of less than minimal demands (Manasse, 1965). Or if it is argued that the psychopath's insistence upon discussing the more externalized aspects of his behavior serves to maintain self-accepting attitudes, then it should be expected that the conduct of the therapeutic interview in a way that forbids this will result in the manifestation of underlying self-derogation (La Barba, 1965). Thus, it might be asserted that the exceptions to the general observation were noted in the presence of just such circumstances nullifying the defensive capabilities of the pathological patterns.

However, whether or not this account is accepted, it will be recalled that for the most part empirical comparisons have revealed that psychotic (usually schizophrenic) subjects tend to display levels of self-acceptance that are at least as favorable as those of presumably normal persons.

MENTAL ILLNESS AND THE THEORY OF DEVIANT BEHAVIOR

The question now arises as to whether the total body of literature reviewed above is compatible with the general theory of deviant behavior under consideration. Briefly, the theoretical model would be applicable to the patterns of mental illness insofar as experiences within the person's membership groups resulted in negative self-attitudes and the subjectively distressful negative self-attitudes were responded to with patterns of mental illness that served self-enhancing functions by facilitating (1) intrapsychic or interpersonal avoidance of the normative experiences associated with the genesis of negative self-attitudes; (2) attacks upon the basis of the person's self-rejection (the normative structure, including his interpersonal nexus); or (3) substitution of alternative response patterns with greater self-enhancing potential than those they replaced.

The empirical findings and clinical formulations detailed above are consistent with the emerging theoretical framework described in Part I if it is understood that nonorganic disorders may be distributed among the two categories described above:—predominantly expressive vs. predominantly instrumental, —and that the theoretical framework is applicable only to the predominantly instrumental disorders. Predominantly expressive disorders reflect severe subjective distress or any behavioral disorganization that might be a concomitant of the subjective distress and, insofar as they are failures to conform to normative expectations, are said to be involuntary, not-motivationally-relevant deviant behaviors. These behavior patterns do not arise out of a loss of motivation to conform to the normative expectations that are violated by these behavior patterns or out of an acquired need to violate these normative expectations toward the goal of gaining an appreciable reduction in (or maintaining an acceptable level of) the person's subjective distress. Since these disorders are not said to be voluntary, motivationally relevant deviant behaviors, these response patterns are not encompassed within the category of deviant behaviors that are said to be explicable by the proposed general theory of deviant behavior. Insofar as the predominantly expressive disorders fall outside of this category of deviant behaviors it is not expected (and, indeed, it is not observed) that these patterns of mental illness would conform to the explanatory model in terms of being functional in reducing prior self-derogation.

In contrast, the residual category of predominantly instrumental disorders do appear to qualify for the category of deviant behaviors that are said to be explainable by the proposed general theory of deviant behavior. These failures to conform to normative expectations are said to be voluntary, motivationally relevant patterns in the sense that they arise out of a loss of motivation to conform to distressful normative expectations or out of an acquired motivation to deviate from the distressful normative expectations in ways that will have the effect of reducing the subject's level of subjective distress or of maintaining the level of subjective distress at an acceptable level (the alternative being a highly probable increase in level of subjective distress). The reduction (or maintenance) of the person's level of distress is said to be accomplished through the patterned responses that are characteristic of the disorder. The patterned responses may take the form of relatively stable and internally consistent sets of beliefs and perceptions about the subject, the environment, and the relationship between the self and environment; predictable affective responses toward self and environment and the relationship between self and environment; and/or other patterned behavioral responses through which the subject alters (or maintains) himself, his environment, or the relationship between self and environment toward the goal of reducing his level of subjective distress (or avoiding a probable increase in subjective distress). Disorders involving the presence of severe subjective distress may be appropriately grouped within this class only if it is assumed that the absence of the stable behavioral responses that otherwise characterize the disorder would result in even more severe subjective distress than that which is currently apparent (and indeed which may be the consequence of these response patterns). This may be the situation in certain of the neuroses, — for example, where anxiety may be unconsciously controlled through the use of any of a variety of psychological mechanisms such as conversion and displacement, which may themselves be productive of subjective distress. However, it is assumed that the interruption of the neurotic pattern in question (for example, a compulsive ritual in an obsessive compulsive neurosis) would increase the level of subjective distress.[7]

   Although the two categories described above do not have exact counter-parts in the diagnostic categories employed in traditional psychiatry, it is possi-ble to distribute these categories among the "predominantly expressive" and "predominantly instrumental" classes by referring to the definitions of the two classificatory schemes. The predominantly expressive category as it is defined here might include such traditionally defined[8] *neurotic disorders* as anxiety neurosis, neurasthenic neurosis, and depressive neurosis; generally the *psychophysiological disorders*, and the *transient situational disturbances*; certain of the *behavior disorders of childhood and adolescence* such as overanx-ious reaction; and certain of the *psychoses not attributed to physical condi-tions*, particularly among the affective disorders such as involutional melan-cholia. The predominantly instrumental category as it is defined here would include other of the traditionally defined *neurotic disorders* such as hysterical neurosis, phobic neurosis, and obsessive compulsive neurosis; generally the *personality disorders*; and several of the *psychoses not attributed to physical conditions*, particularly those disorders of thought and behavior characterized by reality distortion or other apparently self-protective behavior.

   With this distribution of traditional diagnostic categories it is now possible to make judgments with regard to which of the empirical studies reviewed above were dealing with predominantly instrumental (as opposed to predomi-nantly expressive) disorders and to consider whether or not the studies dealing with predominantly instrumental disorders are congruent with the proposed general theory of deviant behavior. Thus, the investigations above that tended to report either no differences in self-attitudes between the mentally disordered and normal subjects or more positive self-attitudes for the mentally ill popula-tion appeared to be dealing primarily with predominantly nonexpressive or instrumental disorders as we have defined them. Further, the studies reporting a higher level of self-derogation for mentally ill subjects relative to normal sub-jects were dealing for the most part with expressive disorders or at least were more likely to be dealing with such disorders than the earlier mentioned studies. This judgment seems warranted in view of the fact that the mentally ill subjects in this group of studies tended to be identified as neurotic or mixed patient groups, which are likely to contain appreciable portions of patients with disor-ders in which the primary characteristic is anxiety with or without other symptomatic distress.

   Thus, the empirical literature is compatible with the view that *predominantly instrumental* psychiatric disorders develop in response to preex-isting highly distressful negative self-attitudes and function to increase the individual's level of self-acceptance. The relatively consistent observation that patients primarily characterized in terms of nonexpressive disorders tend to display at least as positive self-attitudes as normal subjects supports this view, particularly with regard to the self-enhancing consequences of these disorders. However, such observations do not directly demonstrate the hypothesis with regard to the influence of preexisting self-rejecting attitudes on the subsequent development of nonexpressive psychiatric disorders. Such verification would demand longitudinal research designs that would demonstrate that self-derogating individuals compared to self-accepting individuals are more likely to develop instrumental psychiatric disorders in the future; and among the self-rejecting subjects, those people who develop nonexpressive psychiatric disorders are more likely than those people who do not develop such disorders to subsequently change their self-attitudes in a more self-accepting direction. Unfortunately such studies do not exist.

The "expressive" disorders, and therefore the studies that concern these disorders, are not relevant in the context of the theoretical model since they are not among the voluntary, motivationally relevant, deviant responses that the theory attempts to explain. The theory explains deviant patterns as motivated behaviors that are the consequences of earlier self-derogation and that function to reduce self-derogation and otherwise enhance self-attitudes. At best, the investigations that apparently deal with expressive disorders are of interest only insofar as these studies, which report significantly greater self-derogation for neurotic or mixed patient groups compared to normal subjects, may be taken simply as support for the existence of the self-esteem motive. Given the motive to gain, maintain, or regain an acceptable level of self-esteem, it is to be expected that negative self-attitudes would be the occasion for severe subjective distress. The disorders that characterize the neurotic or mixed patient groups are taken to be those that are likely to be expressive of such distress. That is, these disorders are defined in terms of the severe distress and/or the behavioral dysfunctions that accompany it. However, these disorders may not be taken to be motivated behaviors in the service of the self-esteem motive, that is, as patterned responses serving to increase positive self-attitudes. The expressive disorders are viewed as the frequent consequences of either the failure to evolve psychological mechanisms that could successfully maintain, attain, or restore positive self-attitudes or the breakdown of such mechanisms after they had been provisionally established. The severe subjective distress (or concomitant behavioral disorganization) that accompanies the resulting self-rejecting attitudes constitutes the core of the expressive disorders. Thus, the expressive disorders are not so much adaptive responses to self-derogation as *correlates* or reflections of self-rejection.

It is that category of disorders termed "instrumental" that is said to be explicable by the model under consideration. Such patterns of behavior are interpreted as voluntarily motivated (consciously or unconsciously) responses to self-rejecting attitudes. These responses are said to function (unless or until the pattern is disrupted) to change self-attitudes in a more self-accepting direction and, thereby, to reduce the severe subjective distress of self-rejecting attitudes. It should be emphasized, however, that to assert that the psychosis, for example, "becomes a defense against the terrifying and injurious self-image" (Arieti, 1967: 453) is not to propose that the psychotic patient is necessarily free of subjective distress. Rather, it is suggested that the psychosis more or less effectively defends the subject against the kinds of distressful negative self-feelings that are associated with self-devaluation rather than against the distressful feelings associated with perhaps perception of threat from the external environment. Thus, Arieti (1967:457) draws the distinction "between the anxiety which undermines the feeling of inner worth and the self-image, and the anxiety and fear which are just signals of external dangers." For example, the paranoid patient who, through his system of delusions and hallucinations, has become the object of unjustified persecution from others may still experience fear and anxiety. However, through the schizophrenic process one type of anxiety was changed into another (presumably more acceptable) type of anxiety. Rather than feeling distressed about his own inadequacy, the paranoid patient is enabled to experience his distress as associated with the external threat presented by his imagined persecutors.

The applicability of the general theory to predominantly instrumental and predominantly expressive mental disorders was investigated above by distributing a number of studies into two groupings, depending upon whether the subjects fell into one or the other category, and by then examining the patterns of association between self-attitudes and mental illness observed for the studies in each of the two groupings. These studies as a whole tended to reveal a positive association between expressive disorders and self-rejection, and either less or as little self-rejection on the part of persons with instrumental disorders than presumably normal persons. The differential relationships were compatible with the assertion of the differential applicability of the theory of mental illness in that only the observation with regard to the *instrumental disorders* was congruent with the assertion that (voluntary, motivated) patterns of mental illness were responses to prior self-rejecting attitudes that function to decrease the experience of distressful self-rejecting attitudes. Similar conclusions appear to be warranted by studies that simultaneously deal with both categories (expressive and instrumental or nonexpressive) of nonorganic mental disorders. The following two studies are offered as illustrations of this category of investigations.

The assumptions that were made regarding the differential relationships of expressive and nonexpressive (or instrumental) modes of psychopathology to self-rejecting attitudes are congruent with certain of the findings reported by Harrow and his associates (1968). The investigators obtained self-ratings from thirty-four adolescent and young adult psychiatric inpatients one and one-half weeks after hospitalization. The patients consisted of fifteen schizophrenics, seven depressives, six character disorders, and six patients of different diagnoses. Sixteen of the patients had received either a primary or a secondary diagnosis of depression.

A comparison of these sixteen depressed patients with the nondepressed patients revealed that the depressed patients manifested significantly poorer self-ratings than the nondepressed patients. This observation was just what would have been expected on the assumption that depressive patients are expressing the subjective distress evoked by negative self-evaluations and on the assumption that nondepressed patients are more likely to be employing mechanisms (albeit pathological ones) that are instrumental in increasing one's level of self-acceptance.

It was also apparent that the schizophrenic patients (although displaying slightly more positive self-attitudes) were not significantly different from the nonschizophrenic patients in this regard. This again would have been expected, given the assumptions discussed above. Thus, although schizophrenic processes are presumed to function so as to maintain acceptable self-attitudes, so also would many of the disorders contained in the nonschizophrenic category. The latter category, in addition to perhaps including a number of cases of expressive disorders such as depression, would also include a number of disorders that have been classified as instrumental in the enhancement of self-attitudes. Therefore, the differences between the schizophrenic and nonschizophrenic patients with regard to level of self-acceptance would be lessened. However, it might have been expected (as it was in fact observed) that the schizophrenic grouping would be somewhat higher in level of self-ratings since it was a more "pure" group than the nonschizophrenic group in terms of proportion of cases of "instrumental" or nonexpressive psychopathology.

However, it should be noted that the schizophrenic patients, like the other patients, were appreciably more negative in their self-ratings *when compared with normal controls.* This is in contrast to the reports of other investigators as cited above that observed no significant differences between schizophrenic and normal subjects with regard to self-ideal discrepancy. The relatively greater level of self-derogation for this schizophrenic sample may be explainable in terms of the observation that these schizophrenics were "young and non-chronic." Thus, the defensive patterns hypothesized to be associated with schizophrenic processes might be less stable and therefore less effective in reducing self-rejecting attitudes than more chronic, better-established patterns. In this connection it is possible that the schizophrenic patients, lacking well-established defensive patterns compared to more chronic patients, are particularly vulnerable to such adverse influences upon self-attitudes as the stigma associated with mental hospitalization and therapeutic disruption of previously established defensive patterns (judged to be pathological).

In any case the pattern of findings discussed above tend to be supportive of the assumptions regarding qualitative differences between expressive and instrumental mental disorders and the applicability of the general theory of deviant behavior in an explanation of the genesis of instrumental disorders. These assumptions continue to appear warranted when viewed in the light of certain of the results of the following study.

Although the clinical formulations reviewed earlier suggest that the adoption of specified modes of mental illness functions to block out from conscious awareness (or otherwise protects the individual from) self-devaluing experiences, relatively little empirical data are available that bear directly on this point. At best, up to this point only those studies detailed directly above may be offered as supportive of this point of view, and then only as compatible with (rather than demonstrative of) the thesis. However, somewhat more direct evidence for this argument is provided by Friedman (1955) from a study cited by Wylie (1961:252). In this investigation, a measure of "projected self" was a Q sort made by the experimeter on the basis of his global appraisal of the subject's stories in response to Thematic Apperception Test (TAT) cards. The experimenter's sort was correlated with the subject's own self-sort. Friedman assumed that low correlations between phenomenal self and TAT self would indicate that a large portion of personal experience was outside of awareness. From this it was predicted that correlations between phenomenal self and projected self would be higher for normals than for neurotics and paranoid schizophrenics. The expected rank order among the size of correlations was indeed found, but the difference between correlations for normals and neurotic subjects was not significant. However, those of the paranoid schizophrenics were significantly smaller than each of the other two groups. This finding is congruent with the conclusion that the relatively little conscious self-derogation displayed by the paranoid schizophrenic in the studies cited above is explicable in terms of his ability to exclude from his awareness self-devaluing experiences. The relatively high correlations between projected self and phenomenal self for the normal and neurotic subjects (and the lack of differentiation between the two groups in this regard) are also explicable in terms of self-protective mechanisms. The normal subjects who tend to have relatively positive self-attitudes would have little need to distort personal experience for self-protective purposes and therefore would tend to display relatively high correlations between projected self and phenomenal self. Neurotic subjects, who from other studies are known to display relatively negative self-attitudes (and who are expected to include among themselves numerous instances of expressive disorders), apparently are unable to defend themselves against the highly distressful self-rejecting attitudes. Since they are unable to effectively employ self-protective mechanisms (including the ability to exclude self-devaluing experiences from awareness), it is to be expected that the way they consciously view themselves would be correlated with their projected self.

In short, the results of the investigations reviewed above provide some validation of the destinction between expressive and instrumental (nonorganic) mental disorders, and the applicability of the theoretical model to the instrumental disorders only. The research literature is congruent with the expectations that negative self-attitudes predispose a person to adopt *instrumental* patterns of mental illness and that these patterns function to enhance the person's self-attitudes. The self-enhancement is likely to occur by virtue of the frequent observations in clinical formulations that the patterns of mental illness may involve intrapsychic or interpersonal avoidance of previously self-devaluing experiences; attacks upon the experiential basis of the self-rejecting attitudes; and the provision of substitute self-enhancing opportunities. However, it should be noted that, in addition to these self-enhancing consequences, the adoption of such stigmatized patterns may evoke negative attitudinal responses from significant others that could exacerbate the subject's self-rejecting attitudes.

The effectiveness of instrumental modes of psychopathology in decreasing self-rejection is in part a function of the extent to which the person evokes adverse influences upon his self-attitudes as a result of his psychopathology and his ability to protect himself from such adverse influences. Both processes are likely to be at work. Thus, Kaplan and his associates (1964) argue that hospitalization for psychopathological patterns evokes responses from others that are self-threatening in nature. By way of protecting themselves from these threats to their self-esteem, the patients are said to evolve a system of protective behavior patterns. These arguments together with the hypothesized function of nonexpressive psychopathology in reducing prior self-rejection suggest a three-stage process. First, the self-rejecting person adopts a psychopathological pattern as a means of maintaining an acceptable level of self-esteem or of reducing the level of self-rejection. Second, the pathological pattern (quite apart from the direct effects of the pattern upon self-attitudes) evokes circumstances including negative responses by other that may indirectly and adversely affect self-attitudes. Third, in response to these circumstances adversely influencing the person's self-attitudes, he evolves patterns of response that function to minimize the self-devaluating consequences of such circumstances.

Kaplan and his associates (1964), observing male patients on an open psychiatric ward of a Veterans Administration hospital, note two sets of circumstances that might arise in response to the adoption of psychopathological patterns and that might have adverse effects upon the patient's self-evaluation. The first set of circumstances relates to the nature of the therapeutic process, entry into which is certainly one possible consequence of adopting psychopathological patterns. The process of treating the patient might have consequences that, at least on a short-term basis, could adversely affect the patient's self-attitudes. For example, traditional psychotherapeutic techniques might involve the uncovering and interpretation of the patient's characteristic modes of defense through which he maintains an acceptable self-image. The disruption of these defenses might well make the subject vulnerable to self-devaluing experiences and tend to lower his level of self-esteem. The second set of circumstances relates to public and institutional attitudes toward mental illness. Such is the nature of public attitudes toward mental illness that the adoption of psychopathological patterns is likely to evoke negative attitudes from significant others, which in turn could be expected to increase levels of self-rejection among the mentally ill.

The investigators describe a number of patterned responses evolved by the patient groups in response to these two sets of circumstances that were said to function to maintain acceptable levels of self-esteem. Clearly, the effectiveness of psychopathological patterns in reducing self-rejection would be a function both of the tendency to evoke circumstances having adverse consequences for self-attitudes and of the ability to evolve such patterns of response as would contain the potentially negative consequences of these circumstances upon self-attitudes. In any case the self-esteem motive would lead the person to strenuous attempts to evolve such self-protective responses as a defense against the potentially adverse consequences of adopting instrumental patterns of mental illness.

SUMMARY

The present chapter considered the applicability of the evolving general theory of deviant behavior to patterns of mental illness in the light of the literature describing clinical formulations and empirical comparisons between groupings of individuals with pathological and "normal" characteristics. Organically based mental disorders were excluded from consideration as nonvoluntary, nonmotivated behaviors, since the theoretical model at the outset was said to explain only voluntary, motivationally relevant deviant behaviors. Within the nonorganic category, a further distinction was made between predominantly expressive and predominantly instrumental disorders. The expressive disorders were characterized in terms of involuntary, nonmotivationally relevant behavior patterns that are judged to be pathological by virtue of the severity of subjective distress manifested or any behavioral dysfunction that might be the consequence of severe subjective distress. These expressive disorders were not considered to be explicable within the theoretical framework, again because they were not voluntary, motivationally relevant deviant patterns. The empirical studies dealing with neurotic and mixed psychiatric patient groups were judged to be most likely to contain frequent instances of expressive disorders. These studies generally reported a positive association between the psychiatric disorders and self-rejecting attitudes. Although these results were interpretable as demonstrations of the significance of the self-esteem motive (since failure to satisfy the self-esteem motive was associated with subjective distress) they were otherwise irrelevant to a discussion of the applicability of the general theory of deviant behavior to patterns of mental illness.

The instrumental mental disorders were hypothesized to be explicable within the general theory of deviant behavior since these disorders were characterized as voluntary, motivationally relevant deviant behaviors, that is, as behaviors that fail to conform to the normative expectations of the person's membership group as a result of either a lack of motivation to conform or a (conscious or unconscious) motivation to deviate. The theoretical model as applicable to instrumental patterns of mental illness would assert that these patterns are responses to histories of self-rejection and function to enhance self-attitudes.

The literature, including clinical formulations and empirical comparisons, that appears to concern instrumental mental disorders is judged to be congruent with the theoretical model for the explanation of deviant behavior. Clinical formulations suggest self-enhancing functions for schizoid, hypochondriacal, hypersexual, phobic, obsessive-compulsive, paranoid schizophrenic, psychopathic, and homosexual patterns. Empirical comparisions generally between psychotic (most frequently schizophrenic) persons and presumably normal controls tend to report that the mentally ill persons are either more self-accepting than, or equivalently positive in self-attitudes to the "normal" comparison groups. This result is what would have been expected if the instrumental patterns of mental disorder in fact did serve self-enhancing functions. While the nature of the self-enhancing mechanisms generally was not demonstrated, the instrumental patterns were presumed to achieve self-enhancing consequences through intrapsychic or interpersonal avoidance of self-devaluing experiences, attacks upon the normative basis of self-devaluation, and substitution of alternative self-enhancing patterns.

Although the adoption of instrumental patterns of mental disorder might evoke responses that could have adverse consequences for the person's self-attitudes (and thereby counteract the otherwise self-enhancing effects), it is suggested that the person will be motivated to adopt other self-protective mechanisms in order to forestall such adverse consequences.

NOTES

[1] Although certain conceptual issues pertaining directly to the task at hand will be considered briefly, the various dimensions of the problems of conceptualizing and identifying mental illness will not be considered in depth. These problems have been examined in some detail by the author elsewhere (Kaplan, 1972b).

[2] The term "motivation" implies a purposive force toward a pleasurable state and away from a painful state. Consequently a subjectively distressful state could not be said to arise out of a need to achieve the (painful) subjective distress or to avoid a previous state of (pleasurable) freedom from subjective distress.

[3] These disorders are so named by virtue of the fact that the constitutive patterns express the subjective distress rather than serve to alleviate the distress.

[4] Although the "predominantly expressive" and "predominantly instrumental" categories have been described as mutually exclusive categories among which recognized patterns of nonorganic mental disorders may be distributed, it is frequently quite difficult to determine (for numerous reasons) whether a particular disorder belongs in one or the other of the categories. In view of this difficulty it may be more useful for present purposes to think in terms of a continuum, the poles of which are "pure" expressive disorders and "pure" instrumental disorders. Recognized instances of mental disorder could then be judged as properly falling at various points along the continuum, thereby more closely approximating one or the other of the poles constituting ideal types.

[5] While the nonorganic expressive disorders frequently are said to derive from self-derogating experiences in the sense that these patterns are *expressive* of highly distressful negative self-attitudes, they are not regarded as motivationally relevant for the reduction of self-rejecting experiences and for the induction of self-enhancing experiences.

[6] A number of behavioral conditions such as alcoholism, drug addiction, suicide, and aggressive behavior might be judged by others to fall appropriately within the category of instrumental patterns of mental disorder. However, whether or not this judgment is deemed justifiable, the literature dealing with the relationship between these disorders and self-attitudes has been considered in earlier chapters and will not be discussed in any detail in the present chapter. The volume of this literature suggested the advisability of considering each of these conditions separately.

[7] In the case of the expressive disorders the basis for applying the "mental disorder" label to the person's behavior is in the severe subjective distress or any behavioral dysfunction that appears to be a necessary concomitant of the distress. In the case of the instrumental disorders, the basis for applying the "mental disorder" label to the person's behavior tends to be in the cognitive, affective, or other behavioral patterns that in the judgment of others impair the person's ability to function effectively in life roles. These behavioral patterns, although they may have role-impairing consequences, are understood to be more or less functional in reducing subjective distress. Even where subjective distress is apparent in conjunction with these behavioral patterns, the assumption is made that a disruption of the life-role-impairing patterns would result in an increase in subjective distress.

[8] The definitions of psychiatric disorders referred to in the present section are taken from the *Diagnostic and Statistical Manual of Mental Disorders* (second edition), American Psychiatric Association (1968).

Chapter 11

General Summary

This volume was devoted to two tasks. The first was the presentation of core propositions for a general theory of deviant behavior, the second, the examination of the compatibility of the relevant literature concerning specified modes of deviant behavior with the theoretical framework. The emerging theory of deviant behavior was a general one in the sense that it sought to delineate the factors that were *common* influences in the predisposition toward, adoption of, and establishment in any of a range of deviant patterns as opposed to the factors that were uniquely operative in the predisposition toward, adoption of, and establishment in a *particular* pattern of deviant behavior. The patterns of deviant behavior that were said to be explicable within the theoretical framework were characterized as response patterns failing to conform to the normative expectations of the person's (predeviance) membership groups due to a loss of motivation to conform or the acquisition of motivation to deviate from the normative expectations. The general theory thus sought to explain why a person who had not previously done so comes to adopt (and becomes established in) some such pattern of deviant behavior.

The general theoretical model is based upon the premise that the self-esteem motive — defined as the need to maximize the experience of positive self-attitudes and to minimize the experience of negative self-attitudes — is universally and characteristically a dominant motive for the individual. Self-attitudes refer to the person's emotional experiences upon perceiving and evaluating his own attributes and behavior.

165

The general theory of deviant behavior asserts that the development of characteristically negative self-attitudes is a function of the person's history of three analytically distinguishable but empirically interdependent sets of experiences in his membership groups: (1) self-perceptions of failure to possess personally valued attributes or to perform personally valued behaviors (and self-perceptions of the possession of personally disvalued attributes or the performance of disvalued behaviors); (2) self-perceptions of failure to be the object of positive attitudes by personally valued others (and self-perceptions as the object of negative attitudes by personally valued others); and (3) the failure to possess and employ self-protective response mechanisms that function to preclude the experience, or mitigate the effects, of the first two sets of experiences.

The actual association of his experiences in his membership groups with the development of negative self-attitudes is said to influence the person to *perceive* the association between his experiences in the membership groups and the experience of intrinsically distressful negative self-attitudes, a subjective association that is generalized to other aspects of the membership groups' normative structures. In time the subjective association between aspects of the normative structure and the experience of distressful negative self-attitudes (a subjective association that is generalized to other aspects of the membership groups' normative structures) leads to the experience of the normative structure as intrinsically distressful. Given the experience of the normative structure as intrinsically distressing, the individual loses motivation to conform to these patterns and becomes positively motivated to deviate from these distressing experiences in ways that would mitigate the distress.

Since, as a result of his prior experiences in his membership groups, the person is said to be characterized by negative self-attitudes, and on the assumption of an operative self-esteem motive, the person is predisposed to behave in ways that would reduce the experience of negative self-attitudes and increase the experience of positive self-attitudes. Since the development of negative self-attitudes attests to the failure of the normative structure to provide subjectively realistic self-enhancing opportunities, the person is predisposed to seek alternatives to these normative patterns that might permit satisfaction of the self-esteem motive. Thus, the person is predisposed to adopt deviant patterns not only by virtue of the experience of the normative structure as intrinsically distressing (an experience that is traceable to the past association of the normative environment with the genesis of self-rejecting attitudes) but also by virtue of the observation that deviant patterns (given the experience of the normative structure as intrinsically distressful) represent the only possible behavioral responses that could function in the service of the self-esteem motive, that is, to improve self-attitudes.

Deviant patterns are said to function in the service of the self-esteem motive by facilitating some combination of three categories of consequences: (1) intrapsychic or interpersonal *avoidance* of self-devaluing experiences associated with the predeviance membership group; (2) *attacks*, symbolic or otherwise, upon what is perceived as the basis of the person's self-rejecting attitudes, that is, upon representations of the normative group structure; and (3) *substitution* of new group memberships and normative patterns that offer self-enhancing potential for those aspects of the person's membership group that were associated with the genesis of self-rejecting attitudes.

The person thus motivated or predisposed to adopt alternative deviant patterns would be likely to adopt such patterns, in fact, under conditions in which he became aware of the existence of the response pattern as a possibility and came to anticipate that the adoption of that pattern would have, in balance, a relatively high probability of consequences that would increase positive self-attitudes and a relatively low probability of consequences that would increase negative self-attitudes.

The adoption of deviant patterns increases the probability that the categories of self-enhancing effects described above will be experienced since deviant patterns imply the reduction of normative experiences that in the past were associated with the genesis of self-rejecting attitudes, and an increase in the range (beyond that provided by the normative structure) of potentially self-enhancing experiences. The experience of self-enhancing effects in association with the adoption of deviant patterns would tend to confirm the person in the employment of the deviant response patterns.

Although it is possible that the adoption of deviant response patterns might have unanticipated adverse consequences for the person's self-attitudes that might counteract the otherwise beneficent effects of the deviant pattern, the person will be motivated to behave in a self-protective manner in order to forestall such adverse consequences. The ultimate effects of the adoption of the deviant pattern upon the person's self-attitudes would be a function of his ability to effectively employ such self-protective mechanisms. The successful use of these mechanisms would increase the likelihood of continuation of the deviant pattern. However, to the extent that any adverse consequences evoked by the deviant pattern counteracted the otherwise beneficent effects, or indeed served to *increase* the person's experience of self-rejection, the probability of continuation of the *particular* deviant pattern would be greatly decreased. Presumably, in the event that the deviant pattern ceased to be performed, the unresolved need for improved self-attitudes in combination with the factors outlined above would predispose the person to adopt alternative deviant patterns under conditions whereby he became aware of deviant patterns with relatively high self-enhancing potential. In short, the maintenance of the deviant pattern as well as the processes leading to the predisposition toward, and adoption of, the deviant pattern are said to be understood in terms of the person's self-attitudes.

The emerging theoretical model was derived from the consideration of the literature concerning a number of modes of deviant behavior and was further refined and evaluated in the process of examining the literature dealing with a broad range of such deviant patterns. Unfortunately, the literature did not permit a clear test of the hypotheses making up the theory. Among the factors militating against this outcome was the fact that the behavior under consideration frequently could not be demonstrated to be "deviant" in the sense that it was apparently a failure to conform to the normative expectations of the group. Thus, it could only be *assumed* that the behavior was deviant. Another major shortcoming of the literature was that the studies frequently did not permit the establishment of the temporal relationships that are so strategic to the theoretical model. This problem necessitated sometimes tenuous interpretations of the data. However, although the propositions could not be demonstrated, the consideration of the relevant literature dealing with each of several patterns of deviant behavior appeared to permit the conclusion that the literature was congruent with the emerging theoretical model.

The present model for understanding deviant behavior properly falls within that category of theories in which the deviant act is said to be a defense mechanism devised by the personality for the purpose of protecting itself from anxiety or guilt (Cohen, 1966:63-73). More particularly, the model under discussion asserts that the adoption of deviant patterns is intended to protect the personality from subjectively distressful feelings of self-rejection. However, this model should not be thought guilty of two of the criticisms frequently applied to what have been called "psychodynamic problem-solving theories": the failure to consider the role of situational factors in conjunction with personality pre-dispositions; and the failure to account for the choice of a deviant solution in general, and of a particular deviant solution to the resolution of the psychodynamic problem — here, the problem of increasing level of self-acceptance (Cohen, 1966:70-73). Throughout this volume it has been recognized that negative self-feelings are not sufficient predictors of the adoption of deviant patterns. Rather, self-rejection must interact with a number of specifiable social-psychological and sociocultural conditions if an individual is to move predictably from a relatively deviance-free state to the adoption of *deviant* patterns. But insofar as the model is represented as a *general* theory of deviant behavior, the variables influencing the choice of a *particular* deviant solution are referred to only in passing in certain of the chapters as those influencing the person's awareness and subjective probability judgments of the net self-enhancing consequences of the deviant pattern.

In spite of its emphasis upon self-rejecting attitudes, this theory should not be thought of as a one-factory theory. Quite the reverse is the case. It is recognized that the explanation for the adoption of deviant patterns will be found in a complicated maze of variables. It is merely asserted that "self-attitudes" represents a most useful point of reference. Starting with self-attitudes will lead further through the maze than will other starting points. If we sometimes get lost in the maze, we will find our way again by returning to our starting point — "self-attitudes." Each of the several theories of deviant behavior that together reflect this maze have contributed something to our understanding of this phenomenon (Cohen, 1966). However, the final explanation of deviant behavior will have to rest upon an integration of the explanatory factors contained in these several theories with other as yet undetermined factors. Based upon the considerations expressed in this volume, self-attitude theory would appear to offer the best opportunity for achieving such integration.

The potential value of "self-attitudes" in offering an integrating bridge to such factors can be illustrated by consideration of the convergence of a number of different points of view regarding deviant behavior upon this concept. For this purpose a number of sociological theories might be considered since the relevance of self-attitudes to the more psychodynamic theories (Cohen, 1966:54-73) is perhaps more readily apparent.

One noteworthy approach to the understanding of deviant behavior is that of anomie theory (Clinard, 1964) particularly as this theory is interpreted by Merton (1957). The relationship between a disjunction between culturally prescribed goals and institutionalized means for achieving these goals, on the one hand, and deviant modes of adaptation, on the other hand, are clearly interpretable as mediated by self-attitudes. The inability to achieve according to internalized standards of personal worth has adverse implications for self-evaluation and self-feeling. It is the motivation to cope with these subjectively distressful negative self-attitudes that is said to predispose the person to adopt any of several apparently available deviant modes of adaptation.

A number of sociological theories of deviant behavior, including labeling theory (Lemert, 1951; Becker, 1963; Goffman, 1963; Scheff, 1966; Matza, 1969; Schur, 1971), concern the influence upon deviant behavior of the society's responses to deviant behavior. Such effects of societal reactions to deviance upon the adoption and stabilization of deviant response patterns may also be viewed as mediated by the individual's self-attitudes. Depending upon the nature of interacting factors, the relationship between societal reactions to deviance and self-attitudes may have any of a number of effects upon the adoption and stabilization of deviant responses. To the extent that the individual is aware of the existence of an internally consistent structure of negative societal responses to deviant behavior he may anticipate adverse consequences for his self-attitudes and thus be constrained from performing the deviant acts. Thus, the societal response structure (in conditions in which the society constitutes a positive reference group) serves as an effective control against deviant behavior. However, even when the person in fact performs deviant acts the societal reactions to deviance should be expected to influence the stabilization of the deviant response pattern by virtue of the influence of societal responses upon the person's self-attitudes. Depending upon the nature of severity of the societal responses to initial deviance the person may be motivated to withdraw from further participation in his former membership group in order to avoid such negative responses, or alternatively to avoid further deviant acts in anticipation of receiving positive attitudinal responses from other group members and hence self-approval. In the event that the severity of the initial adverse responses motivated the person to avoid further assaults upon his self-attitudes (by removing himself from participation in the group) he would be removed from the influence of the group's social control mechanisms, and the probability of continuing deviant behavior would be increased. The satisfactions gained from avoidance of participation in the group would be increased by virtue of the fact that the person was also removed from the very experiences that led to the genesis of negative self-attitudes and, hence, to the predisposition to deviant modes of adaptation. Insofar as the nature of the societal responses to the person's initial deviance were such as to provide him with a deviant group identity and, thereby, to exclude him from participation in the group (a circumstance that, it was noted above, could be highly compatible with the person's self-acceptance), the person would be influenced to adopt the deviant group's standards for achievement as guides for his own behavior toward the goal of earning the approval of other ("deviant") group members and, ultimately, self-approval.

Other sociological theories that account for deviant behavior partly in terms of such factors as group support and learning experiences[1] are also clearly interpretable in terms of the mediating influence of self-attitudes upon the adoption and stabilization of deviant behavior patterns whether the group in question was one in which the person was *reared* and to which he was motivated to conform, one in which he did not hold membership but the standards of which he accepted as guides for his own behavior, or one in which he *came* to hold membership and the standards of which he came to accept as binding upon him. In the first instance the group in which he was reared would constitute a membership/reference group.[2] In such a group, performance of "deviant" behaviors would be explicable in terms of the person's having learned that approximation to these standards was the appropriate route to acceptance by other group members and to self-acceptance.[3] In the latter two instances, where the person anticipates or comes to hold membership in the group(s) in question, the group is said to become the means by which the person learns and becomes motivated to conform to the deviant patterns. These deviant patterns, which are learned in the process of observing or interacting with group members, have a number of implications for the self-enhancement process. The deviant patterns may represent a substitute set of normative standards, conformity to which earns positive attitudinal responses from other group members and thereby influences more positive self-feelings. The positive support provided by the group reinforces the deviant response pattern. Continued conformity to these standards implies that existing conditions were more favorable to successful achievement by the present set of standards than by a previous set of standards.

Alternatively, or in addition, the group may be the vehicle for showcasing alternative (deviant) behavior patterns that have self-enhancing implications by virtue of their ability to permit withdrawal from, or attacks upon, the person's prior membership group, which, both in fact and subjectively, was associated with a history of experiences leading to self-rejection. Both the avoidance of further self-rejecting experiences and attacks upon the basis of the person's prior self-rejection would be expected to improve the person's self-attitudes, particularly under conditions in which he received emotional support for these behaviors in the context of a new membership group.[4]

These theoretical points of view that variously seek the explanation of deviant behavior in terms of anomie, societal reactions to deviance, cultural transmission, or group support do not constitute an inclusive list of explanations of deviant behavior. They are only a few of the explanations of deviant behavior proposed in recent decades. Nevertheless, the discussions of these theories serve to illustrate how several different points of view might contribute to an integrated theory of deviant behavior through their convergence on a common concept — self-attitudes.

However, the potential value of the model presently under consideration for integrating diverse theories of deviant behavior is not sufficient justification for urging its acceptance. The theoretical model guiding this volume will have to pass two tests if it is to gain acceptance over competing models. First, it will have to be better able than competing theories to incorporate the enormous output of relevant empirical findings, whether or not the investigations productive of these findings were guided by different conceptual schemes. Second, it will have to manifest superiority over competing models in generating hypotheses that are empirically verified. It is hoped that the discussions of the literature in this volume will offer some hope of success for the model under consideration by the first criterion. Its degree of success by the second criterion must necessarily await the test of time and the efforts of interested investigators.

NOTES

[1] A number of such approaches to deviant behavior in terms of group learning and support processes are conveniently reviewed by Cohen (1966:84-106), frequently with discussions of their implications for self-attitudes.

[2] In the terms used in Chapter 1, to hold membership in a group is to imply that the group also functions as a reference group since the person is said to accept the normative expectations of the group as binding upon him and other group members judge the normative expectations to be applicable to the person. However, it is conceivable that a person aspires to membership in a group and therefore adopts the standards of the group as applicable to him although other members of the group do not view these standards as applicable to the person. In this event the group constitutes a reference group but not a membership group for the person.

Instances in which the person does not accept the standards of a group as applicable to him (for example, standards of the wider society) but in which the group members apply the standards to the person may have important implications for the person's performance of "deviant" behaviors since the group may apply negative sanctions to the person in ways that may further isolate him from the positive influence of the group in question. However, insofar as these group processes do not directly concern the cultural transmission and group support arguments presently under consideration they will not be discussed further at this point.

When a group neither is a membership nor a reference group for the individual nor regards the person as a group member, the group cannot be said to have any direct motivational significance for the person at all.

[3] Again, in the terms used in Chapter 1, such behavior would not constitute deviant behavior since the person is said to be conforming to the standards of his membership group unless he simultaneously accepts membership in multiple groups with conflicting standards. In that event he might be said to be simultaneously conforming to the standards of one membership group and deviating from the standards of the others (presumably because of the greater self-enhancing relevance of the former group).

[4] In effect, the former membership group may be said to have become a *negative* reference group.

References

Adler, Alfred, 1927. *The Practice and Theory of Individual Psychology.* New York: Harcourt.

Alexander, Franz, and William Healy, 1935. *Roots of Crime.* New York: Alfred A. Knopf.

Allen, M. K., and R. M. Liebert, 1969. "Effects of live and symbolic deviant-modeling cues on adoption of a previously learned standard," *Journal of Personality and Social Psychology,* 11 (3): 253–260.

American Psychiatric Association, 1968. *Diagnostic and Statistical Manual of Mental Disorders.* Washington, D.C.: American Psychiatric Association.

Anderson, Lorna M., 1969. "Personality characteristics of parents of neurotic, aggressive, and normal preadolescent boys," *Journal of Consulting and Clinical Psychology,* 33 (5): 575–581.

Ansbacher, J. L., and R. R. Ansbacher, 1956. *The Individual Psychology of Alfred Adler.* New York: Basic Books.

Arieti, S., 1967. "Some elements of cognitive psychiatry, "*American Journal of Psychotherapy,* 124 (October): 723–736.

Aronson, E., and D. R. Mettee, 1968. "Dishonest behavior as a function of differential levels of induced self-esteem," *Journal of Personality and Social Psychology,* 9 (June): 121-127.

Becker, Ernest, 1962. *The Birth and Death of Meaning: A Perspective in Psychiatry and Anthropology.* New York: Free Press.

Becker, Howard S., 1963. *Outsiders: Studies in the Sociology of Deviance.* New York: Free Press.

Berg, Norman L., 1971. "Effects of alcohol intoxication on self-concept," *Quarterly Journal of Studies on Alcohol,* 32: 442–453.

Berger, E. M., 1955. "Relationship among acceptance of self, acceptance of others, and MMPI scores," *Journal of Counseling Psychology,* 2: 279–284.

Berkowitz, Leonard, 1970. "Experimental investigations of hostility catharsis," *Journal of Consulting and Clinical Psychology,* 35 (1): 1–7.

Block, J., and H. Thomas, 1955. "Is satisfaction with self a measure of adjustment?" *Journal of Abnormal and Social Psychology,* 51: 254–259.

Blum, R., et al., 1964. *Utopiates: The Use and Users of LSD-25.* New York: Atherton Press.

Braaten, L. J., and C. D. Darling, 1962. "Suicidal tendencies among college students," *Psychiatric Quarterly,* 36: 665–692.

Breed, Warren, 1968. "The suicide process," in N. L. Farberow (ed.), *Proceedings. Fourth International Conference for Suicide Prevention.* Los Angeles: Delmar, 286–291.

Breen, Michael, 1968. "Culture and schizophrenia: a study of Negro and Jewish schizophrenics," *International Journal of Social Psychiatry,* 14: 282–289.

Brehm, M. L., and K. W. Back, 1968. "Self-image and attitudes toward drugs," *Journal of Personality,* 36: 299–314.

Carroll, James L., and Gerald B. Fuller, 1969. "The self and ideal self-concept of the alcoholic as influenced by length of sobriety and/or participation in Alcoholics Anonymous," *Journal of Clinical Psychology*, 25: 363–364.

Chamblis, William, 1964. "The negative self: an empirical assessment of a theoretical assumption," *Sociological Inquiry*, 34: 108–112.

Chase, P. H., 1957. "Self-concepts in adjusted and maladjusted hospital patients," *Journal of Consulting Psychology*, 21: 495–497.

Chodorkoff, G., 1954. "Adjustment and the discrepancy between the perceived and ideal self," *Journal of Clinical Psychology*, 10: 266–268.

Clinard, Marshall B., 1964. *Anomie and Deviant Behavior: A Discussion and Critique*. New York: Free Press.

Cloward, Richard A., and Lloyd E. Ohlin, 1960. *Delinquence and Opportunity: A Theory of Delinquent Gangs*. New York: Free Press.

Cohen, Albert K., 1955. *Delinquent Boys: The Culture of the Gang*. New York: Free Press.

——, 1966. *Deviance and Control*. Englewood Cliffs, N.J.: Prentice-Hall.

Cole, C. W., E. R. Detting, and J. E. Hinkle, 1967. "Non-linearity of self-concept discrepancy — the value dimension," *Psychological Reports*, 21 (August): 58–60.

Coopersmith, Stanley, 1967. *The Antecedents of Self-Esteem*. San Francisco: W.H. Freeman.

Cowen, E. L., and P. N. Tongas, 1959. "The social desirability of trait-descriptive terms: applications to a self-concept inventory," *Journal of Consulting Psychology*, 23: 361–365.

Crowne, Douglas P., and Mark W. Stephens, 1961. "Self-acceptance and self-evaluative behavior: a critique of methodology," *Psychological Bulletin*, 58 (2): 104–121.

Deitz, George E., 1969. "A comparison of delinquents with nondelinquents on self-concept, self-acceptance, and parental identification," *Journal of Genetic Psychology*, 115 (December): 285–295.

Dentler, Robert A., and Lawrence J. Monroe, 1961. "Social correlates of early adolescent theft," *American Sociological Review*, 26 (5): 733–743.

Diller, L., 1954. "Conscious and unconscious self-attitudes after success and failure," *Journal of Personality*, 23: 1–12.

Dinitz, Simon, Frank R. Scarpitti, and Walter C. Reckless, 1962. "Delinquency vulnerability: a cross group and longitudinal analysis," *American Sociological Review*, 27: 515–517.

Dittes, J. E., 1959. "Effect of changes in self-esteem upon impulsiveness and deliberation in making judgements," *Journal of Abnormal and Social Psychology*, 58: 348–356.

——, 1959b. "Attractiveness of group as a function of self-esteem and acceptance by group," *Journal of Abnormal and Social Psychology*, 59: 77–82.

Dosey, Michael A., and Murray Meisels, 1969. "Personal space and self-protection," *Journal of Personality and Social Psychology*, 11 (2): 93–97.

Eisenman, R., 1965. "Usefulness of the concepts of inferiority feelings and life style with schizophrenics," *Journal of Individual Psychology*, 21: 171–177.

Elliot, D. S., 1966. "Delinquency, school attendance, and dropout," *Social Problems*, 13: 307–314.

Engel, Mary, 1959. "The stability of the self-concept in adolescence," *Journal of Abnormal and Social Psychology*, 58: 211–215.

Epstein, S., 1955. "Unconscious self-evaluation in a normal and schizophrenic group," *Journal of Abnormal and Social Psychology*, 50: 65–70.

Erikson, Kai T., 1968. "Patient role and social uncertainty," in Earl Rubington and Martin S. Weinberg (eds.), *Deviance: The Interactionist Perspective*. New York: Macmillan, 337–342.

Farberow, N. L., 1950. "Personality patterns of suicidal mental hospital patients," *Genetic Psychological Monographs*, 42 (1).

———, and E. S. Shneidman, 1961. *The Cry for Help*. New York: McGraw-Hill.

———, E. S. Shneidman, and C. Neuringer, 1966. "Case history and hospitalization factors in suicides of neuropsychiatric hospital patients," *Journal of Nervous and Mental Disease*, 142: 32–44.

Farnham-Diggory, S., 1964. "Self-evaluation and subjective life expectancy among suicidal and nonsuicidal psychotic males," *Journal of Abnormal and Social Psychology*, 69 (6): 628–634.

Fawcett, J., M. Leff, and W. E. Bunney, 1969. "Suicide," *Archives of General Psychiatry*, 21: 129–137.

Feldman, Harvey W., 1968. "Ideological supports to becoming and remaining a heroin addict," *Journal of Health and Social Behavior*, 9 (2): 131–139.

Festinger, L., Jane Torrey, and Ben Willerman, 1954. "Self-evaluation as a function of attraction to the group," *Human Relations*, 7: 161–174.

Fisher, S., and S. Mirin, 1966. "Further validation of the special favorable responses occurring during unconscious self-evaluation," *Perceptual and Motor Skills*, 23: 1097–1098.

Frankel, A. Steven, 1969. "Attitudes toward a group as a function of self-esteem, group achievement level, and success or failure on a group-relevant task," *Proceedings, Seventy-seventh Annual Convention, American Psychological Association*, 351–352.

Freidson, Eliot, 1965. "Disability as a social deviance," in Marvin B. Sussman (ed.), *Sociology and Rehabilitation*, Washington, D.C.: American Sociological Association, 71–99.

French, John R. P., 1968. "The conceptualization and measurement of mental health in terms of self-identity theory," in S. B. Sells (ed.), *The Definition and Measurement of Mental Health*, Washington, D.C.: U.S. Department of Health, Education, and Welfare, Public Health Service, Health Services and Mental Health Administration, National Center for Health Statistics, 136–159.

Friedman, I., 1955. "Phenomenal, ideal and projected conceptions of self," *Journal of Abnormal and Social Psychology*, 51: 611–615.

Ganzler, S., 1967. "Some interpersonal and social dimensions of suicidal behavior," *Dissertation Abstracts*, 28B: 1192–1193.

Geen, Russell G., 1970. "Perceived suffering of the victim as an inhibitor of attack-induced aggression," *Journal of Social Psychology*, 81 (August): 209–215.

Gibby, R. G., Sr., and R. G. Gibby, Jr., 1967. "The effects of stress resulting from academic failure," *Journal of Clinical Psychology*, 23 (January): 35–37.

Glaser, Kurt, 1965. "Attempted suicide in children and adolescents: psychodynamic observations," *American Journal of Psychotherapy*, 19 (April): 220–227.

Goffman, Erving, 1963. *Stigma: Note on the Management of Spoiled Identity.* Englewood Cliffs, N.J.: Prentice-Hall.

Goldfried, Marvin R., 1963. "Feelings of inferiority and the depreciation of others: a research review and theoretical reformulation," *Journal of Individual Psychology,* 19: 27–48.

Gordon, Chad, 1969. "Self-conceptions methodologies," *Journal of Nervous and Mental Disease,* 148 (April): 328–364.

Gough, Harrison G., and Donald R. Peterson, 1952. "The identification and measurement of predispositional factors in crime and delinquency," *Journal of Consulting Psychology,* 16: 207–212.

Gould, Robert E., 1965. "Suicide problems in children and adolescents," *American Journal of Psychotherapy,* 19 (April): 228–246.

Graf, Richard G., 1971. "Induced self-esteem as a determinant of behavior," *Journal of Social Psychology,* 85 (December): 213–217.

Gunderson, E. K., 1965. "Body size, self-evaluation, and military effectiveness," *Journal of Personality and Social Psychology,* 2 (December): 902–906.

———, and L. C. Johnson, 1965. "Past experience, self-evaluation, and present adjustment," *Journal of Social Psychology,* 66: 311–321.

Hahn, Harlan, 1969. "Violence: the view from the ghetto," *Mental Hygiene,* 53 (4): 509–512.

Hall, Peter M., 1966. "Identification with the delinquent subculture and level of self-evaluation," *Sociometry,* 29: 146–158.

Hardyck, J. A., 1968. "Predicting response to a negative evaluation," *Journal of Personality and Social Psychology,* 9 (June): 128–132.

Harrow, Martin, David A. Fox, Kathryn I. Markhus, Richard Stillman, and Carolyn B. Hallowell, 1968. "Changes in adolescents' self-concepts and their parents' perceptions during psychiatric hospitalization," *Journal of Nervous and Mental Disease,* 147 (3): 252–259.

Hartlage, Lawrence C., and Phyllis Hale, 1968. "Self concept decline from psychiatric hospitalization," *Journal of Individual Psychology,* 24: 174–176.

Harvey, O. J., 1962. "Personality factors in resolution of conceptual incongruities," *Sociometry,* 25: 336–352.

Hattem, J. V., 1964. "Precipitating role of discordant interpersonal relationships in suicidal behavior," *Dissertation Abstracts,* 25: 1335–1336.

Havener, P. H., and C. E. Izard, 1962. "Unrealistic self-enhancement in paranoid schizophrenics," *Journal of Consulting Psychology,* 26: 65–68.

Healy, William, and Augusta Bronner, 1936. *New Light on Delinquency and Its Treatment.* New Haven: Yale University Press.

Heilbrun, Alfred B., Jr., 1972. "Style of adaptation to experienced aversive maternal control and interpersonal distancing following failure," *Journal of Nervous and Mental Disease,* 155 (3): 177–183.

Hillson, J. S., and P. Worchel, 1957. "Self-concept and defensive behavior in the maladjusted," *Journal of Consulting Psychology,* 21: 83–88.

Hoffman, Martin, 1964. "Drug addiction and 'hypersexuality': related modes of mastery," *Comprehensive Psychiatry,* 5 (4): 262–270.

Hokanson, J. E., and M. Burgess, 1962. "The effects of three types of aggresion on vascular processes," *Journal of Abnormal and Social Psychology,* 64: 446–449.

————, M. Burgess, and M. F. Cohen, 1963. "Effects of displaced aggression on systolic blood pressure," *Journal of Abnormal and Social Psychology*, 67: 214–218.

————, and R. Edelman, 1966. "Effects of three social responses on vascular processes," *Journal of Personality and Social Psychology*, 3: 442–447.

Horney, Karen, 1945. *Our Inner Conflicts*. New York: Norton.

————, 1950. *Neurosis and Human Growth*. New York: Norton.

Horowitz, Frances D., 1962. "The relationship of anxiety, self-concept, and sociometric status among fourth, fifth, and sixth grade children," *Journal of Abnormal and Social Psychology*, 65 (September): 212–214.

Horowitz, M., 1958. "The veridicality of liking and disliking," in R. Tagiuri and L. Petrullo (eds.), *Person Perception and Interpersonal Behavior*. Stanford: Stanford University Press, 191–209.

Ibelle, Bertram Patterson, 1961. "Discrepancies between self-concepts in paranoid schizophrenics and normals," *Dissertation Abstracts*, 21 (January): 2004–2005.

Jacobs, J., 1967. "Adolescent suicide attempts," *Dissertation Abstracts*, 28A: 801.

————, and J. D. Teicher, 1967. "Broken homes and social isolation in attempted suicide of adolescents," *International Journal of Social Psychiatry*, 13: 139–149.

Jacobson, Leonard I., Stephen E. Berger, and Jim Millham, 1969. "Self-esteem, sex differences, and the tendency to cheat," *Proceedings*, Seventy-seventh Annual Convention, American Psychological Association, 353–354.

James, William, 1890. *Principles of Psychology*. Two volumes, New York: Holt.

Johnson, Homer H., 1966. "Some effects of discrepancy level on responses to negative information about one's self," *Sociometry*, 29 (March): 52–66.

Jones, Edward E., Kenneth J. Gergen, and Keith E. Davis, 1962. "Some determinants of reactions to being approved or disapproved as a person," *Psychological Monographs*, 72 (2): 1–17.

Jones, Stephen C., and Carl Ratner, 1967. "Commitment to self-appraisal and interpersonal evaluations," *Journal of Personality and Social Psychology*, 6 (4): 442–447.

Kamano, D. K., and C. S. Crawford, 1966. "Self-evaluation of suicidal mental hospital patients," *Journal of Clinical Psychology*, 22 (July): 278–279.

Kaplan, E. A., 1967. "Homosexuality — a search for the ego-ideal," *Archives of General Psychiatry*, 16 (May): 355–358.

Kaplan, Howard B., 1971. "Social class and self-derogation: a conditional relationship," *Sociometry*, 34 (1): 41–65.

————, 1972a. "Toward a general theory of psychosocial deviance: the case of aggressive behavior," *Social Science and Medicine*, 6 (5): 593–617.

————, 1972b. *The Sociology of Mental Illness*. New Haven: College and University Press.

————, Ina Boyd, and Samuel W. Bloom, 1964. "Patient culture and the evaluation of self," *Psychiatry*, 7 (2): 116–126.

————, and Joseph H. Meyerowitz, 1970. "Social and psychological correlates of drug abuse: a comparison of addict and non-addict populations from the perspective of self-theory," *Social Science and Medicine*, 4 (2): 203–225.

————, and Alex D. Pokorny, 1969. "Self-derogation and psychosocial adjustment," *Journal of Nervous and Mental Disease*, 149 (5): 421–434.

Kitsuse, J. I., 1964. "Societal reaction to deviant behavior: problems of theory and method," in Howard S. Becker (ed.), *The Other Side: Perspectives on Deviance*. New York: Free Press, 87–102.

Kogan, W. S., R. Quinn, A. F. Ax, and H. S. Ripley, 1957. "Some methodological problems in the quantification of clinical assessment by Q array," *Journal of Consulting Psychology.* 21: 57–62.

Kohn, Paul M., and G. W. Mercer, 1971. "Drug use, drug use attitudes, and the authoritarianism-rebellion dimension," *Journal of Health and Social Behavior,* 12 (2): 125–131.

Korman, Abraham K., 1967. "Self-esteem as a moderator of the relationship between self-perceived abilities and vocational choice," *Journal of Applied Psychology,* 51 (1): 65–67.

Krause, M. S., 1961. "The measurement of transitory anxiety," *Psychological Review,* 68: 178–189.

Kumler, F. R., 1964. "Communication between suicide attemptors and significant others," *Nursing Research,* 13: 268–270.

La Barba, R. C., 1965. "The psychopath and anxiety — a reformulation," *Journal of Individual Psychology,* 21: 167–170.

Lachman, Jordon H., and James M. Cravens, 1969. "The murderers — before and after," *Psychiatric Quarterly,* 43 (1): 1–11.

Lemert, Edwin M., 1951. *Social Pathology.* New York: McGraw-Hill.

―――, 1967. *Human Deviance, Social Problems, and Social Control.* Englewood Cliffs, N.J.: Prentice-Hall.

Leon, Carlos A., 1969. "Unusual patterns of crime during La Violencia in Colombia," *American Journal of Psychiatry,* 125 (11): 1564–1575.

Lester, David. 1970. *Suicidal Behavior: A Summary of Research Findings.* A supplement to Vol. 2 (3) of *Crisis Intervention.* Buffalo: Suicide Prevention and Crisis Service.

Leventhal, H., and S.I. Perloe, 1962. "A relationship between self-esteem and persuasibility," *Journal of Abnormal and Social Psychology,* 64: 385–388.

Long, Barbara H., E. H. Henderson, and R. C. Ziller, 1967. "Self-social correlates of originality in children," *Journal of Genetic Psychology,* 111 (September): 47–57.

―――, Robert C. Ziller, and John Bankes, 1970. "Self-other orientations of institutionalized behavior-problem adolescents," *Journal of Consulting and Clinical Psychology,* 34 (1): 43–47.

Lovald, Keith, and Gertrud Neuwirth, 1968. "Exposed and shielded drinking: drinking as a role behavior and some consequences for social control and self-concept," *Archives of General Psychology,* 19 (July): 95–103.

Ludwig, D. J., and M. L. Maehr, 1967. "Changes in self-concept and stated behavioral preferences," *Child Development,* 38: 453–467.

Maddox, George L., 1968. "Drinking among Negroes: inferences from the drinking patterns of selected Negro male collegians," *Journal of Health and Social Behavior,* 9 (2): 114–120.

Maehr, M. L., J. Mensing, and S. Nafzger, 1962. "Concept of self and the reaction of others," *Sociometry,* 25 (December): 353–357.

Manasse, G., 1965. "Self-regard as a function of environmental demands in chronic schizophrenics," *Journal of Abnormal Psychology,* 70: 210–213.

Margolin N. L., and J. D. Teicher, 1968. "Thirteen adolescent male suicide attemptors," *Journal of the American Academy of Child Psychiatry,* 7: 296–315.

Maris, Ronald W., 1971. "Deviance as therapy: the paradox of the self-destructive female," *Journal of Health and Social Behavior,* 12 (2): 113–124.

Marks, P.A., and W. Seeman, 1963. *The Actuarial Description of Abnormal Personality.* Baltimore: Williams and Wilkins.

Matza, David, 1969. *Becoming Deviant.* Englewood Cliffs, N.J.: Prentice-Hall.

McGuire, Michael T., Stefan Stein, and Jack H. Mendelson, 1966. "Comparative psychosocial studies of alcoholic and nonalcoholic subjects undergoing experimentally induced ethanol intoxication," *Psychosomatic Medicine,* 28 (1): 13–26.

Mead, George Herbert, 1934. *Mind, Self, and Society.* Chicago: University of Chicago Press.

Medinnus, G. R., 1965. "Adolescents' self-acceptance and perceptions of their parents," *Journal of Consulting Psychology,* 29 (April): 150–154.

Merton, Robert K., 1957. *Social Theory and Social Structure.* New York: Free Press.

Miller, D. H., 1968. "Suicidal careers," *Dissertation Abstracts,* 28A: 4720.

Mindlin, Dorothee F., 1964. "Attitudes toward alcoholism and toward self: differences between three alcoholic groups," *Quarterly Journal of Studies on Alcohol,* 25 (March): 136–141.

Mogar, Robert E., Wayne M. Wilson, and Stanley T. Helm, 1970. "Personality subtypes of male and female alcoholic patients," *International Journal of the Addictions,* 5 (1): 99–113.

Morse, Stan, and Kenneth Gergen, 1970. "Social comparison, self-consistency and the concept of self," *Journal of Personality and Social Psychology,* 16 (1): 148–156.

Murphy, Gardner, 1947. *Personality: A Biosocial Approach to Origins and Structure,* New York: Harper.

Mussen, Paul, Stephen Harris, Eldred Rutherford, and Charles Blake Keasey, 1970. "Honesty and altruism among preadolescents," *Developmental Psychology,* 3 (2): 169–194.

Neuringer, C., 1964. "Rigid thinking in suicidal individuals," *Journal of Consulting Psychology,* 28: 54–58.

Nisbett, R. E., and A. Gordon, 1967. "Self-esteem and susceptibility to social influence," *Journal of Personality and Social Psychology,* 5 (March): 268–276.

Nocks, James Jay, and D. Bradley, 1969. "Self-esteem in an alcoholic population," *Diseases of the Nervous System,* 30 (September): 611–617.

Pearson, Manuel M., and Ralph B. Little, 1969. "The addictive process in unusual addictions: a further elaboration of etiology," *American Journal of Psychiatry,* 125 (9): 1166–1171.

Pepitone, A., and C. Wilpizeski, 1960. "Some consequences of experimental rejection," *Journal of Abnormal and Social Psychology,* 60 (May): 359–364.

Pflanz, M., and J. J. Rohde., 1970. "Illness: deviant behavior or conformity," *Social Science and Medicine,* 4: 645–653.

Rado, S. 1956. *Psychoanalysis of Behavior.* New York: Grune and Stratton.

———, 1957. "Narcotic bondage," *American Journal of Psychiatry,* 114: 165–170.

Rasmussen, G., and A. Zander, 1954. "Group membership and self-evaluation," *Human Relations,* 7: 239–251.

Reed, C. F., and C. A. Cuadra, 1957. "The role-taking hypothesis in delinquency," *Journal of Consulting Psychology,* 21: 386–390.

Rogers, A. H., 1958. "The self-concept in paranoid schizophrenia," *Journal of Clinical Psychology,* 14: 365–366.

Rogers, A. H., and T. M. Walsh, 1959. "Defensiveness and unwitting self-evaluation," *Journal of Clinical Psychology,* 15: 302–304.

Rogers, C. R., 1951a. "Perceptual reorganization in client-centered therapy," in R. R. Blake and G. V. Ransey (eds.), *Perception: An Approach to Personality*. New York: Ronald, 307–327.

———, 1951b. *Client-Centered Therapy: Its Current Practice, Implications, and Theory*. Boston: Houghton Mifflin.

———, and Rosalind R. Dymond, 1954. *Psychotherapy and Personality Change*. Chicago: University of Chicago Press.

Rosen, E., 1956a. "Self-appraisal and perceived desirability of MMPI personality traits," *Journal of Counseling Psychology*, 3: 44–51.

———, 1956b. "Self-appraisal, personal desirability and perceived social desirability of personality traits," *Journal of Abnormal and Social Psychology*, 52: 151–158.

Rosen, G. M., and A. O. Ross, 1968. "Relationship of body image to self-concept," *Journal of Consulting and Clinical Psychology*, 32: 100.

Rosenbaum, Milton, and Joseph Richman, 1970. "Suicide: the role of hostility and death wishes from the family and significant others," *American Journal of Psychiatry*, 126 (11): 128–131.

Rosenberg, Morris, 1965. *Society and the Adolescent Self-Image*. Princeton: Princeton University Press.

———, and Roberta G. Simmons, 1971. *Black and White Self-Esteem: The Urban School Child*. Washington, D.C.: American Sociological Association.

Ruebush, B. K., 1963. "Anxiety," in H. W. Stevenson, J. Kagan, and C. Spiker, (eds.), *Child Psychology*. Chicago: University of Chicago Press.

Salzman, L., 1965. "Obsessions and Phobias," *Contemporary Psychoanalysis*, 2: 1–25.

Sarbin, T. R., and B. G. Rosenberg, 1955. "Contributions to role-taking theory: IV, a method for obtaining a qualitative estimate of the self," *Journal of Social Psychology*, 42: 71–81.

Scarpitti, Frank R., 1965. "Delinquent and non-delinquent perceptions of self, values and opportunity," *Mental Hygiene*, 49 (July): 399–404.

Schaps, Eric, and Clinton R. Sanders, 1970. "Purposes, patterns, and protection in a campus drug-using community," *Journal of Health and Social Behavior*, 11 (2): 135–145.

Scheff, Thomas J., 1966. *Being Mentally Ill: A Sociological Theory*. Chicago: Aldine.

Schur, Edwin M., 1971. *Labeling Deviant Behavior: Its Sociological Implications*. New York: Harper & Row.

Schwartz, Michael, Gordon F. N. Fearn, and Sheldon Stryker, 1966. "A note on self conception and the emotionally disturbed role," *Sociometry*, 29 (September): 300–305.

———, and Sheldon Stryker, 1970. *Deviance, Selves, and Others*. Washington, D.C.: American Sociological Association.

———, and Sandra S. Tangri, 1965. "A note on self-concept as an insulator against delinquency," *American Sociological Review*, 30 (December): 922–926.

Sears, R. R., 1970. "Relation of early socialization experiences to self-concepts and gender role in middle childhood," *Child Development*, 41: 267–289.

Secord, P. F., and S. M. Jourard, 1953. "The appraisal of body-cathexis and the self," *Journal of Consulting Psychology*, 15 (5): 343–347.

Sharoff, Robert L., 1969. "Character problems and their relationship to drug abuse," *American Journal of Psychoanalysis*, 29 (2): 189–193.

Shean, Glenn D., and Freddie Fechtmann, 1971. "Purpose in life scores of student marihuana users," *Journal of Clinical Psychology*, 27 (1): 112–113.

Sherwood, John J., 1965. "Self-identity and referent others," *Sociometry*, 28 (March): 66–81.

———, 1967. "Increased self-evaluation as a function of ambiguous evaluations by referent others," *Sociometry*, 30 (December): 404–409.

Shinohara, M., and Richard L. Jenkins, 1967. "MMPI study of three types of delinquents," *Journal of Clinical Psychology*, 23: 156–163.

Short, J. F., R. Rivera, and R. A. Tennyson, 1965. "Perceived opportunities, gang membership and delinquency," *American Sociological Review*, 30 (February): 56–67.

Silverman, I., 1964. "Note on the relationship of self-esteem to subject self-selection," *Perceptual and Motor Skills*, 19 (December): 769–770.

Skelton, W. Douglas, 1969. "Prison riot," *Archives of General Psychiatry*, 21 (September): 359–362.

Smart, Reginald G., and Dianne Fejer, 1969. "Illicit LSD users: their social backgrounds, drug use and psychopathology," *Journal of Health and Social Behavior*, 10 (4): 297–308.

Smith, T. L., and R. M. Suinn, 1965. "A note on identification, self-esteem, anxiety and conformity," *Journal of Clinical Psychology*, 21 (July): 286.

Solomon, Fredric, Walter L. Walker, Garrett J. O'Connor, and Jacob R. Fishman, 1965. "Civil rights activity and reduction in crime among Negroes," *Archives of General Psychiatry*, 12: 227–236.

Stotland, E., S. Thorley, E. Thomas, A. R. Cohen, and A. Zander, 1957. "The effects of group expectations and self-esteem upon self-evaluation," *Journal of Abnormal and Social Psychology*, 54: 55–63.

Suchman, Edward A., 1968. "The 'hang-loose' ethic and the spirit of drug use," *Journal of Health and Social Behavior*, 9 (2): 146–155.

Sullivan, Harry Stack, 1953. *The Interpersonal Theory of Psychiatry*. New York: Norton.

Syngg, D., and A. W. Combs, 1949. *Individual Behavior: A New Frame of Reference*. New York: Harper.

Tabachnick, N., R. E. Litman, M. Osman, W. L. Jones, J. Cohn, A. Casper, and J. Moffat, 1966. "Comparative psychiatric study of accidental and suicidal death," *Archives of General Psychiatry*, 14: 60–68.

Tahka, V., 1966. *The Alcoholic Personality – A Clinical Study*. Helsinki: Finnish Foundation for Alcohol Studies, 13.

Tamkin, A. S., 1957. "Selective recall in schizophrenia and its relation to ego strength," *Journal of Abnormal and Social Psychology*, 55: 345–349.

Tanay, E., 1969. "Psychiatric study of homicide," *American Journal of Psychiatry*, 125: 1252–1258.

Teele, J. E., 1965. "Suicidal behavior, assaultiveness, and socialization principles," *Social Forces*, 43: 510–518.

Tippett, J. S., and E. Silber, 1966. "Autonomy of self-esteem," *Archives of General Psychiatry*, 14: 372–385.

Toch, Hans, 1969. *Violent Men*. Chicago: Aldine Press.

Trow, William Clark, and Alfred S. T. Pu, 1927. "Self-ratings of the Chinese," *School and Society*, 26: 213–216.

Tucker, G. J., and R. F. Reinhardt, 1966. *Suicide Attempts*. Pensacola, Fla.: U.S. Naval Aerospace Medical Institute, NAM I–975.

Usdin, Gene L., 1969. "Civil disobedience and urban revolt," *American Journal of Psychiatry*, 125 (11): 91–97.

Vanderpool, James, A., 1969. "Alcoholism and the self-concept," *Quarterly Journal of Studies on Alcohol*, 30: 59–77.

Videbeck, Richard, 1960. "Self-conception and the reactions of others," *Sociometry*, 23 (December): 351–359.

Wahl, C. W., 1956. "Some antecedent factors in the family histories of 109 alcoholics," *Quarterly Journal of Studies on Alcohol*, 17: 643–654.

Wahler, H. J., 1958. "Social desirability and self ratings of intakes, patients in treatment, and controls," *Journal of Consulting Psychology*, 22: 357–363.

Washburn, Wilber C., 1962. "Patterns of protective attitudes in relation to differences in self-evaluation and anxiety level among high school students," *California Journal of Educational Research*, 13 (2): 84–94.

———, 1963. "The effects of sex differences on protective attitudes in delinquents and non-delinquents," *Exceptional Children*, 30: 111–117.

Weinstock, Allan R., 1967. "Family environment and the development of defense and coping mechanisms," *Journal of Personality and Social Psychology*, 5 (January): 67–75.

White, William F., and Eugene L. Gaier, 1965. "Assessment of body image and self-concept among alcoholics with different intervals of sobriety," *Journal of Clinical Psychology*, 21 (October): 374–377.

———, and Thomas L. Porter, 1966. "Self concept reports among hospitalized alcholics during early periods of sobriety," *Journal of Counseling Psychology*, 13 (3): 352–355.

Whitelock, Paul R., John E. Overall, and Jerry H. Patrick, 1971. "Personality patterns and alcohol abuse in a state hospital population," *Journal of Abnormal Psychology*, 78 (1): 9–16.

Whitlock, F. A., and A. D. Broadhurst, 1969. "Attempted suicide and the experience of violence," *Journal of Biosocial Science*, 1: 353–368.

Williams, A. F., 1965. "Self-concepts of college problem drinkers: (1) a comparison with alcoholics," *Quarterly Journal of Studies on Alcohol*, 26: 589–594.

Wilson, Lowell T., R. W. Miskimins, G. Nicholas Braucht, and K. L. Berry, 1971. "The severe suicide attempter and self-concept," *Journal of Clinical Psychology*, 27 (July): 307–309.

Wood, Arthur L., 1961. "A socio-structural analysis of murder, suicide, and economic crime in Ceylon," *American Sociological Review*, 26 (5): 744–753.

Wylie, Ruth C., 1961. *The Self Concept*. Lincoln: University of Nebraska Press.

———, 1965. "Self-ratings, level of ideal-self ratings, and defensiveness," *Psychological Reports*, 16 (February): 135–150.

Zahn, Margaret, 1973. "Incapacity, impotence and invisible impairment: their effects upon interpersonal relations," *Journal of Health and Social Behavior*, 14 (June): 115–123.

Ziller, R. C., and Lynn H. Golding, 1969. "Political personality," *Proceedings, Seventy-seventh Annual Convention, American Psychological Association*, 441–442.

Zuckerman, M., and I. Monashkin, 1957. "Self-acceptance and psychopathology," *Journal of Consulting Psychology*, 21 (2): 145–148.

Index